Home-Style Soups, Salads *and* Sandwiches

Editors: Julie Schnittka, Geri Truszynski
Food Editor: Mary Beth Jung
Assistant Food Editor: Coleen Martin
Senior Home Economist: Mary Fullmer
Assistant Editor: Kristine Krueger
Art Director: Stephanie Marchese
Production: Ellen Lloyd
Test Kitchen Home Economists: Rochelle Schmidt, Karla Spies
Test Kitchen Assistants: Judith Scholovich, Sherry Smalley
Photography: Scott Anderson, Glenn Thiesenhusen
Photo Studio Coordinator: Anne Schimmel
Illustrations: Jim Sibilski

©1996, Reiman Publications, L.P.
5400 S. 60th St., Greendale WI 53129
International Standard Book Number: 0-89821-174-3
Library of Congress Catalog Card Number: 96-67810
All rights reserved.
Printed in U.S.A.
Fourth Printing, May 2002

PICTURED ABOVE. Deli Club Sandwich and Crunchy Pea Salad (both recipes on page 99).

PICTURED ON OUR COVER. Clockwise from top: Country Vegetable Soup (page 22), Cinnamon Fruit Compote (page 75), Giant Picnic Sandwich (page 95) and Blue Cheese-Bacon Dressing (page 65).

Finally...a Cookbook That Adds *Extra* to the Ordinary

WHETHER for lunch, dinner or snacks in between, soups, salads and sandwiches are mainstays in most homes. Unfortunately, that eventually creates a predicament for even the best of cooks: How do you make those standbys come alive day in and day out?

Sure, some cookbooks include a handful of recipes you can turn to. But that's not much help when a *whole book* devoted to deliciously new ways to make savory soups, satisfying sandwiches and refreshingly crisp salads is what you need.

Wouldn't it be great if there was such a book? Well, now there is. And you're holding it right in your hands!

Their Kitchens to Yours. *Home-Style Soups, Salads and Sandwiches* is packed with *hundreds* of different ideas from great cooks coast to coast. Here at Reiman Publications, we asked readers of our popular *Taste of Home* and *Country Woman* magazines to share their favorite recipes in those three categories. The friendly cooks were happy to oblige!

For instance, Shelley Way receives rave reviews from folks in Douglas, Wyoming when she serves her robust Ravioli Soup (page 17). And Betty Kuhlber of Slippery Rock, Pennsylvania says family and friends alike can't seem to get enough of her hearty Garden Chowder (page 31).

Meanwhile, Mary Prior of St. Paul, Minnesota recalls Creamy Citrus Salad (page 76) was always a hit at family get-togethers when she was little. Now, she receives the same reaction when she takes along this tasty dish.

In Louisville, Kentucky, Elaine Cooley earns kudos from her family whenever she serves her mom's Hot Turkey Sandwiches (page 89). Elaine loves their fast-to-fix convenience!

Those are just a few of the meat and vegetable soups, cream soups, fruit and molded salads and hot sandwiches waiting for you inside this unique book.

Plus, there are complete chapters covering pasta salads, fresh garden vegetable salads and even bean and grain salads. You'll also find robust bean soup and chili recipes, "summer soups" and piled-high cold sandwiches.

No Fuss! You should know, however, that there *is* something you *won't* find in this cookbook. What's that? Required ingredients that send you on a special trip to the store! We've carefully screened the recipes in *Home-Style Soups, Salads and Sandwiches* to ensure they *all* call only for ingredients cooks commonly keep on hand. So you should be able to start on any of them immediately.

If you're especially pressed for time, you're bound to appreciate the separate chapter devoted to quick-and-easy recipes. It features over 35 recipes for shortcut soups, snappy sandwiches and speedy salads that can be tossed together in 30 minutes or less!

Are you or a family member limiting your intake of salt, sugar and fat for any reason? Be sure to note the recipes marked with a check like this ✓. It means they are prepared with less salt, sugar and fat and include *Diabetic Exchanges*—but retain full flavor as well.

With that, simply turn the page...and surprise *your* family with the soup, salad and sandwich "magic" you can now perform in your kitchen—transforming the ordinary into the extraordinary!

Home-Style Soups, Salads and Sandwiches

Bean Soup & Chili Bonanza...6

Meat & Vegetable Soups...16

Comforting Cream Soups...28

Soups for the Summer...38

Hearty Main-Dish Salads...42

Pasta, Bean & Grain Salads...50

Garden Vegetable Medley...58

Fruit & Molded Salads...68

Hot Sandwich Specialties...78

Satisfying Cold Sandwiches...90

Quick & Easy Favorites...98

Index...110

Bean Soup & Chili Bonanza

With this mouth-watering roundup of zesty chilis and robust bean soups and stews, the possibilities for country-style eating are endless!

Chicken Lima Bean Soup

Carol Ann Kaiser, Pendleton, Oregon
(PICTURED AT LEFT)

When I was little, my father could be found in the kitchen during his free time. This soup is one of his most memorable dishes...and one of my most treasured recipes.

- 1 pound dry large lima beans
- 1 broiler/fryer chicken (3 to 3-1/2 pounds)
- 3 quarts water
- 2 celery ribs with leaves, sliced
- 4 chicken bouillon cubes
- 2-1/2 teaspoons salt
- 1/2 teaspoon pepper
- 3 medium carrots, chopped
- 4 cups chopped fresh spinach
- 2 tablespoons minced fresh parsley

In a Dutch oven or soup kettle, combine beans, chicken, water, celery, bouillon, salt and pepper; bring to a boil. Reduce heat; cover and simmer for 2 hours or until beans are tender. Remove chicken; allow to cool. Debone and cut chicken into chunks; return to pan. Add carrots; simmer for 30 minutes or until tender. Stir in spinach and parsley; heat through. **Yield:** 12-14 servings (3-1/2 quarts).

Hunter's Chili

Julie Batterman, Lincoln, Nebraska
(PICTURED AT LEFT)

As soon as hunting season begins here, you can find this spicy chili brewing in our kitchen. It's a great way to warmly welcome folks in from the cold.

- 1 pound fresh bratwurst
- 1 pound ground beef
- 2 cups chopped onion
- 1 large green pepper, chopped
- 1 quart water
- 1 to 2 garlic cloves, minced
- 1 can (6 ounces) tomato paste
- 1 can (28 ounces) diced tomatoes, undrained
- 1 can (8 ounces) tomato sauce
- 2 cans (15 to 16 ounces *each*) kidney beans, rinsed and drained
- 1 can (15-1/4 ounces) whole kernel corn, drained
- 1 can (15 ounces) pinto beans, rinsed and drained
- 2 cans (4 ounces *each*) mushroom stems and pieces, drained
- 3 tablespoons chili powder
- 1 tablespoon paprika
- 1 teaspoon ground cumin
- 1 teaspoon dried oregano
- 1 teaspoon salt
- 1/2 teaspoon pepper
- 1/4 teaspoon cayenne pepper
- 1/4 teaspoon crushed red pepper flakes
- 2 bay leaves

In a 6-qt. Dutch oven or soup kettle over medium heat, brown bratwurst. Remove and thinly slice; return to pan along with beef, onion and green pepper. Cook over medium heat until beef is browned and onion is tender; drain. Add all remaining ingredients. Cover and simmer for 1-2 hours. Remove bay leaves before serving. **Yield:** 14-18 servings (4-1/2 quarts).

Green Chili

Sharon Malleis, Parker, Colorado

Friends and family never seem to tire of this chili. We like this as a meal in itself but also use it to top our favorite Mexican foods like burritos.

- 1 pork shoulder roast (3-1/2 to 4 pounds)
- 1/2 cup all-purpose flour
- 1/2 teaspoon salt
- 1/4 teaspoon pepper
- 1 tablespoon cooking oil
- 4 cans (4 ounces *each*) chopped green chilies
- 2 cans (28 ounces *each*) stewed tomatoes
- 2 garlic cloves, minced
- 1 medium onion, chopped
- 1 jalapeno pepper, seeded and chopped
- 1 to 2 teaspoons minced fresh cilantro *or* parsley
- 1/2 teaspoon ground cumin
Warm flour tortillas, optional

Trim pork and cut into 1/2-in. cubes. In a large bowl or resealable plastic bag, combine flour, salt and pepper. Add pork cubes and toss to coat. In a Dutch oven or soup kettle over medium heat, brown pork in oil; drain. Add chilies, tomatoes, garlic, onion, jalapeno, cilantro and cumin; bring to a boil. Reduce heat; cover and simmer for 1-1/2 to 2 hours or until pork is tender. Serve with tortillas if desired. **Yield:** 10-12 servings (3 quarts).

> **HOT AND HEARTY.** *Pictured at left, top to bottom: Chicken Lima Bean Soup and Hunter's Chili (both recipes on this page).*

Chicken Chili

Lisa Goodman, Bloomington, Minnesota

Loaded with hearty beans and chicken, this zippy chili really warms us up on chilly winter nights.

✓ **This tasty dish uses less sugar, salt and fat. Recipe includes *Diabetic Exchanges*.**

4-1/2 cups chicken broth
    2 cans (15 ounces *each*) black beans, rinsed and drained
1/2 cup *each* chopped green, yellow and sweet red pepper
1/4 cup chopped onion
    1 tablespoon chili powder
1-1/2 teaspoons paprika
    1 to 1-1/2 teaspoons pepper
    1 to 1-1/2 teaspoons crushed red pepper flakes
    1 to 1-1/2 teaspoons ground cumin
1/2 teaspoon salt, optional
Dash cayenne pepper
    2 cups cubed cooked chicken
Shredded cheddar cheese, optional

In a 3-qt. saucepan, bring broth to a boil. Reduce heat; add beans, peppers, onion and seasonings. Cover and simmer 15 minutes. Add chicken; simmer for 30 minutes. Garnish with cheese if desired. **Yield:** 7 servings. **Diabetic Exchanges:** One 1-cup serving (prepared with low-sodium chicken broth, chicken breast and without salt and cheese) equals 1-1/2 starch, 1-1/2 lean meat, 1 vegetable; also, 183 calories, 68 mg sodium, 25 mg cholesterol, 28 gm carbohydrate, 17 gm protein, 2 gm fat.

Hearty Black Bean Chili

Colleen Hilliker, Stevens Point, Wisconsin

Featuring beans, ground beef and chicken, this chili is perfect for those with big appetites.

    1 pound dry black beans
    1 pound ground beef
    2 boneless skinless chicken breast halves, cubed
3/4 cup chopped onion
    3 cups water
    1 can (15 ounces) tomato sauce
    1 can (14-1/2 ounces) diced tomatoes, undrained
    1 tablespoon chili powder
2-1/4 teaspoons salt
1-1/2 teaspoons ground cumin
1/4 teaspoon garlic powder
1/4 teaspoon pepper
Shredded cheddar cheese and thinly sliced green onions, optional

Place beans in a saucepan and cover with water; bring to a boil and boil for 2 minutes. Remove from the heat; soak for 1 hour. Drain and rinse beans. Meanwhile, in a Dutch oven or soup kettle over medium heat, cook beef, chicken and onion until meats are browned and onion is tender; drain. Add water, tomato sauce, tomatoes and seasonings; mix well. Add

beans; bring to a boil. Reduce heat; cover and simmer for 3-1/2 to 4 hours or until beans are tender. Garnish with cheese and green onions if desired. **Yield:** 6-8 servings (2-1/2 quarts).

Oven-Baked Bean Soup

Delores Anderson, Woodburn, Oregon

When I know I have a busy day ahead of me, I reach for this recipe. I just pop this soup in the oven early in the day and have a delicious ready-to-eat meal all set for supper.

    1 pound dry navy beans
1-1/4 pounds fully cooked ham, diced
    3 quarts water
    2 cans (8 ounces *each*) tomato sauce
    1 cup *each* diced onion, celery and carrot
    2 teaspoons chili powder
    2 teaspoons salt
    1 teaspoon dried marjoram
1/4 teaspoon pepper

Combine all ingredients in a 6-qt. ovenproof Dutch oven. Cover and bake at 350° for 4-1/2 to 5 hours or until beans are tender. **Yield:** 14-18 servings (4-1/2 quarts).

Winter Vegetable Soup

Gertrude Vinci, Reno, Nevada

Folks always seem to ask for the recipe whenever I make this flavorful filling soup. And they're surprised to learn that refried beans are a major ingredient!

    1 cup chopped celery
1/2 cup chopped onion
    1 garlic clove, minced
    2 tablespoons olive *or* vegetable oil
1-1/2 quarts water
    1 can (14-1/2 ounces) diced tomatoes, undrained
    3 medium potatoes, peeled and cubed
    2 medium carrots, diced
    1 cup chopped cabbage
    3 tablespoons minced fresh parsley
    2 teaspoons brown sugar
1-1/4 teaspoons salt
    1 teaspoon dried marjoram
1/2 teaspoon dried rosemary, crushed
1/4 teaspoon pepper
1/8 teaspoon cayenne pepper
    2 cans (16 ounces *each*) refried beans with green chilies
    1 can (15 to 16 ounces) kidney beans, rinsed and drained
Hot cooked macaroni

In a Dutch oven or soup kettle, saute celery, onion and garlic in oil for 7 minutes or until tender. Add the next 12 ingredients; bring to a boil. Reduce heat; cover and simmer for 40 minutes. Stir in beans. Cover and simmer for 20 minutes or until vegetables are tender. Serve over macaroni. **Yield:** 12-16 servings (4 quarts).

White Chili

Kaye Whiteman, Charleston, West Virginia

Growing up in a Pennsylvania Dutch area, I was surrounded by excellent cooks and wonderful foods. I enjoy experimenting with new recipes, like this change-of-pace chili.

    1/2 cup chopped onion
      3 garlic cloves, minced
      2 tablespoons cooking oil
  2-1/2 teaspoons ground cumin
    1/2 pound ground turkey
      1 pound uncooked boneless skinless turkey breast, cubed
      3 cups chicken broth
      1 can (15 ounces) garbanzo beans, rinsed and drained
      1 tablespoon minced jalapeno pepper
    1/2 teaspoon dried marjoram
    1/4 teaspoon dried savory
      2 teaspoons cornstarch
      1 tablespoon water
  Shredded Monterey Jack cheese, optional

In a 2-qt. saucepan, saute onion and garlic in oil for 5 minutes or until tender. Stir in cumin; cook for 5 minutes. Add turkey; cook over medium heat until no longer pink. Add broth, beans, jalapeno, marjoram and savory; bring to a boil. Reduce heat; cover and simmer for 45 minutes, stirring occasionally. Uncover; cook 15 minutes more. Dissolve cornstarch in water; stir into chili. Bring to a boil; cook and stir for 2 minutes. Serve topped with cheese if desired. **Yield:** 6 servings.

Country Bean Soup

Donna Higbee, Sandy, Utah

I like to give this mix as a gift, layering the beans in a clear pint jar and attaching the soup directions with a festive ribbon. You'll find it's perfect to serve year-round.

      1 cup *each* dry yellow split peas, green split peas, lentils, black-eyed peas, pinto beans, black beans, kidney beans and great northern beans (enough for four batches of soup)
  1-1/2 quarts water
      1 large onion, chopped
      2 medium carrots, chopped
      1 celery rib, chopped
      1 garlic clove, minced
      1 to 2 teaspoons salt
      1 teaspoon chili powder
    1/4 teaspoon pepper
      1 smoked ham hock
      1 can (8 ounces) tomato sauce

Combine beans, peas and lentils; divide into four equal batches, 2 cups each. Store in an airtight container. *To make one batch of soup:* Place one batch of beans in a large saucepan. Add remaining ingredients; bring to a boil over medium-high heat. Reduce heat; cover and simmer for 3 hours or until beans are tender. Remove ham hock; cut meat into bite-size pieces and return to pan. Heat through. **Yield:** One batch makes 8-10 servings (2-1/2 quarts).

Pasta and Lentil Soup

Marie Herr, Berea, Ohio

I keep these ingredients on hand so I can share this soup with friends who are under the weather. It also makes a quick and easy gift-giving idea.

✓ **This tasty dish uses less sugar, salt and fat. Recipe includes *Diabetic Exchanges*.**

  3-1/2 cups water
    1/2 cup uncooked small pasta (shells, elbow macaroni, etc.)
    1/4 cup dry lentils
      2 tablespoons grated Parmesan cheese
      1 tablespoon dried minced onion
      1 tablespoon chicken bouillon granules
  1-1/2 teaspoons dried vegetable flakes
      1 teaspoon dried parsley flakes
    1/2 teaspoon dried oregano
  Dash garlic powder

Combine all ingredients in a 2-qt. saucepan; bring to a boil over medium heat. Reduce heat; cover and simmer for 25-30 minutes or until pasta and lentils are tender. **Yield:** 4 servings. **Diabetic Exchanges:** One 1-cup serving (prepared with low-sodium bouillon) equals 1 starch, 1 vegetable, 1/2 very lean meat; also, 117 calories, 58 mg sodium, 2 mg cholesterol, 20 gm carbohydrate, 7 gm protein, 1 gm fat.

Southwestern Chili

Jean White, Forsyth, Missouri

I came across this mouth-watering recipe while living in Arizona. Because it doesn't contain tomato sauce, it's quite different than traditional chili, but it's a real family favorite.

      1 pork shoulder roast (2 to 3 pounds)
      1 tablespoon cooking oil
    1/2 cup chopped onion
      1 garlic clove, minced
      1 quart chicken broth
      2 cans (4 ounces *each*) chopped green chilies
      2 tablespoons chili powder
    1/2 teaspoon dried oregano
    1/2 teaspoon salt
    1/2 teaspoon pepper
      2 cans (15-1/2 ounces *each*) hominy, drained
  Warm flour tortillas, optional

Trim pork and cut into 1/2-in. cubes. In a 3-qt. saucepan over medium heat, brown pork in oil; drain. Add onion and garlic; cook for 2 minutes. Add broth, chilies, chili powder, oregano, salt and pepper; bring to a boil. Reduce heat; cover and simmer for 1 hour. Add hominy; simmer for 30 minutes or until pork is tender. Serve with tortillas if desired. **Yield:** 6-8 servings.

LADLE UP SOME LEGUMES. *Clockwise from top right: Mexican Bean Soup, Ham and Bean Soup, Tuscan Soup, Italian Macaroni Soup and Split Pea Soup with Meatballs (all recipes are on pages 12 and 13).*

Italian Macaroni Soup

Mary Scodeller, Lansing, Michigan
(PICTURED ON PAGE 10)

Cold Midwestern winters call for steaming bowls of this robust soup. I like to serve it as a meal with a green salad and lots of fresh Italian bread.

2-1/2 cups chopped fully cooked ham
    1 large onion, finely chopped
    2 to 3 garlic cloves, minced
    3 tablespoons olive *or* vegetable oil
    2 cans (28 ounces *each*) crushed tomatoes
    2 cans (14-1/2 ounces *each*) beef broth
3-1/4 cups water
    1/2 teaspoon salt
    1/2 teaspoon dried basil
    1/4 teaspoon fennel seed
    3 cans (16 ounces *each*) great northern beans, rinsed
      and drained
Hot cooked macaroni
Shredded Parmesan cheese, optional

In a Dutch oven or soup kettle, saute ham, onion and garlic in oil until onion is tender. Add the next six ingredients; bring to a boil. Reduce heat; cover and simmer for 1 hour. Add beans; simmer for 1 hour. Serve over macaroni; garnish with Parmesan cheese if desired. **Yield:** 12-16 servings (about 4 quarts).

Split Pea Soup with Meatballs

Donna Smith, Grey Cliff, Montana
(PICTURED ON PAGE 10)

The addition of tender meatballs add a flavorful twist to ordinary split pea soup. Whenever I prepare this for our church soup suppers, I come home with an empty kettle!

    1 pound dry green split peas
    3 medium carrots, sliced 1/2 inch thick
3/4 cup diced celery
    1 medium onion, diced
    2 quarts water
    3 medium potatoes, cut into 1/2-inch cubes
2-1/2 teaspoons salt
    1/4 teaspoon pepper
MEATBALLS:
3/4 cup finely chopped celery
    1 medium onion, finely chopped
    4 tablespoons cooking oil, *divided*
    1 pound ground pork
1-1/2 cups soft bread crumbs
    2 tablespoons water
    1 teaspoon salt
    1/2 teaspoon dried sage, crushed
    1 egg

In a Dutch oven or soup kettle, combine peas, carrots, celery, onion and water; bring to a boil over medium heat. Reduce heat; cover and simmer for 1 hour. Add potatoes, salt

and pepper; cover and simmer for 30 minutes. Meanwhile, in a large skillet, saute celery and onion in 2 tablespoons oil until tender; transfer to a bowl. Add pork, bread crumbs, water, salt, sage and egg; mix well. Form into 3/4-in. balls. In the same skillet, brown meatballs in remaining oil until no longer pink inside. Add to soup; cover and simmer for 15 minutes. **Yield:** 10-14 servings (3-1/2 quarts).

Tuscan Soup

Rosemary Goetz, Hudson, New York
(PICTURED ON PAGE 10)

I work full-time outside of the home, so I relish recipes like this that can be prepared in a flash.

    1 small onion, chopped
    1 small carrot, sliced
    1 tablespoon olive *or* vegetable oil
    2 cans (14-1/2 ounces *each*) chicken broth
    1 cup water
3/4 teaspoon salt
    1/4 teaspoon pepper
    1 can (15 to 16 ounces) white kidney *or* great
      northern beans, rinsed and drained
2/3 cup uncooked small spiral pasta
    3 cups thinly sliced fresh escarole *or* spinach

In a 2-qt. saucepan over medium-high heat, saute onion and carrot in oil until onion is lightly browned. Add broth, water, salt and pepper; bring to a boil. Stir in beans and pasta; return to a boil. Reduce heat; cover and simmer for 15 minutes or until pasta and vegetables are tender, stirring occasionally. Add escarole; heat through. **Yield:** 4 servings.

Mexican Bean Soup

Vivian Christian, Stephenville, Texas
(PICTURED ON PAGE 11)

For our family's fall birthday bash, I make a big pot of this soup and serve it with plenty of oven-fresh corn bread.

    2 pounds ground beef
    1 medium onion, chopped
    1 quart water
    3 cans (14-1/2 ounces *each*) diced tomatoes,
      undrained
    2 cans (15-1/2 ounces *each*) hominy, drained
    2 cans (15 ounces *each*) ranch-style *or* chili beans
    1 can (15 to 16 ounces) kidney beans, rinsed and
      drained
    1 can (4 ounces) chopped green chilies
    2 envelopes taco seasoning mix
    1 envelope (1 ounce) original ranch dressing mix
    2 tablespoons brown sugar
    1/4 teaspoon cayenne pepper
Shredded cheddar cheese and sour cream, optional

In a Dutch oven or soup kettle, brown beef and onion; drain. Add the next 10 ingredients; bring to a boil. Reduce heat; cover and simmer for 30 minutes. Garnish with cheese and sour cream if desired. **Yield:** 14-16 servings (4 quarts).

Ham and Bean Soup

Mary Detweiler, West Farmington, Ohio
(PICTURED ON PAGE 11)

When I was a cook in a restaurant years ago, this was our best-selling soup. One taste and your family will agree it's a winner!

> 3/4 **pound fully cooked ham, cubed**
> 1 **medium onion, chopped**
> 2 **garlic cloves, minced**
> 2 **tablespoons butter *or* margarine**
> 2 **cans (16 ounces *each*) great northern beans, rinsed and drained**
> 3 **cups chicken broth**
> 2 **cups water**
> 1 **cup diced peeled potatoes**
> 3/4 **cup diced carrots**
> 3/4 **cup diced celery**
> 1/4 **teaspoon pepper**
> 1/2 **cup frozen peas**
> 2 **tablespoons minced fresh parsley**

In a 3-qt. saucepan, saute ham, onion and garlic in butter until onion is tender. Add the next seven ingredients; cover and simmer for 30 minutes or until vegetables are tender. Add peas and cook for 5 minutes. Add parsley. **Yield:** 8 servings (about 2 quarts).

Favorite Chili

Cindi Clinton, Kimball, Nebraska

I received this recipe from a friend and have modified it to suit my family's tastes. Our three children especially like this slightly sweet chili because it's not too spicy.

> 3-1/2 **pounds beef chuck roast, cut into 1/2-inch cubes**
> 1/4 **cup cooking oil**
> 2 **cups chopped onion**
> 3 **medium green peppers, chopped**
> 5 **garlic cloves, minced**
> 2 **cans (28 ounces *each*) diced tomatoes, undrained**
> 2 **cups water**
> 1 **can (12 ounces) tomato paste**
> 1/3 **cup chili powder**
> 1/4 **cup sugar**
> 1 **tablespoon salt**
> 2 **teaspoons dried oregano**
> 3/4 **teaspoon pepper**
> 1 **can (16 ounces) pinto beans, rinsed and drained**
> 1/4 **cup cornmeal**

Shredded cheddar cheese and additional chopped onion, optional

In a Dutch oven or soup kettle, brown beef in oil; drain. Add onion, green peppers and garlic; cook until tender. Add the next eight ingredients; bring to a boil. Reduce heat;

cover and simmer for 2 hours, stirring occasionally. Add beans and cornmeal; simmer for 15 minutes, stirring frequently. Garnish with cheese and onion if desired. **Yield:** 14-16 servings (4 quarts).

Pea Soup for a Crowd

Maria Bosma, Cobourg, Ontario

This soup is perfect for busy days because it bakes in the oven for hours with little fuss. I've served it several times with great success to various church groups.

> 3 **cups (1-1/2 pounds) dry yellow split peas**
> 1 **pound dry navy beans *or* whole yellow peas**
> 2 **pounds smoked pork shoulder *or* picnic ham**
> 3-1/2 **quarts water**
> 4 **celery ribs, chopped**
> 3 **large carrots, shredded**
> 2 **cups chopped onion**
> 1-1/4 **teaspoons salt**
> 1 **teaspoon pepper**

Place peas and beans in a Dutch oven or soup kettle; cover with water. Bring to a boil; boil for 2 minutes. Remove from the heat; let stand 1 hour. Drain beans and discard liquid. Place beans in an 8-qt. roaster. Add remaining ingredients. Cover and bake at 350° for 5-7 hours or until peas are tender and soup is thick, stirring occasionally. Remove pork; allow to cool. Cut into chunks, discarding bone and fat. Return meat to pan; heat through. **Yield:** 20-26 servings (6-1/2 quarts).

Mixed Legume Soup

Marlene Penno, Eden, Manitoba

My brother began growing legumes a few years back, so I've been trying many different recipes. Everyone enjoys the comforting old-fashioned flavor of this vegetable soup.

> 1/2 **pound sliced bacon, diced**
> 1 **cup dry lentils**
> 3/4 **cup dry yellow split peas**
> 3/4 **cup dry green split peas**
> 3 **quarts beef broth**
> 1 **large onion, chopped**
> 1 **cup diced celery**
> 1 **cup diced carrots**
> 1/4 **teaspoon pepper**

In a Dutch oven or soup kettle, cook bacon until crisp; drain. Add all remaining ingredients and bring to a boil. Reduce heat; cover and simmer for 1 to 1-1/2 hours or until the lentils and peas are tender. **Yield:** 12-14 servings (about 3-1/2 quarts).

> **INTERCHANGEABLE INGREDIENTS.** Great northern beans, which stand up well to long slow cooking, can easily be substituted for other white beans—such as navy beans—in most soup recipes.

Sweet Succotash Chili

Kristine Floren, Cranbury, New Jersey

This recipe deliciously combines two of my family's favorite dishes—succotash and chili. I often make it on a weekend for meals throughout the week.

    1 pound dry lima beans
    2 pounds ground beef
    4 medium onions, chopped
    3 tablespoons olive *or* vegetable oil
1/4 cup paprika
    3 tablespoons ground cumin
    3 garlic cloves, minced
    1 teaspoon salt
    1 can (49-1/2 ounces) chicken broth
    1 can (28 ounces) crushed tomatoes
    2 packages (10 ounces *each*) frozen whole kernel corn

Place beans in a Dutch oven or soup kettle; cover with water. Bring to a boil; boil for 2 minutes. Remove from the heat; let stand for 1 hour. Drain beans and discard liquid. In a 6-qt. Dutch oven or soup kettle, cook beef and onions until beef is browned and onions are tender; drain. Add beans, paprika, cumin, garlic and salt. Stir in chicken broth and tomatoes; bring to a boil. Reduce heat; cover and simmer for 1 hour. Add corn; cover and simmer for 1 hour or until beans are tender. **Yield:** 12-16 servings (4 quarts). **Editor's Note:** For added flavor, use hot Hungarian paprika or add 1/2 teaspoon hot pepper sauce.

Dilly Beef Barley Soup

Phyllis Kramer, Little Compton, Rhode Island

My mother and grandmother were wonderful cooks who taught me to create foods that were both attractive and full-flavored. This soup from Mom meets those requirements nicely.

✓ This tasty dish uses less sugar, salt and fat. Recipe includes *Diabetic Exchanges*.

3/4 cup dry baby lima beans
1/2 cup dry yellow split peas
1/2 cup dry green split peas
    4 medium carrots, sliced
    4 celery ribs, sliced
    3 quarts water
    2 pounds boneless beef short ribs, cut into 1-inch cubes
    2 medium onions, chopped
3/4 cup medium pearl barley
    5 chicken bouillon cubes
    4 medium potatoes, peeled and cubed
    1 tablespoon chopped fresh dill *or* 1 teaspoon dill weed
1-1/2 teaspoons salt, optional
1/4 teaspoon pepper

In a Dutch oven or soup kettle, combine beans, peas, carrots, celery and water; bring to a boil. Reduce heat; cover and simmer for 1-1/2 hours. Add beef, onions, barley and

bouillon; bring to a boil. Skim foam. Reduce heat; cover and simmer for 2 hours or until meat and beans are tender. Add potatoes and simmer for 20 minutes. Add dill, salt if desired and pepper; cook for 5 minutes. **Yield:** 15 servings (3-3/4 quarts). **Diabetic Exchanges:** One 1-cup serving (prepared with low-sodium bouillon and without salt) equals 2 starch, 2 meat; also, 272 calories, 54 mg sodium, 44 mg cholesterol, 28 gm carbohydrate, 20 gm protein, 9 gm fat.

Lentil and Brown Rice Soup

Janis Plourde, Smooth Rock Falls, Ontario

The first time I made this soup, I thought our teenage son would turn up his nose. Much to my delight—and surprise—he loved every bite! I know you will, too.

    2 quarts water
3/4 cup dry lentils
1/2 cup uncooked brown rice
    1 envelope onion soup mix
    1 can (14-1/2 ounces) diced tomatoes, undrained
    1 medium carrot, diced
1/2 cup diced celery
    1 tablespoon minced fresh parsley
    4 chicken bouillon cubes
1/2 teaspoon dried basil
1/2 teaspoon dried oregano
1/2 teaspoon salt
1/2 teaspoon pepper
1/4 teaspoon dried thyme
    1 tablespoon cider vinegar, optional

In a Dutch oven or soup kettle, combine all ingredients except vinegar; bring to a boil. Reduce heat; cover and simmer for 35-45 minutes or until lentils and rice are tender, stirring occasionally. Stir in vinegar if desired. **Yield:** 12-14 servings (3-1/2 quarts).

Vegetarian Chili

Polly Habel, Monson, Massachusetts

With the abundance of beans, vegetables and flavor in this spicy chili, you'll never miss the meat! My family has been enjoying this meal for many years.

1/2 cup chopped onion
    1 garlic clove, minced
    1 tablespoon cooking oil
    1 cup chopped carrot
    1 cup chopped celery
3/4 cup chopped green pepper
1/4 cup chopped green onions
    1 cup chopped fresh mushrooms
    1 can (6 ounces) pitted ripe olives, drained and chopped
    1 can (6 ounces) tomato paste
4-1/2 cups water
    1 can (15 to 16 ounces) kidney beans, rinsed and drained

1 can (15 ounces) tomato sauce
1 medium tomato, chopped
1 can (4 ounces) chopped green chilies
3 tablespoons chili powder
1 teaspoon ground cumin
1 teaspoon salt
1/2 teaspoon crushed red pepper flakes, optional
1/4 teaspoon cayenne pepper, optional

In a Dutch oven or soup kettle, saute onion and garlic in oil for 5 minutes. Add carrot, celery, green pepper and green onions; cook for 7 minutes or until crisp-tender. Add mushrooms, olives and tomato paste; blend well. Add remaining ingredients; bring to a boil. Reduce heat; cover and simmer for at least 3 hours. **Yield:** 8-10 servings (2-1/2 quarts).

Sausage Bean Chowder

Phyllis Heberger, Fishers Landing, New York

When the first hint of cooler weather appears at the end of summer, my husband always asks, "Isn't it time to make some soup?" It's his subtle hint for me to make this special chowder!

1 pound bulk pork sausage
2 cans (15 to 16 ounces *each*) kidney beans, rinsed and drained
1 can (28 ounces) diced tomatoes, undrained
1 can (32 ounces) tomato juice
1 cup chopped onion
1 cup chopped green pepper
1 cup diced peeled potatoes
1 teaspoon seasoned salt
1/2 teaspoon garlic salt
1/2 teaspoon dried thyme
1/8 teaspoon pepper
1 bay leaf

In a Dutch oven or soup kettle, brown sausage until no longer pink; drain. Add remaining ingredients; bring to a boil. Reduce heat; cover and simmer for 2 hours. Remove bay leaf. **Yield:** 12-14 servings (about 3 quarts).

Country-Style Stew

LaDonna Reed, Ponca City, Oklahoma

I created this recipe when my husband and I were married almost 20 years ago. As a new bride, I was delighted with the delicious results. This is still our favorite stew.

2 pounds ground beef
1 can (32 ounces) tomato juice
1 quart water
4 medium carrots, sliced
1 large onion, diced
2 cups frozen sliced okra
1-1/2 cups shredded cabbage
1-1/2 cups diced celery
1 cup frozen green beans
1 cup frozen peas

2 cans (14-1/2 ounces *each*) diced tomatoes, undrained
1 can (16 ounces) great northern beans, rinsed and drained
1 can (15-1/2 ounces) black-eyed peas, rinsed and drained
1 can (15-1/4 ounces) lima beans, rinsed and drained
1 can (11 ounces) Mexican-style corn
5 beef bouillon cubes
1 teaspoon seasoned salt
1/2 teaspoon dried oregano
1/2 teaspoon garlic powder
1/2 teaspoon pepper
1/4 teaspoon celery salt

In a Dutch oven or soup kettle, brown beef; drain. Add remaining ingredients; bring to a boil. Reduce heat; cover and simmer for 2 hours or until vegetables are tender. **Yield:** 18-22 servings (5-1/2 quarts).

Black Bean Soup

Audrey Thibodeau, Mesa, Arizona

Here's an economical meal that doesn't skimp on flavor. Hearty black beans make up for the meat, and the peppers add just the right splash of color.

✓ This tasty dish uses less sugar, salt and fat. Recipe includes *Diabetic Exchanges*.

1 pound dry black beans
1-1/2 quarts chicken broth
1 quart water
1-1/2 cups chopped onion
1 cup thinly sliced celery
1 large carrot, chopped
1/2 cup *each* chopped green, yellow and sweet red peppers
2 garlic cloves, minced
3 tablespoons olive *or* vegetable oil
1/4 cup tomato paste
3 tablespoons minced fresh parsley
1 tablespoon chopped fresh oregano *or* 1 teaspoon dried oregano
1 tablespoon chopped fresh thyme *or* 1 teaspoon dried thyme
1-1/2 teaspoons ground cumin
1 teaspoon pepper
3/4 teaspoon salt, optional
3 bay leaves
Chopped tomato, optional

In a Dutch oven or soup kettle, combine beans, broth and water; bring to a boil. Reduce heat; cover and simmer for 1-1/2 hours or until beans are tender. Meanwhile, in a large skillet, saute onion, celery, carrot, peppers and garlic in oil until tender. Add the next seven ingredients; mix well. Add to beans along with bay leaves; bring to a boil. Reduce heat; cover and simmer for 1 hour. Remove bay leaves before serving. Garnish with chopped tomato if desired. **Yield:** 12 servings (3 quarts). **Diabetic Exchanges:** One 1-cup serving (prepared with low-sodium broth and tomato paste and without salt) equals 1-1/2 starch, 1 vegetable, 1 fat; also, 187 calories, 48 mg sodium, trace cholesterol, 30 gm carbohydrate, 11 gm protein, 4 gm fat.

Meat & Vegetable Soups

From chicken dumpling and beef barley to hearty potato and marvelous minestrone, these kettle creations put down-home cooking right at your fingertips.

Spicy Zucchini Soup

Catherine Johnston, Stafford, New York
(PICTURED AT LEFT)

My files are overflowing with recipes I keep meaning to try. So when I encountered a bumper crop of zucchini, I finally reached for this recipe. We look forward to it each summer.

- 1 pound bulk Italian sausage
- 3 cans (28 ounces *each*) diced tomatoes, undrained
- 3 cans (14-1/2 ounces *each*) beef broth
- 2 pounds zucchini, diced
- 2 medium green peppers, diced
- 2 cups thinly sliced celery
- 1 cup chopped onion
- 2 teaspoons Italian seasoning
- 1 teaspoon dried basil
- 1 teaspoon dried oregano
- 1 teaspoon salt
- 1/2 teaspoon sugar
- 1/4 teaspoon pepper
- 1/4 teaspoon garlic powder
- 3 cups cooked macaroni

In a Dutch oven or soup kettle, brown and crumble sausage; drain. Add tomatoes, broth, zucchini, green peppers, celery, onion and seasonings; bring to a boil. Reduce heat; cover and simmer for 1-1/4 to 1-1/2 hours or until vegetables are tender. Add macaroni; heat through. **Yield:** 14-16 servings (4 quarts).

Turkey Soup with Slickers

Christine Fleeman, Salem, Oregon
(PICTURED AT LEFT)

Our grandson calls this "bone soup" because I make it with Thanksgiving turkey bones! The recipe for slickers—half dumplings, half egg noodles—comes from my grandmother.

- 1 leftover turkey carcass (from a 14-pound turkey)
- 5 quarts water
- 1/2 cup chopped onion
- 1/2 cup chopped carrot
- 1/2 cup chopped celery
- 3 tablespoons dried parsley flakes

SOUPER SUPPER. *Pictured at left, top to bottom: Spicy Zucchini Soup, Turkey Soup with Slickers and Ravioli Soup (all recipes on this page).*

- 2 teaspoons salt
- 1/2 teaspoon pepper
- 2 bay leaves
- 1 egg
- 2-1/2 to 3 cups all-purpose flour
- 1/2 teaspoon dill weed
- 1/2 teaspoon poultry seasoning
- 1 cup frozen peas

Place the first nine ingredients in a Dutch oven or soup kettle. Bring to a boil; skim fat. Reduce heat; cover and simmer for 2 hours. Remove bay leaves. Remove carcass; allow to cool. Remove turkey from bones and cut into bite-size pieces; set aside. Pour 1 cup of the broth into a bowl; add egg and beat. Stir in enough flour to form a stiff dough. Turn onto a floured surface; knead 8-10 times or until smooth. Divide dough in half; roll out each piece to 1/8-in. thickness. Cut into 2-in. x 1/4-in. strips. Add dill and poultry seasoning to remaining broth; bring to a gentle boil. Drop slickers into broth; cover and cook for 30-35 minutes or until tender. Add peas and reserved turkey; heat through. **Yield:** 8-10 servings (2-1/2 quarts).

Ravioli Soup

Shelley Way, Douglas, Wyoming
(PICTURED AT LEFT)

My family's love of pasta dishes inspired me to create this thick and hearty soup. People always rave about the rich tomato base and tender pockets of cheese-filled ravioli.

- 1 pound ground beef
- 2 cups water
- 1 can (28 ounces) crushed tomatoes
- 1 can (14-1/2 ounces) beef broth
- 1 can (6 ounces) tomato paste
- 1-1/2 cups chopped onion
- 1/4 cup minced fresh parsley
- 2 garlic cloves, minced
- 3/4 teaspoon dried basil
- 1/2 teaspoon dried oregano
- 1/2 teaspoon onion salt
- 1/2 teaspoon sugar
- 1/2 teaspoon salt
- 1/4 teaspoon pepper
- 1/4 teaspoon dried thyme
- 1/4 cup grated Parmesan cheese
- 1 package (9 ounces) refrigerated cheese ravioli

In a Dutch oven or soup kettle, brown beef; drain. Add the next 14 ingredients; bring to a boil. Reduce heat; cover and simmer for 30 minutes. Stir in the Parmesan cheese. Cook ravioli according to package directions; drain and add to soup. **Yield:** 8-10 servings (2-1/2 quarts).

Sage 'n' Rosemary Pork Stew

Gail Dvorchak, Smock, Pennsylvania

This stew satisfies the appetites of my husband and son, who are real meat-and-potatoes men. It's easy on the family budget, yet is special enough to serve to guests.

3 to 4 pounds pork shoulder, trimmed and cut
    into 3/4-inch cubes
1 tablespoon cooking oil
1 can (49-1/2 ounces) chicken broth
1-1/2 cups water
3/4 cup chopped onion
1-1/4 teaspoons dried rosemary, crushed
3/4 teaspoon salt
1/2 teaspoon dried sage
1/2 teaspoon pepper
4 cups cubed red potatoes
1 package (10 ounces) frozen cut green beans
1-1/2 cups frozen lima beans
1 teaspoon Dijon mustard
1/3 cup all-purpose flour
1/2 cup half-and-half cream

In a Dutch oven or soup kettle over medium heat, brown pork in oil; drain. Add broth, water, onion, rosemary, salt, sage and pepper; bring to a boil. Reduce heat and simmer, uncovered, for 40-45 minutes or until pork is almost tender. Add potatoes, beans and mustard; mix well. Return to a boil; reduce heat and simmer, uncovered, for 40-45 minutes or until vegetables and pork are tender. Combine flour and cream; stir until smooth. Add to stew. Bring to a boil; boil for 2 minutes, stirring constantly. **Yield:** 10-12 servings (3 quarts).

Herbed Fish Soup

Geraldine De Iure, Calgary, Alberta

My husband loves fish prepared in variety of ways, so it's no surprise this soup has become one of his most-requested meals. I think you'll also enjoy its comforting flavor.

✓ This tasty dish uses less sugar, salt and fat. Recipe includes *Diabetic Exchanges*.

1 pound frozen fish fillets (cod, haddock, etc.),
    partially thawed
2 bacon strips, diced, optional
1 cup diced carrots
1 cup sliced fresh mushrooms
1 medium onion, sliced
1 garlic clove, minced
2 tablespoons cooking oil
1/2 cup all-purpose flour
1/4 teaspoon dried thyme
1/4 teaspoon dill weed
Dash pepper
4 cups chicken broth
1 bay leaf
1-1/2 cups frozen cut green beans

Cut fish into bite-size pieces; set aside. Cook bacon in a 3-qt. saucepan until crisp. Remove to paper towels to drain. Discard drippings. In the same pan, saute carrots, mushrooms, onion and garlic in oil until onion is tender. Stir in flour, thyme, dill and pepper until smooth. Stir in broth; bring to a boil. Add bay leaf. Reduce heat; cover and simmer for 12-15 minutes or until carrots are tender. Add fish and beans. Simmer, uncovered, for 5 minutes or until fish is opaque and flakes easily. Remove bay leaf. Garnish individual servings with bacon. **Yield:** 7 servings (about 2 quarts). **Diabetic Exchanges:** One 1-cup serving (prepared with low-sodium broth and without bacon) equals 1 meat, 1 vegetable, 1/2 starch; also, 143 calories, 76 mg sodium, 25 mg cholesterol, 13 gm carbohydrate, 14 gm protein, 4 gm fat.

Southern Garden Soup

Leslie Owens, Poplar Bluff, Missouri

I created this recipe as a way to combine all of my family's favorite produce into one dish. No matter how much I make, this soup never lasts too long around our house.

6-1/4 cups water, *divided*
5 chicken bouillon cubes
2 cups cauliflowerets
1/2 cup small boiling onions
2 pounds fresh asparagus, cut into 1/2-inch pieces
1 can (8 ounces) sliced water chestnuts, drained
1 cup chopped fresh spinach
1/2 cup chopped chives
1/2 teaspoon dried marjoram
1/2 teaspoon salt
1/8 to 1/4 teaspoon pepper
1/8 teaspoon ground nutmeg
3 tablespoons cornstarch

In a 3-qt. saucepan, bring 6 cups water and bouillon to a boil. Add cauliflower and onions; cover and cook for 5 minutes. Add the next eight ingredients; cover and cook for 5 minutes or until asparagus is tender. Dissolve cornstarch in remaining water; stir into soup. Bring to a boil; boil for 2 minutes, stirring constantly. Serve immediately. **Yield:** 8-10 servings (2-1/4 quarts).

Beef Tortellini Soup

Tammy Nadeau, Presque Isle, Maine

Because of its rich spicy flavor, this soup has been a favorite in our home for years. I think you'll agree the tortellini adds an interesting twist.

1 pound ground beef
7 cups beef broth
2 cans (14-1/2 ounces *each*) stewed tomatoes
3/4 cup ketchup
3/4 cup thinly sliced carrots
3/4 cup thinly sliced celery
3/4 cup finely chopped onion

1 tablespoon dried basil
1-1/2 teaspoons seasoned salt
1 teaspoon sugar
1/4 teaspoon pepper
4 bay leaves
1-1/2 cups dried cheese-filled tortellini
Grated Parmesan cheese, optional

In a Dutch oven or soup kettle, brown beef; drain. Add the next 11 ingredients; bring to a boil. Reduce heat; cover and simmer for 30 minutes. Add tortellini; cook for 20-30 minutes or until tender. Remove bay leaves. Garnish individual servings with Parmesan cheese if desired. **Yield:** 10-12 servings (3-1/4 quarts).

Rainy Day Soup

Laine Fengarinas, Palm Harbor, Florida

One rainy day a few years back, this comforting soup was served at a local arts and crafts bazaar. Now family members who are feeling under the weather request it.

✓ **This tasty dish uses less sugar, salt and fat. Recipe includes** *Diabetic Exchanges.*

   1 pound ground turkey
   1 can (46 ounces) V-8 juice
   1 jar (16 ounces) thick and chunky salsa
   1 can (14-1/2 ounces) chicken broth
   1 can (15 to 16 ounces) kidney beans, rinsed and drained
   1 package (10 ounces) frozen mixed vegetables
   4 cups shredded cabbage
   1 cup chopped onion
1/2 cup cubed peeled potatoes
1/3 cup medium pearl barley

In a Dutch oven or soup kettle coated with nonstick cooking spray, brown turkey over medium heat; drain. Add remaining ingredients; bring to a boil. Reduce heat; cover and simmer for 60-70 minutes or until the vegetables and barley are tender. **Yield:** 12 servings (3 quarts). **Diabetic Exchanges:** One 1-cup serving (prepared with ground turkey breast and low-sodium broth and V-8) equals 2 vegetable, 1 very lean meat, 1 starch; also, 168 calories, 400 mg sodium, 12 mg cholesterol, 26 gm carbohydrate, 15 gm protein, 1 gm fat.

Zesty Tortilla Soup

Tammy Leiber, Navasota, Texas

Because everyone in our family enjoys Mexican food, we especially find this soup appealing. It has just the right amount of "zip" without being overwhelming.

   1 medium onion, chopped
   2 garlic cloves, minced
   2 tablespoons cooking oil
   2 pounds beef stew meat, cut into 1-inch cubes
   2 cups water
   1 can (14-1/2 ounces) stewed tomatoes

   1 can (10 ounces) diced tomatoes with green chilies, undrained
   1 can (10-3/4 ounces) condensed tomato soup, undiluted
   1 can (10-1/2 ounces) beef broth
   1 can (10-1/2 ounces) chicken broth
   1 tablespoon Worcestershire sauce
   1 teaspoon ground cumin
   1 teaspoon chili powder
   1 teaspoon salt
   1 teaspoon lemon-pepper seasoning
1/2 teaspoon hot pepper sauce
 10 corn tortillas (6 inches)
Shredded cheddar cheese, sour cream and sliced green onions, optional

In a Dutch oven or soup kettle, saute onion and garlic in oil until onion is tender. Add the next 13 ingredients; bring to a boil. Reduce heat; cover and simmer for 1-1/2 hours or until beef is tender. Tear tortillas into bite-size pieces; add to soup. Simmer, uncovered, for 10 minutes; let stand for 5 minutes. Garnish individual servings with cheese, sour cream and onions if desired. **Yield:** 10 servings (2-1/2 quarts).

> **BETTER BROTH.** Substitute one-third to one-half of the water in your vegetable soup recipe with V-8 juice. It adds a richer, more robust flavor.

Shaker Herb 'n' Meatball Soup

Carolyn Milke, North Canton, Connecticut

Filling soups like this make it easy to get through cold New England winters. The meatballs are extra-easy because they cook in the soup…there's no need for browning beforehand.

   2 quarts beef broth
   2 cans (14-1/2 ounces *each*) diced tomatoes, undrained
   3 medium potatoes, peeled and cubed
   3 medium carrots, sliced
   1 cup shredded cabbage
   1 large onion, chopped
1/2 cup chopped fresh parsley
   6 whole peppercorns
1/2 teaspoon dried marjoram
1/2 teaspoon celery seed
1/2 teaspoon dried thyme
1/8 teaspoon ground cumin
   1 pound lean ground beef
1/2 cup soft bread crumbs
   1 egg, beaten
   1 teaspoon Worcestershire sauce
1/4 teaspoon salt
1/8 teaspoon pepper

In a Dutch oven or soup kettle, combine the first 12 ingredients; bring to a boil. Reduce heat; cover and simmer for 1 hour. In a bowl, combine beef, bread crumbs, egg, Worcestershire sauce, salt and pepper. Shape into 1-in. balls; drop into soup. Cover and simmer for 2 hours. **Yield:** 12-14 servings (3-1/2 quarts).

Tomato Spinach Soup

Erna Ketchum, San Jose, California
(PICTURED AT LEFT)

I first sampled this soup in a local restaurant. After some experimenting with ingredients and seasonings, I finally found a combination my family preferred to the original.

- 2 large yellow onions, cubed
- 2 tablespoons olive *or* vegetable oil
- 1 can (28 ounces) diced tomatoes, undrained
- 1 quart water
- 4 beef bouillon cubes
- 1 cup sliced fresh mushrooms
- 3/4 teaspoon Italian seasoning
- 1/2 teaspoon dried basil
- 1/2 teaspoon salt
- 1/8 teaspoon pepper
- 4 cups loosely packed spinach leaves

Grated Parmesan *or* shredded cheddar cheese, optional

In a Dutch oven or soup kettle, saute onions in oil over medium heat for 10 minutes or until tender. Add the next eight ingredients; bring to a boil. Reduce heat; cover and simmer for 30 minutes. Stir in spinach; simmer for 3-5 minutes or until tender. Garnish individual servings with cheese if desired. **Yield:** 8-10 servings (2-1/2 quarts).

Green Bean Soup

Elvira Beckenhauer, Omaha, Nebraska
(PICTURED AT LEFT)

This soup has been passed down for generations beginning with my great-grandmother. I make it often, especially when I can use homegrown beans, carrots, onions and potatoes.

✓ **This tasty dish uses less sugar, salt and fat. Recipe includes** *Diabetic Exchanges.*

- 1 quart water
- 2 cups fresh green beans, cut into 2-inch pieces
- 1-1/2 cups cubed peeled potatoes
- 1 cup cubed fully cooked ham
- 1/2 cup thinly sliced carrot
- 1 medium onion, diced
- 1 bay leaf
- 1 sprig fresh parsley
- 1 sprig fresh savory *or* 1/4 teaspoon dried savory
- 1 beef bouillon cube
- 1/4 teaspoon pepper
- 1/2 teaspoon salt, optional

In a 2-qt. saucepan, combine water, beans, potatoes, ham, carrot, onion, bay leaf, parsley, savory, bouillon, pepper and salt if desired; bring to a boil. Reduce heat; cover and simmer for 20 minutes or until vegetables are tender. Before

---

EAT YOUR VEGGIES. *Pictured at left, top to bottom: Tomato Spinach Soup and Green Bean Soup (both recipes on this page).*

---

serving, remove bay leaf and parsley and savory sprigs. **Yield:** 6 servings. **Diabetic Exchanges:** One 1-cup serving (prepared with low-fat ham and low-sodium bouillon and without salt) equals 1 lean meat, 1 vegetable, 1/2 starch; also, 107 calories, 175 mg sodium, 19 mg cholesterol, 12 gm carbohydrate, 9 gm protein, 2 gm fat.

Turkey Barley Soup

Jodi Jeude, Carbondale, Colorado

I originally created this recipe as a way to use leftover Thanksgiving turkey. I think you'll agree it's too good to serve only once a year! It makes a hearty meal with home-made bread.

- 1-1/2 cups sliced carrots
- 1-1/2 cups sliced fresh mushrooms
- 1 cup thinly sliced celery
- 1 cup chopped onion
- 2 tablespoons cooking oil
- 9 cups turkey broth
- 2 cups cubed cooked turkey
- 1/2 cup medium pearl barley
- 2 bay leaves
- 1/4 teaspoon pepper

In a 3-qt. saucepan, saute carrots, mushrooms, celery and onion in oil for 20 minutes or until tender. Add remaining ingredients; bring to a boil. Reduce heat; cover and simmer for 50-60 minutes or until barley is tender. Remove bay leaves before serving. **Yield:** 6-8 servings (2 quarts).

Country Tomato-Rice Soup

Kimberly Owen, Burnt Prairie, Illinois

When my husband comes home after being on the road, I like to have a hot pot of this traditional soup waiting for him. It's a wonderful "welcome home" meal on a cold winter day.

- 1-1/2 pounds round steak, cut into 1-inch cubes
- 1 tablespoon cooking oil
- 2 quarts water
- 1 can (28 ounces) diced tomatoes, undrained
- 3 beef bouillon cubes
- 1 teaspoon dried thyme
- 1/2 teaspoon dried marjoram
- 1/2 teaspoon garlic salt
- 1/2 teaspoon pepper
- 5 medium carrots, cut into 1/2-inch pieces
- 5 celery ribs, cut into 1/2-inch pieces
- 1 medium onion, chopped
- 1/2 cup uncooked long grain rice

In a Dutch oven or soup kettle, brown beef in oil. Add water; bring to a boil. Reduce heat; cover and simmer for 30 minutes. Add tomatoes, bouillon and seasonings; cover and simmer for 1 hour. Add carrots, celery, onion and rice. Simmer for 30-40 minutes or until beef and rice are tender. **Yield:** 14 servings (3-1/2 quarts).

Country Vegetable Soup

Pauline Morgan, Igo, California
(PICTURED ON FRONT COVER)

Years ago when money was scarce, I often relied on this economical standby. I sometimes added roast beef when leftovers were available.

- 2 quarts water
- 2 cans (10-1/2 ounces *each*) condensed French onion soup, undiluted
- 1 can (28 ounces) diced tomatoes, undrained
- 3 cups chopped zucchini
- 1 cup diced carrots
- 1 cup sliced celery
- 1 cup diced peeled potato
- 1/2 cup chopped fresh parsley
- 1 garlic clove, minced
- 1 teaspoon beef bouillon granules
- 1 bay leaf
- 1/2 teaspoon *each* dried basil, thyme and marjoram
- 1/4 teaspoon pepper
- 8 bacon strips, cooked and crumbled
- 2 cups broken uncooked wide egg noodles
- 2 cans (15 ounces *each*) butter beans, rinsed and drained
- 1/4 cup grated Parmesan cheese
- 4 cups cubed cooked roast beef, optional

In a Dutch oven or soup kettle, combine water, soup, tomatoes, zucchini, carrots, celery, potato, parsley, garlic, bouillon and seasonings; bring to a boil. Reduce heat; cover and simmer for 1 hour. Add bacon and noodles; simmer for 15 minutes, stirring frequently. Stir in beans, Parmesan cheese and beef if desired; heat through. Remove bay leaf before serving. **Yield:** 18-20 servings (5 quarts).

Potato Onion Soup

Mary Brombaugh, Mt. Pleasant, Iowa

Around our house, soups are always a hearty standby for supper. In this recipe, ground beef and potatoes give a new twist to traditional onion soup.

- 2 large onions, chopped
- 3 tablespoons cooking oil
- 1 pound ground beef
- 1 quart water
- 2 medium potatoes, peeled and diced
- 2 tablespoons red wine vinegar
- 1 tablespoon beef bouillon granules
- 1 teaspoon salt
- 1/2 teaspoon pepper
- 2 tablespoons minced fresh parsley
- 1 cup (4 ounces) shredded Swiss cheese
- 2 tablespoons grated Parmesan cheese
- 7 slices French bread (1 inch thick)

In a Dutch oven or soup kettle over medium heat, saute onions in oil for 10-12 minutes or until golden brown. Remove and set aside. In the same kettle, brown beef; drain. Add the water, potatoes, vinegar, bouillon, salt, pepper and reserved onions; bring to a boil. Reduce heat; cover and simmer for 30 minutes or until potatoes are tender. Stir in parsley. Ladle into ovenproof bowls. Top each with Swiss cheese, a slice of bread and Parmesan cheese. Bake at 375° for 10 minutes or until cheeses are bubbly. **Yield:** 7 servings.

Mulligatawny Soup

Esther Nafziger, La Junta, Colorado

One taste of this traditional curry-flavored soup, and folks will know it didn't come from a can! This soup fills the kitchen with a wonderful aroma while it's simmering.

- 1 medium tart apple, peeled and diced
- 1/4 cup *each* chopped carrot, celery and onion
- 1/4 cup butter *or* margarine
- 1/3 cup all-purpose flour
- 1 teaspoon curry powder
- 1/2 teaspoon sugar
- 1/2 teaspoon salt
- 1/8 teaspoon pepper
- 1/8 teaspoon ground mace
- 6 cups chicken *or* turkey broth
- 1 cup cubed cooked chicken *or* turkey
- 1 medium tomato, peeled, seeded and chopped
- 1/2 cup chopped green pepper
- 2 whole cloves
- 1 tablespoon minced fresh parsley
- 1 cup cooked rice

In a Dutch oven or soup kettle, saute apple, carrot, celery and onion in butter for 5 minutes or until tender. Add flour, curry, sugar, salt, pepper and mace; stir until smooth. Gradually add broth. Bring to a boil; boil for 2 minutes, stirring constantly. Add chicken, tomato, green pepper, cloves and parsley; return to a boil. Reduce heat; cover and simmer for 20-30 minutes. Add rice; simmer for 5 minutes or until heated through. Remove cloves before serving. **Yield:** 6-8 servings (about 2 quarts).

Mexican Beef Soup

Trudi Peters, Aurora, Oregon

As owners of a nursery, we entertain salespeople quite a bit. I like to prepare this spicy soup as a warm way to welcome them into our home. It tastes great with fresh corn bread.

- 1/2 pound ground beef
- 1 medium onion, diced
- 1 cup shredded cooked roast beef
- 3 cans (14-1/2 ounces *each*) diced tomatoes, undrained
- 2 cans (14-1/2 ounces *each*) beef broth
- 1 can (4 ounces) chopped green chilies
- 1/2 cup pitted ripe olives, halved
- 1-1/2 teaspoons ground cumin

1 teaspoon chili powder
1/2 teaspoon dried oregano
1/4 teaspoon cayenne pepper
1-1/2 cups frozen whole kernel corn
1 cup frozen cut green beans
Salt and pepper to taste

In a Dutch oven or soup kettle, brown beef and onion; drain. Add the next nine ingredients; bring to a boil. Reduce heat; cover and simmer for 2 hours. Add corn and beans; cover and simmer for 15 minutes. Season with salt and pepper. **Yield:** 8-10 servings (2-3/4 quarts).

Turkey Noodle Soup

Karen Chinigo, Lisbon, Connecticut

I usually try three new recipes a week. My wonderful husband willingly samples everything I make…even if it is a flop! This old-fashioned soup is one of his favorites.

1 leftover turkey carcass (from a 12- to 14-pound turkey)
3-1/2 quarts water
4 chicken bouillon cubes
1 large onion, halved
4 whole peppercorns
2 bay leaves
1 teaspoon poultry seasoning
1 teaspoon seasoned salt
1/2 to 3/4 teaspoon pepper
1 cup chopped carrots
1 cup chopped celery
1 medium potato, peeled and diced
1/2 cup chopped onion
1 medium turnip, peeled and diced, optional
1 cup uncooked egg noodles

Place the first nine ingredients in a soup kettle or Dutch oven; bring to a boil. Reduce heat; cover and simmer for 1 hour. Strain broth; discard onion, peppercorns and bay leaves. Remove carcass; allow to cool. Remove turkey from bones and cut into bite-size pieces; set aside. Add carrots, celery, potato, chopped onion and turnip if desired to broth; bring to a boil. Reduce heat; cover and simmer for 20 minutes or until the vegetables are tender. Add noodles and reserved turkey. Return to a boil; cook, uncovered, for 10 minutes or until noodles are tender. **Yield:** 12-14 servings (3-1/2 quarts).

Chunky Fish Chowder

Cyndi Reason, Ruidoso, New Mexico

Our kids refused to try this soup when I first served it, but then they saw how much their father and I were enjoying it! I serve it with salad and bread for a complete meal.

3 bacon strips, diced
1 large onion, chopped
1 garlic clove, minced
1 can (14-1/2 ounces) stewed tomatoes
1 quart water

3/4 teaspoon ground cumin
1/2 teaspoon salt
1/4 teaspoon ground turmeric
Dash pepper
2 medium potatoes, peeled and diced
1 pound frozen cod, thawed and cut into 3/4-inch pieces
1 package (10 ounces) frozen whole kernel corn, thawed
1 tablespoon cider vinegar
GARLIC BUTTER:
1/2 cup butter *or* margarine, softened
2 tablespoons chopped fresh parsley
2 tablespoons lemon juice
2 garlic cloves, minced
Fish-shaped crackers, optional

In a 3-qt. saucepan, cook bacon until crisp. Remove with a slotted spoon and set aside. Saute onion and garlic in drippings until tender. Add tomatoes, water, cumin, salt, turmeric and pepper; bring to a boil. Add potatoes; simmer for 15 minutes or until tender. Add fish, corn and vinegar; cook for 10 minutes or until fish is opaque and flakes easily. Stir in bacon. For garlic butter, beat butter, parsley, lemon juice and garlic in a small mixing bowl until fluffy. Top each serving of soup with a dollop of garlic butter; garnish with crackers if desired. **Yield:** 8 servings (2 quarts).

Grandma's Harvest Soup

Ronald Desjardins, St. Andrews West, Ontario

I have fond memories of eating Grandma's soup when I was a child. Now I give my wife a break in the kitchen by making this soup every once in a while. It tastes just like home!

1 smoked ham shank *or* ham hocks (1-1/2 pounds)
3 quarts water
1 tablespoon beef bouillon granules
6 medium potatoes, peeled and chopped
6 medium carrots, sliced
2 medium onions, chopped
1/2 medium head cabbage, chopped
1 small turnip, diced
1-1/2 teaspoons salt
1/4 teaspoon pepper

Place ham shank, water and bouillon in a Dutch oven or soup kettle; bring to a boil. Reduce heat; cover and simmer for 1-1/2 hours. Remove shank; allow to cool. Add potatoes, carrots, onions, cabbage and turnip to broth; cover and simmer for 1 hour or until vegetables are tender. Using a potato masher, coarsely mash vegetables. Remove meat from shank; cut into bite-size pieces and add to soup. Stir in salt and pepper; heat through. **Yield:** 16-18 servings (4-1/4 quarts).

SKIMMING OFF THE TOP. Before freezing homemade soup, refrigerate it until the fat rises to the surface. Skim off the fat. Line individual soup bowls with plastic freezer bags; add soup and freeze. When solid, remove the bag from the bowl. These individual servings will stack nicely in your freezer.

Taco Soup

Tammie Lightner, Bynum, Montana
(PICTURED AT LEFT)

This is a fun dish to serve when entertaining. Folks can fill their bowls with whatever garnish ingredients they like and then top it with the soup. It's like a taco in a bowl!

- 2 cans (28 ounces *each*) diced tomatoes, undrained
- 1 quart water
- 1 tablespoon chicken bouillon granules
- 1-1/2 teaspoons chili powder
- 1/2 teaspoon ground cumin
- 8 ounces Monterey Jack *or* cheddar cheese, cubed
- 1 medium tomato, chopped
- 1 medium avocado, chopped
- 1 can (2-1/4 ounces) sliced ripe olives, drained
- 1/4 cup sliced green onions
- 3 cups tortilla chips

In a blender or food processor, puree tomatoes until smooth; pour into a 3-qt. saucepan. Add the water, bouillon, chili powder and cumin; bring to a boil. Reduce heat; cover and simmer for 20 minutes. In soup bowls, layer cheese, tomato, avocado, olives, onions and chips. Top with hot soup and serve immediately. **Yield:** 8 servings (2 quarts).

Meatless Minestrone

Margaret Shauers, Great Bend, Kansas

This recipe for traditional Italian soup may have quite a few ingredients, but it couldn't be easier to prepare. Plus it's packed with flavor and nutrition.

✓ This tasty dish uses less sugar, salt and fat. Recipe includes *Diabetic Exchanges*.

- 1 medium onion, chopped
- 3/4 cup sliced celery
- 2 medium carrots, sliced
- 3 tablespoons butter *or* margarine
- 2 cans (14-1/2 ounces *each*) stewed tomatoes
- 2 cans (14-1/2 ounces *each*) chicken broth
- 2 cups water
- 4 cups shredded cabbage
- 1 medium potato, peeled and diced
- 2 garlic cloves, minced
- 1 tablespoon dried basil
- 2-1/4 teaspoons dried oregano
- 2 teaspoons dried parsley flakes
- 1/2 teaspoon pepper
- Pinch cayenne pepper
- 1 can (15 to 16 ounces) kidney beans, rinsed and drained
- 1/2 cup cooked rice

In a Dutch oven or soup kettle, saute onion, celery and carrots in butter until vegetables are tender. Add tomatoes, broth, water, cabbage, potato and seasonings; bring to a boil. Reduce heat; cover and simmer for 1 hour. Stir in beans and rice; heat through. **Yield:** 9 servings (2-1/4 quarts).
Diabetic Exchanges: One 1-cup serving (prepared with margarine, no-salt-added tomatoes and low-sodium broth) equals 1-1/2 starch, 1 vegetable, 1 fat; also, 166 calories, 87 mg sodium, 0 cholesterol, 27 gm carbohydrate, 7 gm protein, 6 gm fat.

Russian Borscht

Ginny Bettis, Montello, Wisconsin

With beets, carrots, cabbage and tomatoes, this recipe is great for gardeners like myself. Not only is it delicious, its bright crimson color is eye-catching on the table.

- 2 cups chopped fresh beets
- 2 cups chopped carrots
- 2 cups chopped onion
- 4 cups beef broth
- 1 can (16 ounces) diced tomatoes, undrained
- 2 cups chopped cabbage
- 1/2 teaspoon salt
- 1/2 teaspoon dill weed
- 1/4 teaspoon pepper
- Sour cream, optional

In a 3-qt. saucepan, combine beets, carrots, onion and broth; bring to a boil. Reduce heat; cover and simmer for 30 minutes. Add tomatoes and cabbage; cover and simmer for 30 minutes or until cabbage is tender. Stir in salt, dill and pepper. Top each serving with sour cream if desired. **Yield:** 8 servings (2 quarts).

Beef Barley Soup

Elizabeth Kendall, Carolina Beach, North Carolina

This hearty barley soup is a favorite menu item in our house throughout the year. Everyone savors the flavor.

- 1 pound round steak, cut into 1/2-inch cubes
- 1 tablespoon cooking oil
- 3 cans (14-1/2 ounces *each*) beef broth
- 2 cups water
- 1/3 cup medium pearl barley
- 1 teaspoon salt
- 1/8 teaspoon pepper
- 1 cup chopped carrots
- 1/2 cup chopped celery
- 1/4 cup chopped onion
- 3 tablespoons chopped fresh parsley
- 1 cup frozen peas

In a Dutch oven or soup kettle, brown beef in oil; drain. Add broth, water, barley, salt and pepper; bring to a boil. Reduce heat; cover and simmer for 1 hour. Add carrots, celery, onion and parsley; simmer for 45 minutes or until vegetables are tender. Add peas; simmer for 15 minutes. **Yield:** 9 servings (2-1/4 quarts).

FIESTA BOWL. *Pictured at left: Taco Soup (recipe on this page).*

Oriental Friendship Soup

Cyndi Stanton, Wellsville, New York

After we completed our chores, Mom would warm us up with lots of hot soup. My love of soup continues today.

>1 large onion, thinly sliced
>2 tablespoons cooking oil
>1-1/2 pounds sirloin steak, thinly sliced
>1 cup sliced celery
>2 cans (14-1/2 ounces *each*) beef broth
>1 tablespoon cornstarch
>2 tablespoons soy sauce
>1 can (14 ounces) chop suey vegetables, drained
>2 cups cooked fine egg noodles
>1 package (10 ounces) fresh spinach, torn
>1/4 teaspoon pepper
>Chow mein noodles, optional

In a Dutch oven or soup kettle, saute onion in oil until tender. Remove and set aside. In the same pan, stir-fry beef, a few slices at a time, until no longer pink. Add celery; stir-fry for 2-4 minutes or until crisp-tender. Return onion and meat to pan. Add broth. In a small bowl, combine cornstarch and soy sauce; mix well. Add to pan. Bring to a boil; cook and stir for 2 minutes or until bubbly. Stir in vegetables, egg noodles, spinach and pepper; heat through. Garnish with chow mein noodles if desired. **Yield:** 6 servings.

Chicken Soup Base

Martha Taylor, California, Missouri

My widowed father isn't much of a cook. So I keep plenty of this delicious base on hand to serve as is or use in a variety of recipes.

>1 broiler/fryer chicken (3-1/2 to 4 pounds)
>3 quarts water
>1 cup chopped broccoli
>1 cup shredded carrots
>1 cup frozen peas
>1 small onion, chopped
>1/2 cup chopped celery
>1/4 cup chicken bouillon granules
>1 tablespoon chopped fresh parsley

Place chicken and water in a Dutch oven or soup kettle; bring to a boil. Skim fat. Reduce heat; cover and simmer for 2 hours or until chicken is tender. Remove chicken; allow to cool. Add enough water to broth to measure 3 qts. Remove chicken from bones; cut into bite-size pieces and return to pan. Add remaining ingredients; cover and simmer for 10 minutes or until vegetables are tender. If desired, pour into 1-pint freezer containers and freeze for future use. **Yield:** 10-14 servings (6-3/4 pints base). **For Chicken Potato Soup:** In a saucepan, combine 1 pint thawed soup base, 1/2 cup cubed peeled potatoes, and salt and pepper to taste. Cover and cook over medium heat until potatoes are tender. **For Cream of Chicken Soup:** In a saucepan, combine

1/4 cup all-purpose flour and 1 cup milk; mix until smooth. Stir in 1 pint thawed soup base. Bring to a boil; boil for 2 minutes, stirring constantly. Add 1/2 teaspoon chicken bouillon granules, and salt and pepper to taste; mix well.

Texas Turkey Soup

Betty Bakas, Lakehills, Texas

I'm not really fond of soup, so I was a little hesitant to try this recipe. But after some adjustments over the years, I've come to love this one-of-a-kind turkey soup.

>2 quarts turkey broth
>4 cups cubed cooked turkey
>2 large white onions, halved
>2 celery ribs, sliced
>3 medium carrots, sliced
>1 cup *each* frozen corn, cut green beans and peas
>2 bay leaves
>1/2 to 1 teaspoon dried tarragon
>3/4 teaspoon garlic powder
>1/4 to 1/2 teaspoon hot pepper sauce
>Salt and pepper to taste
>1-1/2 cups uncooked noodles
>1 tablespoon cornstarch
>1 tablespoon water

In a Dutch oven or soup kettle, combine broth, turkey, vegetables and seasonings; bring to a boil. Reduce heat; cover and simmer for 20-30 minutes or until vegetables are tender. Return to a boil; add noodles. Reduce heat; cover and simmer for 15-20 minutes or until noodles are tender. Combine cornstarch and water until smooth; add to soup. Bring to a boil; boil for 2 minutes, stirring constantly. Remove bay leaves. **Yield:** 10-12 servings (3 quarts).

Hamburger Soup

Terry Dunn, Kenai, Alaska

Folks always comment on the great blend of spices and the hearty addition of cabbage in this soup.

✓ This tasty dish uses less sugar, salt and fat. Recipe includes *Diabetic Exchanges*.

>1 pound ground beef *or* turkey
>1 large onion, chopped
>4 large potatoes, peeled and cubed
>4 large carrots, grated
>4 celery ribs, chopped
>1/2 small head cabbage, shredded
>1/4 cup uncooked long grain rice
>1 quart water
>1 can (28 ounces) diced tomatoes, undrained
>1 can (8 ounces) tomato sauce
>1 can (15 to 16 ounces) kidney beans, rinsed and drained
>2 bay leaves
>1 teaspoon dried basil
>1 teaspoon dried thyme
>3/4 teaspoon pepper

1/2 teaspoon dill weed
    1 to 2 teaspoons salt, optional

In a Dutch oven or soup kettle, brown meat and onion; drain. Add remaining ingredients; bring to a boil. Reduce heat and simmer, uncovered, for 2-3 hours. Remove bay leaves before serving. **Yield:** 14 servings (3-1/2 quarts). **Diabetic Exchanges:** One 1-cup serving (prepared with ground turkey breast and no-salt-added tomato sauce and without salt) equals 1 starch, 1 very lean meat, 1 vegetable; also, 140 calories, 123 mg sodium, 10 mg cholesterol, 22 gm carbohydrate, 15 gm protein, 2 gm fat.

Manhattan Clam Chowder

Joan Hopewell, Pennington, New Jersey

I typically serve this chowder with a tossed salad and hot rolls. It's easy to make and tastes wonderful on a cold winter evening. My family's enjoyed it for over 30 years.

    1 cup chopped onion
2/3 cup chopped celery
    2 teaspoons minced green pepper
    1 garlic clove, minced
    2 tablespoons butter *or* margarine
    2 cups hot water
    1 cup cubed peeled potato
    1 can (28 ounces) diced tomatoes, undrained
    2 cans (6-1/2 ounces *each*) minced clams, undrained
    1 teaspoon salt
1/2 teaspoon dried thyme
1/4 teaspoon pepper
Pinch cayenne pepper
    2 teaspoons minced fresh parsley

In a 3-qt. saucepan over low heat, saute onion, celery, green pepper and garlic in butter for 20 minutes, stirring frequently. Add water and potato; bring to a boil. Reduce heat; cover and simmer for 15 minutes or until potato is tender. Add the next six ingredients; heat through. Stir in parsley. Serve immediately. **Yield:** 6-8 servings (about 2 quarts).

Gingersnap Goulash

Diane Hoffman, Brunswick, Nebraska

A friend shared this authentic recipe with me years ago. I think you'll enjoy the extra spice from the addition of gingersnaps. It wonderfully captures the flavor of sauerbraten.

1-1/2 pounds beef stew meat, cut into 1-inch cubes
    2 quarts water
    1 cup chopped onion
    12 gingersnap cookies, crumbled
    2 tablespoons Worcestershire sauce
    2 tablespoons brown sugar
    1 teaspoon salt
1/4 teaspoon pepper
    1 bottle (14 ounces) ketchup

In a Dutch oven or soup kettle, combine the first eight ingredients; bring to a boil. Reduce heat; cover and simmer

for 1 hour or until meat is tender. Add ketchup; cover and simmer for 1 hour, stirring occasionally. **Yield:** 8-10 servings (2-1/2 quarts).

Roast Beef Soup

Kathy Jensen, Edmonds, Washington

If your family's like mine, you have to disguise leftovers in order for anyone to eat them! This special soup turns leftovers into a lively meal.

    2 pounds cooked roast beef, cut into 1-inch cubes
1-1/4 cups chopped onion
    2 tablespoons cooking oil
4-1/2 cups water
    1 jar (12 ounces) au jus gravy
    1 cup leftover beef gravy *or* 1 can (10-1/4 ounces) beef gravy
    1 envelope brown gravy mix
    2 bay leaves
1/4 teaspoon garlic salt
1/4 teaspoon pepper
1/4 teaspoon hot pepper sauce
    1 cup dry lentils, rinsed
    1 cup leftover cooked vegetables *or* 1 cup frozen vegetables

In a 3-qt. saucepan, saute beef and onion in oil until onion is tender. Add the next eight ingredients; cover and simmer for 1 hour. Stir in lentils; cover and simmer for 30 minutes. Add vegetables; cover and simmer for 10 minutes or until lentils and vegetables are tender. Remove bay leaves. **Yield:** 6-8 servings (2 quarts).

Asparagus Soup

Betty Jones, Kohler, Wisconsin

Each spring, my husband takes our dogs and searches for wild asparagus. He's been so successful that I finally developed this recipe. We look forward to this special soup every year.

    1 cup chopped onion
    6 green onions, sliced
    3 tablespoons butter *or* margarine
1-1/2 cups sliced fresh mushrooms
    1 pound fresh asparagus, cut into 1/2-inch pieces
    1 can (49-1/2 ounces) chicken broth
1/2 cup chopped fresh parsley
1/2 teaspoon salt
1/2 teaspoon dried thyme
1/4 teaspoon pepper
1/8 teaspoon cayenne pepper
    2 cups cooked wild rice
    3 tablespoons cornstarch

In a 3-qt. saucepan, saute onions in butter for 4 minutes. Add mushrooms and cook until tender. Add asparagus, broth and seasonings; cover and simmer for 30 minutes. Add rice. Dissolve cornstarch in water; stir into soup. Bring to a boil; boil for 2 minutes, stirring constantly. **Yield:** 8-10 servings (2-1/4 quarts).

Comforting Cream Soups

Warmly welcome family and friends in from the cold with the appealing aroma of a rich, old-fashioned cream soup slowly simmering on the stove.

Fresh Tomato Soup

Marilyn De Zort, Fairfield, Montana
(PICTURED AT LEFT)

This is one of the best recipes I have because it can be put together in no time. When tomato season is here, you'll find me making this pretty and pleasing soup often.

1 cup chopped onion
1/4 cup butter *or* margarine
3 pounds fresh tomatoes, peeled, seeded and chopped
2 tablespoons tomato paste
1 tablespoon sugar
1 teaspoon salt
1 teaspoon dried basil
1/2 teaspoon dried thyme
1/4 teaspoon pepper
1/4 cup all-purpose flour
4 cups chicken broth, *divided*
1 cup whipping cream

In a 3-qt. saucepan over medium heat, saute onion in butter until tender. Add tomatoes, tomato paste, sugar, salt, basil, thyme and pepper; simmer for 10 minutes, stirring occasionally. Combine flour and 3/4 cup broth; form a smooth paste. Add to tomato mixture with remaining broth. Bring to a boil; boil for 2 minutes, stirring constantly. Reduce heat; cover and simmer for 30 minutes or until tomatoes are tender. Remove from the heat. Stir in cream; serve immediately. **Yield:** 4-6 servings.

Creamy Wild Rice Soup

Patricia Batchelder, Fond du Lac, Wisconsin
(PICTURED AT LEFT)

Whenever I make this soup in the morning, it's gone by evening! Friends and family alike rave about the unbeatable combination of down-home flavors.

3/4 cup uncooked wild rice
1 tablespoon cooking oil
1 quart water
1/2 teaspoon salt
1 medium onion, chopped

> **SMOOTH AND SOOTHING.** *Pictured at left, top to bottom: Fresh Tomato Soup and Creamy Wild Rice Soup (both recipes on this page).*

1 celery rib, diced
1 medium carrot, diced
1/2 cup butter *or* margarine
1/2 cup all-purpose flour
3 cups chicken broth
2 cups half-and-half cream
1 cup diced fully cooked ham
1/2 teaspoon dried rosemary
1/4 teaspoon pepper

In a soup kettle or Dutch oven over medium heat, saute rice in oil for 5 minutes. Add water and salt; bring to a boil. Reduce heat; cover and simmer for 35 minutes (rice will not be completely cooked). Drain, reserving 1-1/2 cups cooking liquid; set rice and liquid aside separately. In the same kettle, saute onion, celery and carrot in butter until onion is transparent. Reduce heat; stir in flour and cook until bubbly. Gradually add broth and cooking liquid; stirring constantly. Bring to a boil; boil for 2 minutes, stirring constantly. Add cream, ham, rosemary, pepper and rice. Reduce heat; cover and simmer for 30-35 minutes or until rice is tender. **Yield:** 8 servings (2 quarts).

Cheesy Clam Chowder

Laurie Jolliffe, Fort Morgan, Colorado

I never thought I'd be able to duplicate the excellent taste of hearty clam chowders found in many restaurants, but this recipe proved me wrong. The dill makes it extra-special.

2 cups chicken broth
2 cans (6-1/2 ounces *each*) chopped clams, undrained
3 medium potatoes, peeled and cubed
4 medium carrots, sliced
4 celery ribs, sliced
1 medium onion, chopped
1 tablespoon lemon juice
1 tablespoon minced fresh dill *or* 1 teaspoon dill weed
1 garlic clove, minced
1/2 teaspoon ground nutmeg
1 teaspoon salt
1/2 teaspoon pepper
2 cups half-and-half cream
1 cup cubed process American cheese
1 cup (4 ounces) shredded Monterey Jack cheese
6 bacon strips, cooked and crumbled

In a soup kettle or Dutch oven, combine the first 12 ingredients; bring to a boil. Reduce heat; simmer for 20 minutes or until the vegetables are tender. Add cream and cheeses; heat through until cheese is melted. Stir in bacon just before serving. **Yield:** 8 servings (about 2 quarts).

Sausage Soup

Sonya Atkins, Farmington, Missouri

When I substituted turkey sausage for the pork sausage in my mother-in-law's recipe, we loved the result.

✓ This tasty dish uses less sugar, salt and fat. Recipe includes *Diabetic Exchanges*.

　　1 pound bulk turkey breakfast sausage
　　1 cup chopped onion
　　3 cups water
　　2 chicken bouillon cubes
　　4 cups cubed peeled potatoes
　1/2 teaspoon salt, optional
　1/4 teaspoon pepper
　1/4 teaspoon dried sage
　　1 can (15-1/4 ounces) whole kernel corn, drained
　　1 can (15 ounces) cream-style corn
1-1/2 cups half-and-half cream *or* evaporated skim milk
Chopped sweet red pepper

In a soup kettle or Dutch oven over medium heat, cook sausage and onion until sausage is no longer pink and onion is tender; drain. Add water and bouillon; bring to a boil. Add potatoes, salt if desired, pepper and sage; return to a boil. Reduce heat; cover and simmer for 25-30 minutes or until potatoes are tender. Stir in corn and cream; heat through. Garnish with red pepper. **Yield:** 10 servings (2-1/2 quarts). **Diabetic Exchanges:** One 1-cup serving (prepared with low-sodium bouillon and evaporated skim milk and without salt) equals 2 starch, 1 meat; also, 221 calories, 608 mg sodium, 20 mg cholesterol, 29 gm carbohydrate, 14 gm protein, 7 gm fat.

Corn Chowder

Bonnie Miller, Devils Lake, North Dakota

When I was growing up, my grandmother would often serve steaming bowls of corn chowder. I tried to capture that wonderful flavor and came up with this recipe.

　　1 quart water
　　4 cups diced peeled potatoes
　　1 cup chopped celery
　1/2 cup chopped onion
　1/2 cup shredded carrot
　　1 can (15-1/4 ounces) whole kernel corn, drained
　　1 can (15 ounces) cream-style corn
　　1 can (10-3/4 ounces) condensed cream of mushroom soup, undiluted
　　2 cups chopped fully cooked ham
　　1 jar (4-1/2 ounces) sliced mushrooms, drained
1-1/4 cups milk
　1/2 teaspoon salt
　1/2 teaspoon pepper
　　6 bacon strips, cooked and crumbled

In a soup kettle or Dutch oven, combine the first five ingredients; bring to a boil. Reduce heat; cover and simmer for 12-15 minutes or until vegetables are tender. Add corn,

soup, ham, mushrooms, milk, salt and pepper; heat through, stirring occasionally. Stir in bacon just before serving. **Yield:** 12-14 servings (about 3 quarts).

Crab Bisque

Kathy Waller, Fort Collins, Colorado

I've enjoyed cooking and baking ever since my 4-H days in rural Iowa. The zesty seasonings in this bisque nicely complement the subtle flavor of crab.

　1/2 cup chopped celery
　　2 tablespoons chopped onion
　1/4 cup butter *or* margarine
　1/4 cup all-purpose flour
2-1/2 cups milk
　　2 beef bouillon cubes
　　1 cup half-and-half cream
　　1 can (6 ounces) crabmeat, drained
　1/2 cup sliced fresh mushrooms
　1/2 teaspoon dried basil
　1/4 teaspoon garlic powder
　1/4 to 1/2 teaspoon Creole seasoning
　1/8 to 1/4 teaspoon pepper

In a 3-qt. saucepan over medium heat, saute celery and onion in butter until tender. Stir in flour; gradually add milk. Bring to a boil; boil for 2 minutes, stirring constantly. Add bouillon, cream, crab, mushrooms, basil, garlic powder, 1/4 teaspoon Creole seasoning and 1/8 teaspoon pepper. Reduce heat; cover and simmer for 45 minutes, stirring frequently. Season to taste with remaining Creole seasoning and pepper if desired. **Yield:** 4 servings.

Stroganoff Soup

Karen Shiveley, Springfield, Minnesota

My husband and I share a love for all kinds of soup and came up with this delicious recipe together. It really does taste like beef Stroganoff. With a crusty roll, it's a satisfying meal in itself.

　1/2 pound sirloin steak *or* beef tenderloin, cut into thin strips
　1/2 cup chopped onion
　　1 tablespoon butter *or* margarine
　　2 cups water
1-1/2 cups milk
　1/4 cup tomato paste
　　2 teaspoons beef bouillon granules
　　1 can (8 ounces) mushroom stems and pieces, drained
　　1 teaspoon salt
　1/8 teaspoon pepper
　　1 can (12 ounces) evaporated milk
　1/3 cup all-purpose flour
　　2 cups cooked wide egg noodles
　1/2 cup sour cream

In a 3-qt. saucepan over medium heat, cook beef and onion in butter until meat is browned. Stir in water, milk, tomato paste and bouillon. Add mushrooms, salt and pepper; bring to a boil. Reduce heat; cover and simmer for 20-30 minutes or until meat is tender. Combine evaporated milk and flour; stir until smooth. Gradually add to soup, stirring constantly. Bring to a boil; boil for 2 minutes, stirring constantly. Add noodles and heat through. Remove from the heat; stir in sour cream. **Yield:** 6 servings.

Zesty Chili-Cheese Soup

Janne Rowe, Wichita, Kansas

With green chilies, corn and cheese, this slightly spicy soup has a Mexican flair. You're sure to like the extra "zip" it brings to your dinner table.

- 1 cup chopped onion
- 2 tablespoons cooking oil
- 2 tablespoons butter *or* margarine
- 3 garlic cloves, minced
- 2 tablespoons all-purpose flour
- 3 cups chicken broth
- 3 cups frozen whole kernel corn
- 2 cans (4 ounces *each*) chopped green chilies
- 1 cup seeded chopped tomatoes
- 1 can (12 ounces) evaporated milk
- 3 cups (12 ounces) shredded sharp cheddar *or* Monterey Jack cheese
- 1 teaspoon ground cumin

In a soup kettle or Dutch oven over medium heat, saute onion in oil and butter until tender. Add garlic and saute for 1 minute. Add flour; cook and stir for 2 minutes. Stir in broth, corn, chilies and tomatoes; bring to a boil. Reduce heat and simmer, uncovered, for 15 minutes, stirring occasionally. Add remaining ingredients; heat, stirring frequently, until the cheese is melted (do not boil). **Yield:** 8 servings (about 2 quarts).

Garden Chowder

Betty Kuhlber, Slippery Rock, Pennsylvania

My family loves to eat, so I'm encouraged to spend lots of time in the kitchen! Featuring garden-fresh produce, this chowder quickly disappears both at home and at potlucks.

- 1/4 cup chopped onion
- 1/2 cup chopped celery
- 1/4 cup butter *or* margarine
- 1/4 cup all-purpose flour
- 1/2 teaspoon salt
- 1/4 teaspoon pepper
- 2 cups chicken broth
- 1 medium tomato, peeled and diced
- 1 cup broccoli florets
- 1 cup chopped carrots
- 1 cup frozen corn
- 1 cup thinly sliced zucchini
- 2 cups half-and-half cream
- 1/4 cup grated Parmesan cheese

In a 3-qt. saucepan over medium heat, saute onion and celery in butter for 5 minutes. Add flour, salt and pepper; stir to form a smooth paste. Gradually add broth, stirring constantly. Bring to a boil; boil and stir for 2 minutes or until thickened. Add tomato, broccoli, carrots, corn and zucchini; return to a boil. Reduce heat; cover and simmer for 40 minutes or until vegetables are tender. Add cream and cheese; heat through. **Yield:** 4-6 servings.

Cream of Zucchini Soup

Jan Poechman, Walkerton, Ontario

Because this soup is very easy to prepare, I reach for it often in the summer when I'm busy playing volleyball and baseball. It's also a great way to use up excess zucchini.

- 2 cups sliced zucchini
- 1/2 cup chopped onion
- 1/2 cup chopped carrot
- 1 tablespoon butter *or* margarine
- 2 cups chicken broth
- 3/4 teaspoon dried tarragon
- 1/2 teaspoon salt
- 1/4 teaspoon pepper
- 1/4 to 1/2 teaspoon garlic powder
- 2 cups milk

Paprika and additional zucchini, optional

In a large saucepan over medium heat, saute zucchini, onion and carrot in butter for 5 minutes. Add broth, tarragon, salt, pepper and garlic powder; bring to a boil. Reduce heat; cover and simmer for 15-20 minutes or until vegetables are tender. Puree in a blender or food processor; return to pan. Add milk; heat through. Garnish with paprika and zucchini if desired. **Yield:** 4 servings.

Chicken Bisque

Mary Wagner, Woodburn, Oregon

When the weather starts turning cooler, we like to sit down to dinner with this colorful rich bisque. Add hot rolls and a salad, and you have a hearty meal.

- 2 quarts chicken broth
- 2 cups cubed cooked chicken
- 1 jar (4 ounces) diced pimientos, undrained
- 1/4 cup chopped green onions
- 1 teaspoon dried tarragon
- 1/2 teaspoon salt
- 1/2 teaspoon pepper
- 2 chicken bouillon cubes
- 1/2 cup butter *or* margarine
- 1 cup all-purpose flour

In a soup kettle or Dutch oven, combine the first eight ingredients; bring to a gentle boil. In a small saucepan, melt butter. Stir in flour; cook and stir for 2 minutes. Gradually add to boiling soup, stirring constantly until smooth. Return to a boil. Reduce heat; simmer, uncovered, for 15 minutes. **Yield:** 8-10 servings (2-1/2 quarts).

Chunky Potato Soup

Betty Ann Walery, Joplin, Montana
(PICTURED AT LEFT)

This special soup is a true family favorite. I received the recipe from my sister and then passed it on to my daughters. It's perfect served with leftover ham.

    2 cups water
    2 chicken bouillon cubes
    3 cups cubed peeled potatoes
    1/2 cup chopped onion
    1/2 cup thinly sliced celery
    3/4 teaspoon salt
    1/2 teaspoon pepper
    2 cups milk, *divided*
    2 tablespoons all-purpose flour
    1 cup (8 ounces) sour cream
    2 tablespoons chopped fresh parsley
    1 tablespoon chopped chives

In a 3-qt. saucepan over medium heat, combine water, bouillon, potatoes, onion, celery, salt and pepper; bring to a boil. Reduce heat; cover and simmer for 15-20 minutes or until potatoes are tender. Add 1-3/4 cups milk. Combine flour with remaining milk; stir to form a smooth paste. Add to soup, stirring constantly. Bring to a boil; boil and stir for 2 minutes or until thickened and bubbly. Add a small amount of hot liquid to sour cream; stir to mix. Gradually add to soup, stirring constantly; heat through but do not boil. Add parsley and chives just before serving. **Yield:** 4-6 servings.

Golden Autumn Soup

Janet Willick, St. Michael, Alberta
(PICTURED AT LEFT)

Here's a great way to use the freshest produce harvested in fall. It's a hot and hearty soup that I like to make for everyday dinners and special-occasion suppers.

✓ **This tasty dish uses less sugar, salt and fat. Recipe includes *Diabetic Exchanges*.**

    5 medium parsnips, peeled and chopped
    5 medium carrots, sliced
    2 medium onions, chopped
    1 medium sweet potato, peeled and chopped
    1 medium turnip, peeled and chopped
    2 celery ribs, sliced
    2 bay leaves
    3 cans (14-1/2 ounces *each*) chicken broth
    2 cups half-and-half cream *or* evaporated skim milk
    1 teaspoon dried tarragon
    1/4 teaspoon pepper

A HARVEST OF CREAMY GOODNESS. *Pictured at left, top to bottom: Chunky Potato Soup and Golden Autumn Soup (both recipes on this page).*

In a soup kettle or Dutch oven, combine the first eight ingredients; simmer for 30 minutes or until vegetables are tender. Remove bay leaves. Let cool for 20 minutes. Puree in small batches in a blender; return to kettle. Add cream, tarragon and pepper; heat through. **Yield:** 12 servings (3 quarts). **Diabetic Exchanges:** One 1-cup serving (prepared with low-sodium broth and evaporated skim milk) equals 1 starch, 1 vegetable; also, 101 calories, 100 mg sodium, 1 mg cholesterol, 19 gm carbohydrate, 6 gm protein, 1 gm fat.

Dilly Cheese Soup

Darlene Jons, Bonesteel, South Dakota

My grandkids will tell you they can't stop with just one bowl of this simple satisfying soup. Even the youngest ones beg me to make it! It's been a family favorite for over 50 years now.

    4-1/2 cups water
    4 medium potatoes, peeled and cubed
    1/2 cup uncooked long grain rice
    3 to 4 tablespoons minced fresh dill
    2 tablespoons chopped onion
    1 to 2 chicken bouillon cubes
    1/4 teaspoon salt
    1/4 teaspoon pepper
    8 ounces process American cheese, cubed
    1/2 cup sour cream

In a soup kettle or Dutch oven, combine the first eight ingredients; bring to a boil. Reduce heat; cover and simmer for 15 minutes or until potatoes are tender. Add the cheese and sour cream; heat and stir just until cheese is melted. **Yield:** 6-8 servings (2 quarts). **Editor's Note:** Recipe can be easily doubled.

Carrot Soup

Julie Anderson, Wausau, Wisconsin

This nice creamy soup really hits the spot...whether you serve it by itself, with sandwiches or as a first course. My family enjoys it often here on our acre in the country.

    1 medium onion, chopped
    2 tablespoons butter *or* margarine
    2-1/2 cups chicken broth
    1 pound carrots, sliced
    2 large potatoes, peeled and cubed
    1-1/2 cups milk
    1/4 teaspoon salt
    1/4 teaspoon pepper
Shredded Swiss cheese and minced fresh parsley, optional

In a 3-qt. saucepan, saute onion in butter until tender. Add broth, carrots and potatoes; bring to a boil. Reduce heat and simmer for 15-20 minutes or until vegetables are tender. Puree on low speed in a blender; return to pan. Stir in milk, salt and pepper; heat through but do not boil. Garnish with cheese and parsley if desired. **Yield:** 6 servings.

Chicken and Dumpling Soup

Joey Ann Mostowy, Bruin, Pennsylvania

Our five kids are grown and live away from the farm, but they visit often with their families. So I stay in practice in the kitchen! I frequently serve this soup for Sunday dinner.

    6 pieces bone-in chicken
1-1/2 quarts water
    2 celery ribs, cut into chunks
    1 medium onion, cut into chunks
1/2 cup diced green pepper
    1 garlic clove, minced
    1 tablespoon minced fresh dill
    1 teaspoon salt
1/2 teaspoon pepper
    1 can (10-3/4 ounces) condensed cream of potato soup, undiluted
    1 can (10-3/4 ounces) condensed cream of chicken soup, undiluted
    1 package (10 ounces) frozen mixed vegetables, thawed
    1 tube (7-1/2 ounces) refrigerated buttermilk biscuits

In a soup kettle or Dutch oven, combine the first nine ingredients; bring to a boil. Reduce heat; cover and simmer for 50-60 minutes or until chicken is tender. Remove chicken; allow to cool. Debone and cut into chunks; set aside. Strain broth and set aside. In a large saucepan, combine soups. Gradually add broth, stirring constantly. Add mixed vegetables and chicken; cook over medium heat for 20-30 minutes or until vegetables are tender. On a floured board, pat biscuits to 1/4-in. thickness; cut into 1/4-in. strips. Bring soup to boil; drop in strips. Cover and cook for 15-18 minutes. **Yield:** 8-10 servings (2-1/2 quarts).

Knoephla Soup

Lorraine Meyers, Willow City, North Dakota

While I was growing up, my mom would make this traditional German soup. It tasted so good on chilly fall days. Knoephla (pronounced nip-fla) Soup is still a warm and comforting meal for my family.

1/2 cup butter *or* margarine
    3 medium potatoes, peeled and diced
    1 small onion, grated
    3 cups milk
1-1/2 quarts water
    6 teaspoons chicken bouillon granules
KNOEPHLA:
1-1/2 cups all-purpose flour
    1 egg, beaten
    5 to 6 tablespoons milk
1/2 teaspoon salt

In a large skillet, melt butter; cook potatoes and onion for 20-25 minutes or until tender. Add milk; heat through but do not boil. Set aside. In a soup kettle or Dutch oven, bring

water and bouillon to a boil. Meanwhile, combine knoephla ingredients to form a stiff dough. Roll into a 1/2-in. rope. Cut into 1/4-in. pieces and drop into boiling broth. Reduce heat; cover and simmer for 10 minutes. Add the potato mixture; heat through. **Yield:** 8-10 servings (2-1/2 quarts).

Garlic Oatmeal Soup

Muriel Ellis, Campbellford, Ontario

This one-of-a-kind soup has a superb garlic and cheese flavor that appeals to everyone. Try serving it with crusty bread for a mouth-watering meal.

    1 quart water, *divided*
1/2 cup quick-cooking oats
    3 chicken bouillon cubes
    2 garlic cloves, minced
    1 cup (4 ounces) shredded cheddar cheese
1/4 teaspoon dried basil
1/4 teaspoon salt
Dash pepper

In a small saucepan over medium heat, bring 1 cup water to a boil. Add oats and cook for 1 minute, stirring occasionally. Cover and set aside for 5 minutes. Add bouillon, garlic and remaining water; bring to a boil. Reduce heat and simmer for 10 minutes, stirring occasionally. Add cheese, basil, salt and pepper; cook and stir until cheese is melted. **Yield:** 4 servings. **Editor's Note:** 1 cup cold leftover oatmeal may be substituted for 1/2 cup oats and 1 cup water.

Swiss-Barley Mushroom Soup

Germaine Stank, Pound, Wisconsin

In this recipe, hearty barley and rich Swiss cheese add a flavorful twist to traditional mushroom soup. You'll find one batch of this filling soup goes a long way.

1/2 pound fresh mushrooms, sliced
1/2 cup chopped onion
1/2 cup butter *or* margarine, melted
1/2 cup all-purpose flour
    3 cups water
1/2 cup quick-cooking barley
    3 chicken bouillon cubes
    3 cups milk
    2 cups (8 ounces) shredded Swiss cheese
    2 tablespoons Worcestershire sauce
    1 tablespoon dried parsley flakes
1/4 teaspoon pepper

In a 3-qt. saucepan, saute mushrooms and onion in butter until tender. With a slotted spoon, transfer mushrooms and onion to a bowl; set aside. Stir flour into pan drippings; cook over medium heat until lightly browned. Stir in water until smooth. Add barley; bring to a boil. Reduce heat; simmer, uncovered, stirring constantly, for 15 minutes or until barley is tender. Add bouillon, milk, cheese, Worcestershire sauce, parsley and pepper; cook and stir until bouillon is dissolved and cheese is melted. Add the mushroom mixture; heat through. **Yield:** 6 servings.

Confetti Soup

Nancy Olson, Belgrade, Minnesota

I created this recipe when I was trying to think of something new and interesting to serve my family. They never cared much for vegetables until they tried this delicious soup.

- 1 cup diced carrots
- 1 cup diced rutabaga
- 1/2 cup chopped celery
- 1/2 cup broccoli florets
- 1/2 cup cauliflowerets
- 1/2 cup chopped onion
- 3 tablespoons water
- 3 tablespoons butter *or* margarine, optional
- 1 cup cubed process American cheese
- 1 cup frozen whole kernel corn
- 1/2 cup frozen peas
- 1/2 cup diced fully cooked ham
- 5 cups milk
- 1-1/2 teaspoons salt
- 1/2 teaspoon pepper
- 1/4 teaspoon sugar

In a microwave-safe 3-qt. baking dish, combine carrots, rutabaga, celery, broccoli, cauliflower, onion, water and butter if desired. Cover and microwave on high for 14 minutes or until vegetables are just tender, stirring three times during cooking. Stir in cheese, corn, peas and ham; cover and let stand for 1 minute. Add milk, salt, pepper and sugar; cover and microwave on medium-high, stirring three times, for 8-10 minutes or until cheese is melted and soup is heated through (do not boil). **Yield:** 8 servings (2 quarts).

Spinach Bisque

Mary Lou Allaman, Kirkwood, Illinois

When my grandchildren were only 3 years old, they tried this "yummy" soup at a local restaurant and fell in love with it, so I immediately asked for the recipe. They still call it "Yummy Soup".

- 5 packages (10 ounces *each*) frozen chopped spinach, thawed and well drained
- 3 cups half-and-half cream
- 3 packages (8 ounces *each*) cream cheese, cubed
- 1 can (14-1/2 ounces) chicken broth
- 1 cup (4 ounces) shredded cheddar cheese
- 3/4 cup grated Parmesan cheese
- 2 garlic cloves, minced
- 1 teaspoon salt
- 1/2 teaspoon pepper

In a Dutch oven or soup kettle, combine spinach and

cream. Cover and cook over medium-low heat until heated through. Add remaining ingredients. Cook, uncovered, stirring constantly, until cheese is melted and soup is hot. **Yield:** 14 servings (3-1/2 quarts).

Chicken and Bacon Chowder

Nancy Schmidt, Delhi, California

The original recipe for this chowder called for ground beef. One day I decided to use chicken instead. Everyone agreed they liked it even better. You're sure to enjoy it, too.

- 1 pound sliced bacon
- 3 cups diced celery
- 1/2 cup diced onion
- 4 cups diced peeled potatoes
- 3 cups chicken broth
- 2 cups diced carrots
- 3 cups diced cooked chicken
- 2 cans (10-3/4 ounces *each*) condensed cream of mushroom soup, undiluted
- 2 cups half-and half cream
- 1/2 teaspoon salt
- 1/2 teaspoon pepper

In a soup kettle or Dutch oven, cook bacon until crisp. Drain, reserving 2 tablespoons drippings. Crumble bacon and set aside. Saute celery and onion in drippings until tender. Add potatoes, broth and carrots; bring to a boil. Reduce heat; cover and simmer for 20 minutes or until vegetables are tender. Stir in remaining ingredients and heat through. **Yield:** 12 servings (3 quarts).

Broccoli-Cauliflower Cheese Soup

Janet Hall, Pleasant Valley, Iowa

Even people who aren't particularly fond of broccoli and cauliflower can't resist this tempting soup. On busy days, you'll appreciate its ease of preparation.

- 3 quarts water
- 8 chicken bouillon cubes
- 2-1/2 cups diced peeled potatoes
- 1 cup chopped celery
- 1/2 cup chopped onion
- 2 packages (10 ounces *each*) frozen chopped broccoli
- 1 package (16 ounces) frozen cauliflowerets
- 2 cans (10-3/4 ounces *each*) condensed cream of chicken soup, undiluted
- 1 pound process American cheese, cubed
- 1/2 teaspoon dried thyme
- 1/4 teaspoon pepper

In a soup kettle or Dutch oven, combine the first five ingredients; cook over medium heat for about 20 minutes or until vegetables are tender. Add broccoli and cauliflower; cook over medium heat for 10 minutes. Stir in the soup, cheese, thyme and pepper; simmer for 20 minutes, stirring occasionally. **Yield:** 18-20 servings (about 5-1/2 quarts).

Spinach Cheese Soup

Susan Bontrager, Middlebury, Indiana
(PICTURED AT LEFT)

A friend brought a pot of this steaming soup to our home after our first child was born. Three kids later, I'm still getting requests to make it frequently.

- 1 large onion, chopped
- 4 garlic cloves, minced
- 1 tablespoon olive *or* vegetable oil
- 6 cups chicken broth
- 8 ounces uncooked linguine
- 1 package (10 ounces) frozen chopped spinach, thawed and well drained
- 2 cups cubed cooked chicken
- 6 cups milk
- 3 cups (12 ounces) shredded Swiss cheese
- 3 cups (12 ounces) shredded brick *or* Monterey Jack cheese

In a soup kettle or Dutch oven, saute onion and garlic in oil until tender. Add broth; bring to a boil. Add linguine and cook for 8-10 minutes or until tender. Reduce heat. Add spinach and chicken; heat through but do not boil. Stir in milk; heat through. Add cheeses and stir just until melted. Serve immediately. **Yield:** 14-16 servings (4 quarts).

Macaroni and Cheese Soup

Emma Head, Sunrise Beach, Missouri
(PICTURED AT LEFT)

I've worked in the food service industry for too many years to count and have made this one-of-a-kind soup at many different jobs. It's always been a big hit.

- 3 quarts water
- 5 teaspoons chicken bouillon granules
- 1-1/2 cups sliced celery
- 2 large carrots, shredded
- 1 large onion, chopped
- 1 medium green pepper, chopped
- 2-1/2 cups uncooked elbow macaroni
- 1 cup butter *or* margarine
- 3/4 cup all-purpose flour
- 6 cups milk
- 1 pound process American cheese, cubed

In a soup kettle or Dutch oven, bring water and bouillon to a boil. Add celery, carrots, onion and green pepper; cook for 4 minutes or until tender. Add macaroni. Cover and return to a boil; boil for 2 minutes. Remove from the heat; let stand for 8-10 minutes or until macaroni is just tender. Meanwhile, melt butter in a saucepan. Add flour, stirring until smooth.

CHEESE, PLEASE! *Pictured at left, clockwise from top: Macaroni and Cheese Soup , Swiss 'n' Cheddar Broccoli Soup and Spinach Cheese Soup (recipes on this page).*

Gradually add milk, stirring constantly. Bring to a boil; cook and stir for 2 minutes. Stir in cheese until melted; add to undrained macaroni mixture. **Yield:** 20 servings (5 quarts).

Swiss 'n' Cheddar Broccoli Soup

Ada Lee Cook, Vernon, Texas
(PICTURED AT LEFT)

With two varieties of cheese—Swiss and cheddar—this soup is doubly delicious! I'm sure it will become a favorite in your home.

- 4 cups water, *divided*
- 4 teaspoons chicken bouillon granules
- 2 packages (10 ounces *each*) frozen chopped broccoli
- 4 cups milk
- 1/2 teaspoon salt
- 1/4 teaspoon pepper
- 1/8 teaspoon ground nutmeg
- 1/2 cup all-purpose flour
- 1-1/4 cups (5 ounces) shredded Swiss cheese
- 3/4 cup shredded cheddar cheese

In a large saucepan, combine 3 cups water and bouillon; heat until bouillon is dissolved. Add broccoli; cover and cook over low heat until tender, about 8 minutes. Stir in milk, salt, pepper and nutmeg. Combine flour and remaining water; stir into soup. Cook and stir over medium heat for 3 minutes or until thick and bubbly. Remove from the heat. Add cheeses; stir until melted. **Yield:** 8 servings (2 quarts).

Potato Clam Chowder

Betty Ann Morgan, Upper Marlboro, Maryland

I ran across this recipe in one of my antique cookbooks. It's a timeless classic I like to prepare for friends and family throughout the year, but especially during the holidays.

- 2 bacon strips, diced
- 1 cup chopped onion
- 2 tablespoons all-purpose flour
- 2 cans (6-1/2 ounces *each*) minced clams
- 1 cup water
- 1/2 teaspoon salt
- 1/4 to 1/2 teaspoon dried thyme
- 1/4 teaspoon dried savory
- 1/8 teaspoon pepper
- 4 medium potatoes, peeled and cubed
- 2 cups milk
- 2 tablespoons minced fresh parsley

In a 3-qt. saucepan or Dutch oven, cook bacon until crisp. Remove bacon; set aside. Saute onion in drippings until tender. Add flour; stir until smooth. Drain clams, reserving juice; set clams aside. Gradually add water and clam juice to pan; cook and stir over medium heat until smooth and bubbly. Add salt, thyme, savory, pepper and potatoes; bring to a boil. Reduce heat; cover and simmer for 25 minutes or until potatoes are tender, stirring often. Add bacon, clams, milk and parsley; heat through. **Yield:** 6 servings.

Soups for the Summer

In the midst of summer's heat, you can't beat this interesting assortment of refreshing soups. You'll reach for them season after season!

Fresh Fruit Soup

Beulah Goodenough, Belleville, New Jersey
(PICTURED AT LEFT)

On a hot summer day, nothing can top the flavor of the season's finest fruits. This recipe is both fast and festive.

- 2 cups water
- 2 tablespoons quick-cooking tapioca
- 1 can (6 ounces) frozen orange juice concentrate, thawed
- 1 to 2 tablespoons sugar
- 1 tablespoon honey
- 1/8 teaspoon almond extract
- Pinch salt
- 2-1/2 cups fresh fruit (blueberries, raspberries, sliced strawberries, halved grapes, etc.)

In a 2-qt. saucepan, combine water and tapioca; let stand for 10 minutes. Bring to a boil; boil for 2 minutes, stirring constantly. Remove from the heat; stir in orange juice concentrate, sugar, honey, extract and salt. Chill. Add fruit; chill until ready to serve. **Yield:** 4 servings.

Low-Fat Gazpacho

Shirley McCabe, Grand Junction, Colorado
(PICTURED AT LEFT)

This soup often appears on my menu when I'm entertaining. It's a real favorite because I can make it ahead.

✓ This tasty dish uses less sugar, salt and fat. Recipe includes *Diabetic Exchanges*.

- 1 can (46 ounces) light and tangy V-8 juice
- 2 large tomatoes, chopped and seeded
- 1 large cucumber, peeled, seeded and chopped
- 3 celery ribs, chopped
- 1 large green pepper, chopped
- 1/2 cup chopped green onions
- 1/3 cup red wine vinegar
- 1 tablespoon Worcestershire sauce
- 1 teaspoon salt, optional
- 1/2 teaspoon pepper

In a large bowl, combine all ingredients. Cover and chill overnight. **Yield:** 12 servings (3 quarts). **Diabetic Exchanges:** One 1-cup serving (prepared without salt) equals 2 vegetable; also, 39 calories, 411 mg sodium, 0 cholesterol, 9 gm carbohydrate, 1 gm protein, trace fat.

Cold Cucumber Soup

Shirley Dufresne, Grants Pass, Oregon
(PICTURED AT LEFT)

I love trying to duplicate restaurant dishes at home. Friends and family tell me they like the results!

✓ This tasty dish uses less sugar, salt and fat. Recipe includes *Diabetic Exchanges*.

- 2 large cucumbers, peeled and seeded
- 1-1/4 cups sour cream
- 1 cup chicken broth
- 1 small onion, cut into wedges
- 4 sprigs fresh parsley, stems removed
- 2 sprigs fresh dill, stems removed *or* 1 teaspoon dill weed
- 1 tablespoon lemon juice
- 3/4 teaspoon salt, optional
- 1/4 teaspoon white pepper

Cut cucumbers into large chunks; place in a blender with remaining ingredients. Puree; pour into a bowl. Cover and refrigerate for at least 8 hours. **Yield:** 4 servings. **Diabetic Exchanges:** One 1-cup serving (prepared with fat-free sour cream and low-sodium broth and without salt) equals 1 starch, 1 vegetable; also, 112 calories, 126 mg sodium, 5 mg cholesterol, 20 gm carbohydrate, 5 gm protein, trace fat.

Beet Borscht

Courtney Bird, Papillion, Nebraska

After a busy day, I like to unwind by creating something delicious for dinner. This recipe proves great meals can be quick.

- 2 cans (15 ounces *each*) diced beets
- 1 can (10-3/4 ounces) condensed cream of chicken soup, undiluted
- 1 can (10-1/2 ounces) condensed beef consomme, undiluted
- 4 dill pickle spears
- 1 cup (8 ounces) sour cream
- 1 jar (16 ounces) shredded sweet-and-sour red cabbage, undrained

Drain one can of beets; place beets in a blender, Add soup, consomme, pickles and sour cream; process until smooth. Pour into a large bowl. Add undrained can of beets and cabbage. Chill at least 4 hours. **Yield:** 8-10 servings (2-1/2 quarts).

> **ALREADY COOLED OFF.** *Pictured at left, top to bottom: Low-Fat Gazpacho, Fresh Fruit Soup and Cold Cucumber Soup (all recipes on this page).*

Christmas Soup

Marg Peters, Hanley, Saskatchewan

In addition to serving it as a summertime meal, I put this traditional Mennonite soup on our Christmas lunch table along with an assortment of cold sandwiches and salads.

> **4 quarts plus 1/2 cup water,** *divided*
> **3 packages (8 ounces** *each***) mixed dried fruit (4 cups)**
> **1 cup raisins**
> **1 cinnamon stick (3 inches)**
> **1-1/2 cups sugar**
> **6 tablespoons cornstarch**
> **1 package (3 ounces) cherry gelatin**
> **1 can (16 ounces) pitted tart cherries, undrained**

In a Dutch oven or soup kettle, bring 4 qts. water, dried fruit, raisins and cinnamon stick to a boil. Reduce heat; cover and simmer for 30 minutes or until fruit is tender. Combine sugar, cornstarch and remaining water; mix well. Add to kettle. Return to a boil; boil for 2 minutes, stirring constantly. Remove from the heat; stir in gelatin until dissolved. Add cherries. Remove cinnamon stick. Chill. **Yield:** 12 servings (3 quarts).

Icy Olive Soup

Theresa Goble, Muscatine, Iowa

When summer turns up the heat, I reach for this cool, refreshing soup. The color of the olives contrasts nicely with the creamy yogurt base.

> **2 cups (16 ounces) plain yogurt**
> **2 cans (10-1/2 ounces** *each***) condensed chicken broth, undiluted**
> **2 cans (2-1/4 ounces** *each***) sliced ripe olives, drained**
> **1 cup coarsely chopped cucumber**
> **1/2 cup chopped green onions**
> **1/2 cup chopped green pepper**
> **1/2 cup sliced stuffed olives**
> **1/8 teaspoon white pepper**
> **Seasoned croutons, optional**

In a large bowl, stir yogurt until smooth. Whisk in broth. Add the next six ingredients; mix well. Cover and chill for 4 hours. Stir before serving. Garnish with croutons if desired. **Yield:** 6 servings.

Pineapple Peach Soup

Teresa Lynn, Kerrville, Texas

I like to take this one-of-a-kind soup along to potlucks and other get-togethers. It is usually different than what other people bring, and everyone raves about the flavors.

> **6 medium fresh peaches, peeled and sliced**

> **1 can (8 ounces) crushed unsweetened pineapple, undrained**
> **1/4 cup white grape juice**
> **1/4 cup lemon juice**
> **2 tablespoons honey**
> **3/4 teaspoon ground cinnamon**
> **1/4 teaspoon ground nutmeg**
> **1 medium cantaloupe, peeled, seeded and cubed**
> **1 cup orange juice**
> **Fresh strawberries and whipped cream, optional**

In a 3-qt. saucepan, combine peaches, pineapple, grape juice, lemon juice, honey, cinnamon and nutmeg; bring to a boil over medium heat. Reduce heat and simmer, uncovered, for 10 minutes. Remove from the heat; cool to room temperature. Add three-fourths of the cantaloupe and the orange juice; puree in batches in a blender. Pour into a large bowl. Add remaining cantaloupe. Cover and refrigerate for at least 3 hours. Garnish with strawberries and whipped cream if desired. **Yield:** 8-10 servings (2-1/4 quarts).

Raspberry Orange Soup

Patti McPheeters, Gothenburg, Alabama

If you're looking for a new and interesting recipe to offer company, you'll love this one. Not only is this soup delicious and easy, it's also impressive to serve.

> **2 cans (11 ounces** *each***) mandarin oranges**
> **2 cups apple juice**
> **1 cup orange juice**
> **1/2 cup grape juice**
> **1/2 cup lemon juice**
> **1/4 cup quick-cooking tapioca**
> **2 packages (10 ounces** *each***) frozen raspberries in syrup**
> **Whipped cream and ground nutmeg, optional**

Drain oranges, reserving syrup; set oranges aside. In a 2-qt. saucepan, combine syrup, juices and tapioca; let stand for 5 minutes. Bring to a boil over medium heat; boil for 5 minutes, stirring occasionally. Remove from the heat; stir in raspberries until thawed. Add oranges. Chill for at least 8 hours. Garnish with whipped cream and a pinch of nutmeg if desired. **Yield:** 8 servings (2 quarts).

Cherry Dumpling Soup

Sharon Skildum, Maple Grove, Minnesota

My husband grew up with this dish, but his mother never wrote down the recipe. So when we got married, I had to create my own. Luckily, my husband deemed my version a success!

> **1 can (15 ounces) dark sweet cherries**
> **2 cups water**
> **1/3 cup plus 1 teaspoon sugar,** *divided*
> **1/2 teaspoon ground cinnamon**
> **1/2 cup all-purpose flour**
> **1 teaspoon baking powder**

1/4 cup milk
1 tablespoon vegetable oil
1 tablespoon cornstarch
1 tablespoon cold water

Drain cherries, reserving juice; set cherries aside. In a 2-qt. saucepan, combine juice, water, 1/3 cup sugar and cinnamon; bring to a boil over medium heat, stirring occasionally. For dumplings, combine flour, baking powder and remaining sugar in a small bowl. Add milk and oil, stirring just until moistened. Drop by teaspoonfuls into boiling soup. Reduce heat; cover and simmer for 10 minutes. Dissolve cornstarch in cold water; stir into soup. Add cherries. Bring to a boil; boil for 1-2 minutes. Reduce heat; cover and simmer for 3-4 minutes. **Yield:** 4-6 servings.

Succulent Strawberry Soup

Paula Pelis, Rocky Point, New York

This creamy fruit soup makes a perfect summertime treat for family and friends. The strawberry base with a hint of orange appeals to all palates!

2 quarts fresh strawberries, *divided*
1/2 cup water
5 tablespoons sugar
1 tablespoon all-purpose flour
1 teaspoon grated orange peel
1 cup whipping cream
Fresh mint and additional strawberries, optional

Mash half of the strawberries with a potato masher or fork; set aside. In a blender, combine remaining strawberries, water, sugar, flour and orange peel; process until smooth. Pour into a 2-qt. saucepan. Bring to a boil over medium heat; boil for 2 minutes, stirring constantly. Add mashed strawberries. Reduce heat; simmer, uncovered, for 10 minutes, stirring constantly. Chill for at least 1 hour. Stir in cream. Cover and chill overnight. Garnish with mint and strawberries if desired. **Yield:** 4 servings.

Shrimp Blitz

Jeannette Aiello, Placerville, California

On a hot summer day, this refreshing soup really hits the spot. I've made it for special-occasion luncheons as well as for casual dinners with friends.

1 bottle (8 ounces) clam juice
1 package (8 ounces) cream cheese, softened
1 garlic clove
1 package (5 ounces) frozen cooked salad shrimp, thawed
1 bottle (32 ounces) tomato juice
1 medium ripe avocado, diced
1/2 cup chopped cucumber
1/3 cup chopped green onions
2 tablespoons red wine vinegar
2 teaspoons sugar

1 teaspoon dill weed
1/2 teaspoon salt
1/4 teaspoon hot pepper sauce
1/8 teaspoon pepper

In a blender, combine clam juice and cream cheese; process until smooth. Pour into a large bowl. Add remaining ingredients; mix well. Cover and chill for at least 4 hours. **Yield:** 8 servings (2 quarts).

Ruby-Red Rhubarb Soup

Alice Hill, Lindon, Colorado

Even folks who don't care for rhubarb can't resist the sweet, tangy taste of this soup. With its eye-catching color, this dish is an attractive addition to any table.

4 cups sliced fresh *or* frozen rhubarb
1 quart plus 1 tablespoon water, *divided*
2/3 cup sugar
1 tablespoon cornstarch
1/2 teaspoon red food coloring, optional
1 egg yolk, beaten
1/2 cup whipping cream

In a 2-qt. saucepan, combine rhubarb, 1 qt. of water and sugar; bring to a boil. Reduce heat; cover and simmer for 20 minutes or until rhubarb is tender. Cool for 15 minutes. Place in a blender; process until smooth. Return to pan. Dissolve cornstarch in remaining water; stir into rhubarb mixture. Bring to a boil; boil for 2 minutes, stirring constantly. Add food coloring if desired; mix well. Add a small amount of soup to egg yolk, stirring constantly; return to pan. Chill. Just before serving, beat cream until very soft peaks form; fold into soup. **Yield:** 6 servings.

Blue Cheese Tomato Soup

Mary Stiner, Fremont, New Hampshire

This recipe comes in handy when I want to serve a fancier soup without a lot of extra fuss. Because it's so rich and flavorful, you can enjoy this as a meal in itself.

1 bottle (32 ounces) tomato juice, *divided*
1 package (3 ounces) cream cheese, *softened*
2 to 4 ounces crumbled blue cheese, *divided*
1 small onion, coarsely chopped
1 tablespoon Worcestershire sauce
1 tablespoon sugar
2 teaspoons lemon juice
1/2 teaspoon pepper
1/4 teaspoon salt
Toasted garlic bread, optional

In a blender or food processor, combine 2 cups tomato juice, cream cheese, half of the blue cheese, onion, Worcestershire sauce, sugar, lemon juice, pepper and salt; process until smooth. Pour into a large bowl; stir in remaining tomato juice. Chill at least 1 hour. Top with garlic bread if desired and remaining blue cheese. **Yield:** 6 servings.

Hearty Main-Dish Salads

Looking for a little lighter fare for lunch or dinner? Loaded with lots of meat, pasta, fruits and vegetables, these superb salads make enticing entrees.

Ham Salad

Patricia Reed, Pine Bluff, Arkansas
(PICTURED AT LEFT)

I first made this for a shower…everyone raved about it. Now when I go to a potluck, I take it, and copies of the recipe.

   3/4 cup mayonnaise
   1/2 cup finely chopped celery
   1/4 cup thinly sliced green onions
     2 tablespoons minced chives
     1 tablespoon honey
     2 teaspoons spicy brown mustard
   1/2 teaspoon Worcestershire sauce
   1/2 teaspoon seasoned salt
     5 cups diced fully cooked ham *or* turkey
   1/3 cup chopped pecans and almonds, toasted
Cantaloupe wedges, optional

In a large bowl, combine the first eight ingredients; mix well. Fold in ham. Refrigerate. Add nuts and toss. Serve over cantaloupe if desired. **Yield:** 4-6 servings.

Turkey and Ham Salad with Greens

Joyce Mackey, Perrysburg, New York
(PICTURED AT LEFT)

There's no better way to "beef up" ordinary greens than with two types of meat! You'll prepare this recipe often.

   1/4 cup vegetable oil
     2 tablespoons white wine vinegar, *divided*
   1/4 teaspoon salt, *divided*
   1/4 teaspoon pepper, *divided*
     4 cups thinly sliced salad greens
   1/3 cup mayonnaise
     4 teaspoons spicy brown mustard
   1/4 teaspoon dried thyme
2-1/2 cups cubed cooked turkey
     2 cups julienned fully cooked ham
     1 cup halved seedless green grapes
   1/4 cup thinly sliced green onions
   1/4 cup slivered almonds, toasted

COUNTRY-STYLE CUISINE. *Pictured at left, top to bottom: Ham Salad, Tuna-Stuffed Tomatoes and Turkey and Ham Salad with Greens (recipes on this page).*

Combine oil, 1 tablespoon vinegar, 1/8 teaspoon salt and 1/8 teaspoon pepper; toss with greens. Arrange on a platter or individual plates. In a bowl, combine mayonnaise, mustard, thyme and remaining vinegar, salt and pepper. Add turkey, ham, grapes and onions; toss to coat. Spoon over greens. Garnish with almonds. **Yield:** 4-6 servings.

Tuna-Stuffed Tomatoes

Patricia Collins, Imbler, Oregon
(PICTURED AT LEFT)

Each summer, I look forward to making this salad when I have a bumper crop of tomatoes in my garden.

     1 can (12 ounces) tuna, drained and flaked
     4 ounces cheddar cheese, cut into 1/4-inch cubes
   1/2 to 3/4 cup mayonnaise
   1/2 cup chopped celery
   1/4 cup chopped onion
     2 tablespoons chopped dill pickle
     1 tablespoon dill pickle juice
   1/4 teaspoon salt
   1/8 teaspoon *each* celery seed and pepper
     5 medium tomatoes, cored
Bacon bits, optional

In a bowl, combine tuna, cheese, mayonnaise, celery, onion, pickle, pickle juice, salt, celery seed and pepper. Chill. Cut tomatoes, not quite through, into quarters; place on individual plates and spread apart. Spoon 1/2 cup salad into each. Garnish with bacon bits if desired. **Yield:** 5 servings.

Shoestring Salad

Karen Cape, Green Bay, Wisconsin

This super salad is delicious and easy to prepare—just right for a busy mother of four!

     1 can (12 ounces) tuna, drained and flaked
     1 cup shredded carrot
     1 cup chopped celery
   1/2 cup mayonnaise
   1/4 cup chopped onion
     1 to 2 tablespoons prepared mustard
     1 cup shoestring potato sticks

In a medium bowl, combine the first six ingredients. Fold in potato sticks just before serving. **Yield:** 3-4 servings.

Fruit 'n' Spice Salad

Carol Kitchens, Ridgeland, Mississippi

If you're looking for a new dish for a summer lunch, you'll love this salad. The meat and rice make it a hearty meal, while the apples add a refreshing crunch.

- 4 cups cooked long grain *or* wild rice
- 3 cups cubed fully cooked ham *or* turkey
- 1 small Granny Smith apple, cubed
- 1 small Red Delicious apple, cubed
- 1/2 cup sliced green onions
- 1/2 cup seedless green grapes, halved
- 1/2 cup seedless red grapes, halved
- 1/4 cup raisins
- 1/4 cup olive *or* vegetable oil
- 1/4 cup white wine vinegar
- 1 teaspoon sugar
- 1/4 teaspoon curry powder
- 1/4 teaspoon ground cinnamon
- 1/4 teaspoon salt
- 1/4 cup slivered almonds

In a large bowl, combine rice, ham, apples, onions, grapes and raisins. In a small bowl, combine oil, vinegar, sugar, curry, cinnamon and salt; pour over rice mixture and toss to coat. Chill for at least 2 hours. Just before serving, add almonds and toss. **Yield:** 6-8 servings.

Tarragon Chicken Salad

Valerie Gonsalves-Perry, Harwich, Massachusetts

This is a perfect salad to serve for a special luncheon because it's made ahead of time. Another plus is the short list of everyday ingredients.

- 3/4 cup sour cream
- 3/4 cup mayonnaise
- 1 cup finely chopped celery
- 1/4 cup minced fresh tarragon *or* 1 tablespoon dried tarragon
- 5 cups cubed cooked chicken

In a medium bowl, combine sour cream, mayonnaise, celery and tarragon; stir in chicken. Refrigerate for 2-3 hours. **Yield:** 4-6 servings.

Dijon Ham Salad

Marcia Bloore, Mishawaka, Indiana

This special recipe was handed down to me from my dear mother. So whenever I make this, it not only brings wonderful flavor to my table, it brings back tasty memories as well.

- 1/3 cup cider vinegar
- 1/4 cup vegetable oil

- 3 tablespoons sugar
- 2 tablespoons Dijon mustard
- 1-1/2 teaspoons garlic salt
- 3/4 teaspoon pepper
- 1/8 to 1/4 teaspoon hot pepper sauce
- 3 cups cubed fully cooked ham
- 3 cups cooked rice
- 1-1/2 cups thinly sliced celery
- 1/2 cup chopped green pepper
- 1/2 cup chopped red onion
- 2 tablespoons chopped pimientos
- 1 can (15 to 16 ounces) kidney beans, rinsed and drained

In a saucepan over medium heat, bring the first seven ingredients to a boil; boil for 1 minute or until sugar is dissolved. Cool; chill. In a large bowl, combine ham, rice, celery, green pepper, onion, pimientos and beans. Add dressing; toss to coat. Chill for at least 1 hour. **Yield:** 8-10 servings.

Spectacular Shrimp Salad

Diane Martin, Brown Deer, Wisconsin

A few years back, I was asked to bring a salad to a potluck. I didn't want to bring an ordinary dish, so I created this recipe. Everyone was pleased with the light vinegar-and-oil dressing.

- 1 medium cucumber
- 1/2 pound frozen medium cooked shrimp, thawed
- 1 can (15 ounces) garbanzo beans, rinsed and drained
- 1/4 cup minced fresh parsley
- 1/3 cup olive *or* vegetable oil
- 2 tablespoons cider vinegar
- 1 garlic clove, minced
- 1/8 teaspoon salt
- 1/8 teaspoon lemon-pepper seasoning

Leaf lettuce, optional

Slice cucumber in quarters lengthwise; cut into thin pieces and place in a bowl. Add shrimp, beans and parsley. In a small bowl, combine oil, vinegar, garlic, salt and lemon pepper; pour over salad and toss to coat. Chill for at least 1 hour. Serve over lettuce if desired. **Yield:** 4 servings.

Chicken Salad Oriental

Vivian Miller, Sonora, California

Our family enjoys sampling a variety of salads, but this one is at the top of their list. It's an interesting twist on traditional chicken salad.

✓ **This tasty dish uses less sugar, salt and fat. Recipe includes *Diabetic Exchanges*.**

- 1-1/2 cups cubed cooked chicken
- 1-1/2 cups cooked rice
- 1 package (10 ounces) frozen green beans, thawed
- 1 cup fresh bean sprouts
- 1 medium green pepper, chopped
- 1 small onion, chopped
- 2 tablespoons minced fresh parsley

DRESSING:
- 1/3 cup sour cream
- 2 tablespoons water
- 2 tablespoons soy sauce
- 1/2 teaspoon garlic powder
- 1/2 teaspoon salt, optional
- 1/4 teaspoon ground ginger
- 1/8 teaspoon pepper

In a large bowl, combine the first seven ingredients. Whisk dressing ingredients together in a small bowl. Pour over salad; toss to coat. Refrigerate 8 hours or overnight. **Yield:** 6 servings. **Diabetic Exchanges:** One 1-cup serving (prepared with chicken breast, fat-free sour cream and low-sodium soy sauce and without salt) equals 1 starch, 1 very lean meat, 1 vegetable; also, 139 calories, 194 mg sodium, 69 mg cholesterol, 23 gm carbohydrate, 9 gm protein, 1 gm fat.

Mexican Chicken Salad

Kay Goldman, Punta Gorda, Florida

This salad was served at a local spring festival and was enjoyed by all. The slightly spicy seasonings add just the right amount of festive flair.

- 4 cups chopped cooked chicken
- 2 cups (8 ounces) shredded cheddar cheese
- 1 can (15 to 16 ounces) kidney beans, rinsed and drained
- 1 can (4 ounces) chopped green chilies
- 1/2 cup sliced ripe olives
- 1/2 cup sour cream
- 1/2 cup mayonnaise
- 1 envelope taco seasoning mix
- 2 tablespoons chopped sweet red pepper
- 2 tablespoons chopped green pepper
- 1 medium onion, chopped
- 5 to 6 cups shredded lettuce
- 2 medium tomatoes, chopped
- 4 cups corn chips

In a large bowl, combine the first 11 ingredients; mix well. Cover and chill until ready to serve. Serve on a bed of lettuce; top with tomatoes and corn chips. **Yield:** 8 servings.

Beef and Pasta Salad

Jo Ann Satsky, Bandera, Texas

My husband and I like zesty pasta salads and have tried many different types. This delightful dish can be eaten warm or cold, so it's a perfect meal anytime of year.

- 3 cups rotini pasta, cooked and drained
- 1 green pepper, julienned
- 1 cup halved cherry tomatoes
- 1/2 cup sliced ripe olives
- 1 pound boneless top sirloin, cut into strips
- 2 tablespoons cooking oil
- 1 bottle (8 ounces) Italian salad dressing
- 1-1/2 cups (6 ounces) shredded provolone *or* mozzarella cheese

In a large bowl, combine pasta, green pepper, tomatoes and olives. In a skillet over medium-high heat, stir-fry sirloin in oil until cooked as desired; drain. If serving salad hot, add dressing to skillet and bring to a boil. Pour over pasta mixture; toss to coat. Add cheese; serve immediately. If serving salad cold, let beef cool for 15 minutes. Add beef, dressing and cheese to pasta mixture; toss to coat. Chill for at least 1 hour. **Yield:** 6 servings.

Submarine Sandwich Salad

Julie Vogl, Cumberland, Iowa

If your family's like mine, they won't be able to resist this salad loaded with meat, produce...even bread! The recipe can be easily doubled, so I often prepare it for potlucks.

- 5 to 6 cups torn lettuce
- 1 to 2 hard rolls, cubed
- 1 medium tomato, chopped
- 1/2 cup thinly sliced red onion
- 1/2 cup shredded Swiss cheese
- 2 ounces *each* ham, turkey and salami, julienned
- 1/2 cup sliced pepperoni

DRESSING:
- 1/3 cup vegetable oil
- 2 tablespoons tarragon *or* white wine vinegar
- 1/4 to 1/2 teaspoon dried oregano
- 1/4 teaspoon salt
- 1/8 teaspoon garlic powder
- Dash pepper

Combine lettuce, rolls, tomato, onion, cheese, ham, turkey, salami and pepperoni in a large bowl. In a small bowl, combine dressing ingredients; mix well. Pour over salad; toss to coat. Serve immediately. **Yield:** 6 servings.

Hot Turkey Pecan Salad

Ethel Brown, Decatur, Illinois

As a way to use leftovers from the holidays, I substituted turkey for chicken in this traditional hot salad. My family always says this country-stye dish reminds them of home.

- 2 cups cubed cooked turkey *or* chicken
- 2 cups thinly sliced celery
- 1/2 cup sliced stuffed olives
- 1/2 cup chopped pecans
- 1 tablespoon finely chopped onion
- 1 cup mayonnaise
- 2 tablespoons lemon juice
- 1/2 teaspoon salt
- 3/4 to 1 cup crushed potato chips
- 1/2 cup shredded cheddar cheese

In a large bowl, combine turkey, celery, olives, pecans and onion. Combine mayonnaise, lemon juice and salt; pour over turkey mixture and toss to coat. Pour into a greased 8-in. square baking dish. Sprinkle with potato chips and cheese. Bake, uncovered, at 375° for 20-25 minutes or until bubbly. **Yield:** 4 servings.

Spicy Grilled Chicken Salad

Brenda Eichelberger, Williamsport, Maryland
(PICTURED AT LEFT)

After working in the garden all day, I don't feel much like spending hours in the kitchen. So I'll frequently prepare this fabulous, filling salad for supper.

✓ **This tasty dish uses less sugar, salt and fat. Recipe includes** *Diabetic Exchanges.*

> 1 can (8 ounces) sliced pineapple
> 3 tablespoons vegetable oil
> 2 tablespoons soy sauce
> 1 tablespoon vinegar
> 1 tablespoon honey
> 1/4 teaspoon ground ginger
> 1/4 teaspoon cayenne pepper
> 4 boneless skinless chicken breast halves (1 pound)
> 1/2 to 1 teaspoon seasoned *or* black pepper
> 5 cups torn salad greens
> 1 small green pepper, julienned
> 1 small sweet red pepper, julienned
> 1 cup sliced fresh mushrooms
> 1 small onion, sliced into rings

Drain pineapple, reserving 2 tablespoons juice. In a jar with tight-fitting lid, combine the juice, oil, soy sauce, vinegar, honey, ginger and cayenne; shake well. Brush some over pineapple slices; set aside. Sprinkle both sides of chicken with pepper; grill or broil for 4-5 minutes on each side or until juices run clear. Slice into strips. Grill or broil pineapple, turning to brown both sides, for 2-3 minutes or until heated through. To serve, toss greens, peppers, mushrooms and onion in a large bowl and top with chicken and pineapple; or arrange on four plates. Drizzle with remaining dressing. **Yield:** 4 servings. **Diabetic Exchanges:** One serving (prepared with unsweetened pineapple and low-sodium soy sauce and served with 2 tablespoons dressing) equals 3 lean meat, 2 vegetable, 1 fat, 1 fruit; also, 323 calories, 659 mg sodium, 73 mg cholesterol, 21 gm carbohydrate, 29 gm protein, 14 gm fat.

Salad in a Bread Bowl

Barbara Hayes, Meadville, Pennsylvania
(PICTURED AT LEFT)

When I made salads in the past, I always served fresh-from-the-oven bread. Now this fun recipe combines these two great foods into one!

> 1 loaf (1 pound) frozen white bread dough, thawed
> 8 cups torn lettuce

MOUTH-WATERING MEALS. *Pictured at left, top to bottom: Spicy Grilled Chicken Salad and Salad in a Bread Bowl (both recipes on this page).*

> 1 cup quartered cherry tomatoes
> 1 cup cauliflowerets
> 1 cup quartered thinly sliced cucumber
> 1/2 cup thinly sliced celery
> 1/2 cup thinly sliced carrots
> 1 pound ground beef
> 1/2 cup chopped onion
> Italian salad dressing *or* dressing of your choice

Divide bread dough into four equal portions; pat each into an 8-in. circle. Coat the outside of four 5-in. x 2-in. round ovenproof bowls with nonstick cooking spray; place upside down on a baking sheet. Shape dough circles around bowls. Cover and let rise in a warm place for 1 hour. Bake at 350° for 25-30 minutes or until golden brown. Meanwhile, combine lettuce, tomatoes, cauliflower, cucumber, celery and carrots; set aside. In a skillet over medium heat, brown beef and onion; drain. Place 2-1/2 cups of lettuce mixture into each bread bowl. Top with 1/4 cup beef mixture. Serve with dressing. **Yield:** 4 servings.

EDIBLE BOWLS. Hollow out large fresh tomatoes or green peppers and fill with homemade tuna, egg or chicken salad for a tasty and attractive main meal.

Haystack Salad

Mrs. Simon Miller, Shreve, Ohio

This recipe comes in handy when it's too hot to be in the kitchen. It really is an all-in-one meal that appeals to the entire family.

> 2 pounds ground beef
> 2 cups spaghetti sauce
> 2 tablespoons taco seasoning mix
> 1/4 cup butter *or* margarine
> 1/4 cup all-purpose flour
> 1/8 teaspoon garlic powder
> 1/8 teaspoon white pepper
> 2-1/4 cups milk
> 8 ounces process American cheese, cubed
> 2 cups hot cooked long grain rice
> 1 head iceberg lettuce, chopped
> 4 medium tomatoes, chopped
> 1 medium onion, chopped
> 1 can (15 to 16 ounces) kidney beans, rinsed and drained
> 1-1/2 cups (6 ounces) shredded cheddar cheese
> 1 bag (9 ounces) tortilla chips, crushed
> 1 cup (8 ounces) sour cream

In a large skillet, brown beef until no longer pink; drain. Add spaghetti sauce and taco seasoning; simmer, uncovered, for 10 minutes. Meanwhile, for cheese sauce, melt butter in a medium saucepan. Stir in flour, garlic powder and pepper. Gradually add milk. Bring to a boil; boil for 2 minutes, stirring constantly. Add American cheese; cook and stir until melted. Remove from the heat. On eight plates, layer rice, lettuce, tomatoes, onion, beans, cheddar cheese and tortilla chips in the order given. Top with meat mixture, sour cream and cheese sauce. **Yield:** 8 servings.

Grill-Side Turkey Salad

Barbara Young, Bethesda, Maryland

I've enjoyed cooking for as long as I can remember…I even majored in home economics in college. I'm now in my mid-70's and enthusiastically cook and bake with my granddaughter.

✓ This tasty dish uses less sugar, salt and fat. Recipe includes *Diabetic Exchanges*.

- 2 turkey breast tenderloins (1-1/2 pounds)
- 2 teaspoons dried tarragon, *divided*
- 1/2 cup thinly sliced celery
- 1/2 cup chopped green pepper
- 1/2 cup chopped red onion
- 2 tablespoons vegetable oil
- 1 tablespoon soy sauce
- 1 tablespoon lemon juice
- 1 tablespoon red wine vinegar
- 1/8 teaspoon pepper
- 1/4 teaspoon salt, optional

Lettuce leaves
Chopped salted peanuts, optional

Sprinkle each tenderloin with 1/2 teaspoon tarragon. Grill, uncovered, over medium-hot coals for 8-10 minutes per side or until a meat thermometer reads 170°-180°. Cool to room temperature. Cut into cubes; place in a large bowl. Add celery, green pepper and onion. In a small bowl, combine oil, soy sauce, lemon juice, vinegar, pepper, salt if desired and remaining tarragon; mix well. Pour over turkey mixture; toss to coat. Refrigerate for at least 3 hours. Serve on lettuce leaves; sprinkle with peanuts if desired. **Yield:** 4 servings. **Diabetic Exchanges:** One 1-1/4-cup serving (prepared with low-sodium soy sauce and without salt and peanuts) equals 5 very lean meat, 1 fat, 1 vegetable; also, 258 calories, 261 mg sodium, 53 mg cholesterol, 4 gm carbohydrate, 41 gm protein, 9 gm fat.

Sweet and Savory Turkey Salad

Suzanne Jones, Twinsburg, Ohio

My mother found this recipe while searching for something different to serve at my bridal shower. The apricots and figs make the dressing unique and tasty.

- 1/3 cup vegetable oil
- 3 tablespoons lemon juice
- 3 tablespoons white wine vinegar
- 2 to 3 tablespoons Dijon mustard
- 3 tablespoons minced red onion
- 3 tablespoons poppy seeds
- 1 tablespoon honey
- 1/4 teaspoon salt
- 1 to 2 teaspoons grated orange peel
- 1/2 cup finely chopped dried apricots
- 1/2 cup finely chopped dried figs
- 5 cups shredded cooked turkey *or* cubed fully cooked ham

- 4 celery ribs, sliced
- 4 ounces cheddar cheese, julienned
- 3/4 cup coarsely chopped pecans, toasted

In a small bowl, whisk oil, lemon juice, vinegar, mustard, onion, poppy seeds, honey and salt. Stir in orange peel, apricots and figs; cover and let stand for 1 hour at room temperature. In a large bowl, combine turkey, celery, cheese and dressing. Refrigerate for several hours. Stir in pecans just before serving. **Yield:** 6-8 servings.

Crunchy Tossed Salad with Chicken

Ileene Nodland, Dunn Center, North Dakota

I like to prepare this in summer when the men are late getting in from the fields. Chicken and a zesty dressing turn simple greens into a satisfying main meal.

- 6 cups torn lettuce
- 3 cups cubed cooked chicken
- 1 cup sliced celery
- 1 cup shredded carrots
- 1/4 cup sliced green onions
- 3/4 cup mayonnaise
- 1/4 cup milk
- 2 tablespoons tarragon *or* white wine vinegar
- 3 to 4 teaspoons prepared mustard
- 1/2 teaspoon pepper
- 2 cups shoestring potato sticks

In a large bowl, combine lettuce, chicken, celery, carrots and onions. Combine mayonnaise, milk, vinegar, mustard and pepper in a small bowl. Pour over salad; toss until lightly coated. Add potato sticks; serve immediately. **Yield:** 4-6 servings.

Hearty Luncheon Salad

Shannon Cooper, South Gibson, Pennsylvania

The real star of this recipe is by far the dressing, which adds an appealing sweet touch to the greens. This salad can be made ahead—that makes it a "keeper" in my book.

- 4 cups torn fresh spinach
- 4 cups torn iceberg lettuce
- 1/2 to 1 cup sliced fresh mushrooms
- 1/2 to 1 cup shredded carrots
- 1/2 cup thinly sliced red onion
- 4 hard-cooked eggs, quartered
- 3 boneless skinless chicken breast halves, cooked and sliced
- 9 bacon strips, cooked and crumbled
- 1/2 cup chow mein noodles
- 1/3 cup sugar
- 3 tablespoons vinegar
- 1-1/2 teaspoons prepared mustard
- 1-1/2 teaspoons onion powder
- 1/2 teaspoon celery seed
- 1/2 teaspoon salt

1/4 teaspoon pepper
1/2 cup vegetable oil

In a large bowl, toss spinach, lettuce, mushrooms, carrots and onion. Arrange eggs around edge of bowl. Place chicken in center of bowl. Sprinkle with bacon and chow mein noodles. In a blender or food processor, combine sugar, vinegar, mustard, onion powder, celery seed, salt and pepper; with unit running, add oil in a slow steady stream. Pour over salad; toss. Serve immediately. **Yield:** 10 servings.

Fruited Turkey Salad

Dorothy Rieke, Julian, Nebraska

During my spare time, I can be found in the kitchen…I love trying new recipes. In this recipe, sunflower seeds add a special crunch to turkey salad.

✓ This tasty dish uses less sugar, salt and fat. Recipe includes *Diabetic Exchanges*.

   4 cups cubed cooked turkey
   1 can (20 ounces) pineapple chunks, drained
   1 cup seedless green grapes, halved
   1 cup sliced celery
   2 tablespoons vegetable oil
   2 tablespoons orange juice
   2 tablespoons lemon juice
   1 tablespoon minced fresh parsley
1/2 teaspoon salt, optional
1/2 cup mayonnaise
1/2 cup salted sunflower seeds, optional

In a large bowl, combine turkey, pineapple, grapes and celery. Whisk together oil, orange juice, lemon juice, parsley and salt if desired in a small bowl. Pour over salad; toss to coat. Chill for 2 hours. Just before serving, add mayonnaise and sunflower seeds if desired; mix well. **Yield:** 7 servings.
Diabetic Exchanges: One 1-cup serving (prepared with turkey breast, unsweetened pineapple and fat-free mayonnaise and without salt and sunflower seeds) equals 2 very lean meat, 1 fat, 1 fruit; also, 184 calories, 280 mg sodium, 49 mg cholesterol, 18 gm carbohydrate, 13 gm protein, 6 gm fat.

Turkey Cashew Salad

Phyllis Barkey, Warren, Michigan

This salad has appeared at many bridal and baby showers, and I finally received the recipe. The salty crunchy cashews work nicely with the sweet tangy dressing.

   1 cup small ring pasta
   4 cups cubed cooked turkey *or* chicken
   1 cup thinly sliced celery
   1 cup seedless green grapes, halved
   1 cup mayonnaise
   2 tablespoons orange juice
   2 tablespoons vinegar
   1 tablespoon olive *or* vegetable oil

1-1/2 teaspoons grated orange peel
  3/4 teaspoon salt
  1/4 teaspoon ground ginger
  3/4 cup salted cashews

Cook pasta according to package directions; drain. Rinse in cold water; place in a large bowl. Add the turkey, celery and grapes. In a small bowl, combine mayonnaise, orange juice, vinegar, oil, orange peel, salt and ginger. Pour over salad; toss to coat. Chill for at least 1 hour. Stir in cashews just before serving. **Yield:** 8 servings.

Perfect Chicken Salad

Lora Schnurr, Fort Wayne, Indiana

My godchild doesn't care for vegetables, but he loved this salad…even the peas and carrots! I hope you'll try this original recipe soon. You'll find it appeals to all palates.

   2 cups cubed cooked chicken
1/2 cup frozen peas, thawed
1/4 cup chopped ripe olives
   2 tablespoons shredded carrot
   2 tablespoons minced onion
DRESSING:
1/2 cup mayonnaise
   1 tablespoon yellow *or* spicy brown mustard
1/4 teaspoon Worcestershire sauce
1/4 teaspoon seasoned salt
1/8 teaspoon pepper

In a medium bowl, combine chicken, peas, olives, carrot and onion. Mix dressing ingredients in a small bowl; pour over salad and toss to coat. Refrigerate until ready to serve. **Yield:** 2-3 servings.

Turkey Chutney Salad

Sharon McMahan, Arroyo Grande, California

This one-of-a-kind salad features an appealing assortment of fruit and flavors. One forkful and I think you'll agree the taste is unbeatable.

1-1/2 cups mayonnaise
  1/2 cup prepared chutney
   1 to 2 teaspoons curry powder
  1/4 teaspoon salt
   4 cups diced cooked turkey
   1 cup sliced celery
   1 can (8 ounces) pineapple chunks, drained
  1/2 cup golden raisins
   2 firm red apples, cubed
   2 medium bananas, sliced
  1/2 cup chopped pecans, toasted
  1/2 cup flaked coconut, toasted, optional

In a large bowl, combine mayonnaise, chutney, curry and salt. Stir in turkey, celery, pineapple and raisins. Chill for at least 2 hours. Just before serving, stir in apples, bananas, pecans and coconut if desired. **Yield:** 10-12 servings.

Pasta, Bean & Grain Salads

Toss aside traditional green salads and liven up family meals and potlucks with filling varieties featuring satisfying staples. Then get ready to serve up seconds.

Three-Bean Garden Salad

Mary Kaye Rackowitz, Marysville, Washington
(PICTURED AT LEFT)

This comes from a recipe I originally found in a bean cookbook. It took quite a few failures to come up with this winning combination. I hope you enjoy it as much as we do!

- 1 package (10 ounces) frozen lima beans
- 1 can (15 to 16 ounces) kidney beans, rinsed and drained
- 1 package (9 ounces) frozen cut green beans, thawed
- 8 ounces fresh mushrooms, sliced
- 1 pint cherry tomatoes, halved
- 1/4 cup thinly sliced green onions

DRESSING:
- 2/3 cup lemon juice
- 1/3 cup sugar
- 1/3 cup olive *or* vegetable oil
- 1-1/4 teaspoons salt
- 3/4 teaspoon Italian seasoning
- 1/2 teaspoon dried basil
- 1/2 teaspoon pepper

Cook lima beans according to package directions. Rinse in cold water; drain and place in a medium bowl. Add kidney and green beans, mushrooms, tomatoes and onions. Combine dressing ingredients. Pour over salad; mix gently to coat. Cover and chill for at least 5 hours, stirring occasionally. **Yield:** 10-12 servings.

Antipasto Pasta Salad

Bernadette Nelson, Arcadia, California
(PICTURED AT LEFT)

I love trying new recipes, and this one for pasta salad tops all other varieties I've tried. With beans, cheese, sausage and vegetables, it's a hearty complement to any meal.

- 1 pound penne *or* tube pasta, cooked and drained
- 1 green *or* sweet red pepper, julienned
- 1 can (15 ounces) garbanzo beans, rinsed and drained

DELIGHTFULLY DIFFERENT. *Pictured at left, top to bottom: Antipasto Pasta Salad, Three-Bean Garden Salad (recipes on this page) and Citrus Black Bean and Rice Salad (recipe on page 52).*

- 4 ounces Monterey Jack cheese, julienned
- 4 ounces mozzarella cheese, julienned
- 4 ounces brick *or* provolone cheese, julienned
- 1 bunch green onions, sliced
- 4 ounces thinly sliced hard salami, julienned
- 1 can (2-1/4 ounces) sliced ripe olives, drained
- 3 ounces thinly sliced pepperoni
- 1 to 2 tablespoons minced fresh chives
- 2 plum tomatoes, sliced and halved

BASIL VINAIGRETTE:
- 2/3 cup vegetable oil
- 1/3 cup red wine vinegar
- 3 tablespoons minced fresh basil *or* 1 tablespoon dried basil
- 1 garlic clove, minced
- 1/4 teaspoon salt

In a large bowl, combine the first 12 ingredients. Combine dressing ingredients in a small bowl. Pour over salad; toss to coat. Cover and refrigerate. Toss before serving. **Yield:** 18 servings.

Quick Pantry Salad

Mary Christiansen, Columbia Falls, Montana

One morning a few years back, I suddenly remembered I needed to bring a salad for that day's Bible study luncheon. I headed to the pantry, pulled together ingredients and created this recipe.

- 4-1/2 cups cooked elbow macaroni
- 1 can (15 to 16 ounces) kidney beans, rinsed and drained
- 1 can (15-1/4 ounces) whole kernel corn, drained
- 2 cups cubed cooked turkey *or* chicken
- 1 small cucumber, seeded and chopped
- 2 celery ribs, thinly sliced
- 1 cup shredded carrots
- 1/2 cup chopped green pepper
- 1/2 cup chopped onion
- 1/2 cup frozen peas, thawed
- 6 hard-cooked eggs, chopped
- 1 cup mayonnaise *or* salad dressing
- 1/4 cup milk
- 1/2 teaspoon salt
- 1/4 to 1/2 teaspoon poultry seasoning
- 1/4 to 1/2 teaspoon ground cumin
- 1/4 teaspoon pepper

In a large bowl, combine the first 11 ingredients. Combine mayonnaise, milk and seasonings in a small bowl. Pour over salad and toss to coat. Serve immediately or refrigerate until ready to serve. **Yield:** 16-18 servings.

Citrus Black Bean and Rice Salad

Billie Jean Culwell, San Diego, California
(PICTURED ON PAGE 50)

I developed this salad from a couple of other recipes that weren't quite tangy enough for my family. The citrus flavor is a nice change of pace from most bean salads.

MARINATED BEANS:
- 1/3 cup olive *or* vegetable oil
- 2 to 3 garlic cloves, minced
- 2 tablespoons lime juice
- 2 tablespoons minced fresh parsley *or* cilantro
- 4 teaspoons brown mustard
- 1 teaspoon ground cumin
- 1/2 teaspoon pepper
- 1/4 teaspoon hot pepper sauce
- 1 can (15 ounces) black beans, rinsed and drained

VEGETABLE COMBO:
- 2 medium tomatoes, diced
- 1 small sweet red pepper, julienned
- 1/2 cup sliced celery
- 1/2 cup sliced green onions

ORANGE RICE:
- 1-1/4 cups uncooked converted rice
- 1 tablespoon olive *or* vegetable oil
- 1 cup chicken broth
- 1/2 cup orange juice
- 1/2 teaspoon salt
- 1/8 teaspoon pepper
- 2 tablespoons minced fresh parsley *or* cilantro
- 1 tablespoon grated orange peel

In a bowl, whisk together the first eight ingredients. Add beans; toss to coat. Cover and chill for at least 1 hour. Combine tomatoes, red pepper, celery and onions in another bowl; cover and chill. Meanwhile, in a skillet over high heat, saute rice in oil until golden brown, about 3 minutes. Add broth, juice, salt and pepper; bring to a boil. Reduce heat; cover and simmer for 20 minutes or until rice is tender and liquid is absorbed. Place in a large bowl; add parsley and orange peel. Cover and chill for at least 30 minutes. When ready to serve, combine beans, vegetables and rice. **Yield:** 8-10 servings.

Turkey Shrimp Salad

Christine Wallat, Greenfield, Wisconsin

It's tradition for my family to have this salad on New Year's Day. I like to serve it with mugs of hot tomato soup and warm French bread.

- 12 cups cooked elbow macaroni
- 6 cups cubed cooked turkey
- 2 cups cooked deveined salad shrimp
- 1 cup thinly sliced celery
- 1/2 cup thinly sliced green onions
- 1 can (20 ounces) pineapple chunks, drained
- 1 can (16 ounces) sliced peaches, drained and diced

- 1 can (14 ounces) sweetened condensed milk
- 1/2 cup lemon juice
- 1/2 cup vegetable oil
- 1/4 cup Dijon mustard
- 1/2 teaspoon salt
- 1/8 teaspoon lemon-pepper seasoning
- Hard-cooked eggs, sliced, optional
- Orange slices, optional

In a large bowl, combine the first seven ingredients. Combine milk, lemon juice, oil, mustard, salt and lemon pepper in a small bowl; mix well. Pour over salad and toss to coat. Cover and chill for at least 2 hours. Garnish with eggs and oranges if desired. **Yield:** 20-22 servings.

Elbow Macaroni Medley

Carolyn Fields, Royston, Georgia

I'm a firm believer that folks can't have too many cookbooks …although my husband may disagree! Of course, he never complains when one of my books yields a tasty dish like this.

- 1 box (7 ounces) elbow macaroni
- 3 hard-cooked eggs, chopped
- 1-1/2 cups cubed cheddar cheese
- 1-1/2 cups chopped celery
- 1 medium green pepper, chopped
- 1 jar (2 ounces) sliced pimientos, drained
- 3/4 cup mayonnaise
- 4 teaspoons lemon juice
- 3/4 teaspoon salt
- 1/4 teaspoon pepper
- 8 bacon strips, cooked and crumbled

Cook macaroni according to package directions; drain and rinse in cold water. Place in a large bowl; add the next five ingredients. Combine mayonnaise, lemon juice, salt and pepper in a small bowl. Pour over salad and toss. Cover and chill for at least 1 hour. Just before serving, add bacon and toss. **Yield:** 6-8 servings.

Two-Bean Tuna Salad

Amelia Meaux, Crowley, Louisiana

My parents owned a restaurant for years, so it's no surprise I love to cook. The light vinaigrette dressing nicely complements the tuna and beans in this salad.

- 1 can (15 to 16 ounces) kidney beans, rinsed and drained
- 1 can (15 ounces) garbanzo beans, rinsed and drained
- 1 can (6 ounces) tuna in water, drained and flaked
- 2/3 cup chopped celery
- 1/2 cup sliced stuffed olives
- 1/3 cup sliced green onions
- 1/4 cup chopped green pepper
- 1/4 cup minced fresh parsley

DRESSING:
- 1/3 cup olive *or* vegetable oil

2 tablespoons lemon juice
2 tablespoons white wine vinegar
1 teaspoon paprika
1/2 teaspoon ground mustard
1/2 teaspoon salt
1/4 teaspoon sugar
1/4 teaspoon pepper

In a large bowl, combine the first eight ingredients. In a jar with tight-fitting lid, combine dressing ingredients. Pour over salad; toss to coat. Cover and chill for at least 2 hours. **Yield:** 6-8 servings.

Ham, Turkey and Wild Rice Salad

Jamie Schmidt, Gaylord, Minnesota

As a nutritionist, I'm always trying to get my family to enjoy—or at least eat!—foods that are good for them. They love the combination of flavors in this salad.

5 cups cooked wild rice
1/2 cup Western salad dressing
1 cup cubed fully cooked ham
1 cup cubed cooked turkey
1 cup thinly sliced celery
1 cup frozen peas, thawed
2/3 cup thinly sliced radishes
1/2 cup finely chopped onion
1 cup mayonnaise
2 teaspoons prepared mustard
1/4 to 1/2 teaspoon curry powder
1/2 teaspoon salt
1/4 teaspoon pepper

In a large bowl, combine rice and dressing; cover and chill overnight. Add ham, turkey, celery, peas, radishes and onion. Combine mayonnaise, mustard, curry, salt and pepper; mix well. Stir into salad. Cover and refrigerate for at least 2 hours. **Yield:** 8-10 servings.

Minty Bean Salad

Jeannette Shields, Brandon, Vermont

Each September, a women's group at our church sponsors a salad supper. Everyone is delighted when they see this extra-special dish on the table.

1 pound dry navy *or* great northern beans
3 chicken bouillon cubes
6 cups water
2 large tomatoes, coarsely chopped
1 can (6 ounces) pitted ripe olives, drained and halved
1/2 cup olive *or* vegetable oil
1/2 cup lemon juice
1/3 cup chopped fresh mint *or* 2 tablespoons dried mint
1 tablespoon sugar
2 teaspoons salt
1/2 teaspoon garlic salt
1/4 teaspoon pepper

Place beans and enough water to cover in a large saucepan. Bring to a boil; boil for 1 minute. Remove from the heat; let stand for 1 hour. Drain and discard liquid. Add bouillon and water; bring to a boil. Reduce heat; cover and simmer for 1 hour or until beans are just tender. Drain; cool slightly. Add remaining ingredients; mix gently. Cover and chill for at least 1 hour. **Yield:** 8-10 servings.

Garbanzo Bean Salad

Laura Welcome, New Market, Maryland

I received the greatest compliment when I took this salad to our daughter's preschool potluck…and came home with an empty bowl! I've given the recipe away many times over the years.

2 cans (15 ounces *each*) garbanzo beans
1 medium green pepper, chopped
1 medium sweet red pepper, chopped
1 medium red onion, thinly sliced
1 jar (4-1/2 ounces) marinated artichoke hearts, drained and sliced
1/4 cup sliced ripe olives
1/4 cup sliced stuffed olives
DRESSING:
3-1/2 tablespoons red wine *or* cider vinegar
3 tablespoons olive *or* vegetable oil
2 garlic cloves, minced
1/2 teaspoon salt
1/8 teaspoon pepper

In a large bowl, combine the first seven ingredients. For dressing, combine all ingredients in a jar with tight-fitting lid. Pour over salad; toss to coat. Cover and chill for at least 2 hours or overnight. **Yield:** 8-10 servings.

Ham and Blue Cheese Pasta Salad

Carla Kirby, Clayton, Missouri

When I first saw this recipe, it piqued my interest. It flopped at first, but after some adjustments, this salad's become a real winner in our home.

2 cups julienned fully cooked ham
1/3 cup crumbled blue *or* feta cheese
1/3 cup minced fresh parsley
1 garlic clove, minced
1-1/2 teaspoons minced fresh rosemary *or* 1/2 teaspoon dried rosemary, crushed
1/4 teaspoon pepper
6 cups (12 ounces) bow tie pasta
1/3 cup olive *or* vegetable oil
1 cup coarsely chopped pecans, toasted
Grated Parmesan cheese

In a bowl, combine ham, cheese, parsley, garlic, rosemary and pepper. Cook pasta; drain. Immediately add to ham mixture and toss. Add oil and nuts; mix well. Sprinkle with Parmesan cheese. Serve immediately. **Yield:** 8-10 servings.

Black-and-White Bean Salad

Margaret Andersen, Greeley, Colorado
(PICTURED AT LEFT)

This zippy bean salad goes perfectly with a barbecued meal and is also great for a buffet or potluck. Best of all, it can be prepared in no time.

1 can (16 ounces) great northern beans, rinsed and drained
1 can (15 ounces) black beans, rinsed and drained
1-1/4 cups chopped seeded tomato
1-1/2 cups diced sweet red *or* yellow pepper
3/4 cup thinly sliced green onions
1/2 cup salsa
3 tablespoons red wine *or* cider vinegar
2 tablespoons minced fresh parsley *or* cilantro
1/4 teaspoon salt
1/8 teaspoon pepper

Combine the first five ingredients in a large bowl. In a small bowl, combine salsa, vinegar, parsley, salt and pepper. Pour over bean mixture; toss to coat. Cover and refrigerate for at least 1 hour. **Yield:** 6-8 servings.

Turkey Pasta Salad

Jean Roche, Walnut Creek, California
(PICTURED AT LEFT)

When you're looking for a side dish to round out your barbecue, nothing compares to this meaty pasta salad. It also makes a simple yet satisfying meal in itself.

DRESSING:
1 cup vegetable oil
1/2 cup red wine *or* cider vinegar
1/4 cup honey
1/4 cup Dijon mustard
SALAD:
1 package (12 ounces) tri-colored spiral pasta
3 cups broccoli florets
3 cups cubed cooked turkey breast
1/2 cup thinly sliced green onions
1/2 cup chopped sweet red pepper

Whisk all dressing ingredients together in a small bowl; set aside. Cook pasta according to package directions; drain. Place in a large bowl. While pasta is warm, stir in 1/2 cup dressing. Cover and chill. Add broccoli, turkey, onions, red pepper and remaining dressing; toss to coat. Cover and chill 3-4 hours or overnight. **Yield:** 12-14 servings.

SPECTACULAR SPREAD. *Pictured at left, top to bottom: Black-and-White Bean Salad, Turkey Pasta Salad and Italian Market Salad (all recipes on this page).*

Italian Market Salad

B.N. Desai, North Fort Myers, Florida
(PICTURED AT LEFT)

With zesty dressing, pepperoni and cheese, this easy salad is a great addition to a spaghetti-and-meatballs dinner. It's a convenient dish that can be made the night before.

2 cups cooked rice
1-1/2 cups cubed fully cooked ham
2 cups cubed mozzarella cheese
1 medium green pepper, diced
2 ounces thinly sliced pepperoni
2 green onions, sliced
1/2 cup Italian salad dressing
1 can (2-1/4 ounces) sliced ripe olives, drained, optional
2 medium tomatoes, chopped, optional

In a large bowl, combine the first seven ingredients. Cover and chill. Just before serving, stir in olives and tomatoes if desired. **Yield:** 6-8 servings.

RICE WISDOM. Cooked wild rice will keep in the refrigerator for up to 1 week. So you can make it ahead to use in satisfying salads later on.

Fiesta Black Bean Salad

Jackie Barmoy, Sitka, Alaska

After building up hearty appetites, the crew on my husband's commercial fishing boat enjoys sitting down to this slightly spicy salad. It's a real crowd-pleaser.

✓ This tasty dish uses less sugar, salt and fat. Recipe includes *Diabetic Exchanges*.

2 cans (15 ounces *each*) black beans, rinsed and drained
1 can (11 ounces) whole kernel corn, drained
1 medium tomato, seeded and diced
1/4 cup thinly sliced green onions
DRESSING:
1/4 cup vegetable oil
2 tablespoons cider vinegar
1 tablespoon fresh lime juice
2 tablespoons minced fresh cilantro *or* parsley
1/2 teaspoon garlic powder
1/4 to 1/2 teaspoon ground turmeric
1/4 teaspoon cayenne pepper
Dash pepper

In a large bowl, combine the first four ingredients. In a small bowl, whisk together dressing ingredients. Pour over black bean mixture. Cover and chill for at least 2 hours. **Yield:** 12 servings. **Diabetic Exchanges:** One 1/2-cup serving equals 1 starch, 1 vegetable, 1 fat; also, 131 calories, 93 mg sodium, 0 cholesterol, 18 gm carbohydrate, 5 gm protein, 5 gm fat.

Four-Bean Salad

Penny Orner, Rockton, Pennsylvania

Most people are surprised to hear this salad gets its sweet flavor from honey instead of sugar. This natural ingredient gives basic bean salad a tasty new twist.

- 1/2 cup vegetable oil
- 1/2 cup honey
- 1/2 cup vinegar
- 1 tablespoon water
- 1/8 teaspoon salt
- 1/8 teaspoon pepper
- 1 can (15 to 16 ounces) kidney beans, rinsed and drained
- 1 can (15 ounces) garbanzo beans, rinsed and drained
- 1 can (14-1/2 ounces) wax beans, drained
- 1 can (14-1/2 ounces) green beans, drained
- 1/4 cup chopped onion
- 1 jar (2 ounces) chopped pimientos, drained

In a medium bowl, combine the first six ingredients; mix well. Add remaining ingredients; toss to coat. Cover and chill for at least 6 hours. **Yield:** 8-10 servings.

Pesto Pasta Salad

Tam Baden, Anacortes, Washington

We grow a large crop of basil each summer and make dozens of jars of pesto sauce to use in dishes such as this salad. You'll love the combination of garlic and herbs.

- 1 package (16 ounces) spiral pasta, cooked, drained and cooled
- 1 cup julienned fully cooked ham
- 1 cup julienned carrots
- 1 cup thinly sliced celery
- 1 cup frozen peas, thawed
- 1 cup sliced fresh mushrooms
- 1 cup julienned zucchini
- 1 cup cubed Monterey Jack cheese
- 1/2 cup grated Parmesan cheese
- 1/2 cup thinly sliced green onions
- 1/3 cup chopped radishes
- 1 can (6 ounces) medium pitted ripe olives, drained and halved
- 1 jar (2 ounces) chopped pimientos, drained

PESTO DRESSING:
- 3 to 5 garlic cloves
- 2 cups loosely packed fresh basil leaves
- 3/4 cup grated Parmesan *or* Romano cheese
- 1/4 cup slivered almonds
- 3/4 teaspoon salt
- 1/2 teaspoon dried tarragon
- 1/4 teaspoon pepper
- 1/8 teaspoon sugar

- 1 cup olive *or* vegetable oil
- 1/2 cup white wine vinegar
- 1 cup whole almonds, toasted

In a large bowl, combine the first 13 ingredients; set aside. For dressing, process garlic in a blender or food processor until finely chopped. Add basil, cheese, slivered almonds, salt, tarragon, pepper and sugar. Process 15-30 seconds or until coarsely chopped. With the motor running, gradually add oil until mixture is smooth. Add vinegar and process until blended. Pour over salad; toss to coat. Just before serving, add whole almonds. **Yield:** 18-20 servings.

Greek Rice Salad

Barbara Nowakowski, North Tonawanda, New York

I love cooking. My husband even had to build another room especially for the cookbooks I collected! No matter how many salad recipes I try, this is still at the top of my list.

✓ This tasty dish uses less sugar, salt and fat. Recipe includes *Diabetic Exchanges*.

- 4 cups cooked brown rice
- 2 cups julienned cooked turkey breast
- 2 cups halved cherry tomatoes
- 1 cup halved ripe olives
- 3/4 cup plain yogurt
- 3 to 4 tablespoons minced fresh mint
- 2 tablespoons red wine vinegar
- 1/2 teaspoon lemon-pepper seasoning
- 1/2 cup crumbled feta cheese, optional

Combine rice, turkey, tomatoes and olives. In a small bowl, combine yogurt, mint, vinegar and lemon pepper; mix well. Pour over rice mixture; toss to coat. Sprinkle with cheese if desired. **Yield:** 8 servings. **Diabetic Exchanges:** One 1-cup serving (prepared with fat-free yogurt and without feta cheese) equals 1-1/2 starch, 1 meat; also, 174 calories, 258 mg sodium, 15 mg cholesterol, 25 gm carbohydrate, 11 gm protein, 3 gm fat.

Lemon Lentil Salad

Renate Kheim, St. Louis, Missouri

I love lentils but never had a recipe that really enhanced their flavor...until I found this one! The touch of lemon juice gives this dish a light, refreshing appeal.

- 5 tablespoons olive *or* vegetable oil, *divided*
- 1 tablespoon lemon juice
- 2 teaspoons red wine vinegar
- 2 teaspoons sugar
- 1 teaspoon Dijon mustard
- 1/2 teaspoon dried thyme
- 1/4 teaspoon salt
- 1/4 teaspoon pepper
- 1 garlic clove, minced
- 3 cups water
- 1 cup dry lentils
- 1 bay leaf
- 1 large tomato, diced

1/2 cup minced fresh parsley
2 to 3 green onions, sliced

In a small bowl, combine 4 tablespoons oil, lemon juice, vinegar, sugar, mustard, thyme, salt, pepper and garlic; set aside. In a medium saucepan, bring water, lentils, bay leaf and remaining oil to a boil. Reduce heat; simmer, uncovered, for 30 minutes. Remove from the heat. Let stand 30 minutes; drain if necessary. Remove bay leaf. Add tomato, parsley, onions and dressing; mix gently. Cover and chill for at least 2 hours. **Yield:** 4-6 servings.

Fruity Pasta Salad

Naomi Giddis, Longmont, Colorado

Pasta salad takes on a whole new taste with fruit, marsh-mallows and cream. Folks will find it hard to turn down a hearty helping of this old-fashioned salad.

    1 can (20 ounces) pineapple chunks
    2 eggs, lightly beaten
    3 tablespoons lemon juice
    2 tablespoons sugar
    1 tablespoon butter *or* margarine
 1/4 teaspoon salt
1-1/4 cups whipping cream, whipped
 6 to 7 cups cooked cooled spiral pasta
    1 can (11 ounces) mandarin oranges, drained
    2 medium apples, diced
    2 cups miniature marshmallows
    1 cup halved seedless green grapes
 1/4 cup maraschino cherries

Drain pineapple, reserving 3 tablespoons juice in a sauce-pan. Set pineapple aside. To juice, add eggs, lemon juice, sugar, butter and salt; cook and stir over medium heat for 3-4 minutes or until thickened. Cool to room temperature. Fold in whipped cream. In a large bowl, combine pasta, oranges, apples, marshmallows, grapes and pineapple. Fold in dressing. Chill. Garnish with cherries. **Yield:** 12-14 servings.

Tuna Rice Salad

Larraine Stadt, South St. Paul, Minnesota

Most of my recipes—including this one—were developed from my experiments with leftovers. This salad is also delicious prepared with leftover chicken or turkey instead of tuna.

    3 cups cooked rice
 1/4 cup olive *or* vegetable oil
4-1/2 teaspoons vinegar
 1/4 teaspoon salt
Dash pepper
    1 can (6 ounces) tuna, drained and flaked
    2 medium tomatoes, chopped
    1 small cucumber, peeled, seeded and diced
    2 tablespoons chopped onion
Lettuce leaves
    2 hard-cooked eggs, sliced
Stuffed olives and lemon wedges, optional

Place rice in a medium bowl. Combine oil, vinegar, salt and pepper; pour over rice and toss to coat. Stir in tuna, tomatoes, cucumber and onion. Line a serving platter with lettuce; top with salad. Garnish with eggs, olives and lemon if desired. **Yield:** 6 servings.

Curried Turkey and Rice Salad

Jena Coffey, St. Louis, Missouri

I adapted this recipe from one of my many cookbooks, and the entire family was pleased with the outcome.

4-1/2 cups chicken broth
    2 cups uncooked long grain rice
    1 to 2 teaspoons curry powder
 1/2 teaspoon ground ginger
 1/2 teaspoon ground turmeric
 1/4 cup olive *or* vegetable oil
 1/4 cup lemon juice
    2 cups cubed cooked turkey
    1 cup golden raisins
    1 can (8 ounces) water chestnuts, drained and chopped
 1/2 cup chopped green pepper
 1/2 cup chopped sweet red pepper
 1/2 cup mayonnaise
 1/2 cup sour cream
 1/2 cup slivered almonds, toasted
Salt and pepper to taste

In a saucepan, bring broth to a boil; add rice, curry, ginger and turmeric. Reduce heat; cover and simmer for 25 minutes or until all of the broth is absorbed. Remove from the heat. Add oil and lemon juice; mix well. Transfer to a large bowl; cover and chill. Just before serving, add remaining ingredients and mix well. **Yield:** 8-10 servings.

Spicy Spaghetti Salad

Diane Hixon, Niceville, Florida

You'll appreciate the convenience of this dish, especially when you need to prepare a pasta salad in a jiffy.

    1 package (7 ounces) spaghetti
    1 can (10 ounces) diced tomatoes with green chilies, undrained
 1/2 cup mayonnaise
 1/2 cup chopped stuffed olives
 1/4 cup chopped celery
 1/4 cup chopped onion
    2 garlic cloves, minced
 1/4 teaspoon salt
 1/4 teaspoon ground cumin

Break spaghetti in half and cook according to package directions. Meanwhile, combine remaining ingredients in a large bowl. Drain spaghetti; rinse in cold water. Add to tomato mixture and toss. Cover and refrigerate for at least 2 hours. **Yield:** 4 servings.

Garden Vegetable Medley

Packed with fresh produce, crisp vegetable dishes are the perfect way to spotlight a bountiful harvest. And a savory selection of dressings tastefully tops off any salad.

Spinach Salad with Honey-Bacon Dressing

Cheryl Koutney, Shelton, Washington
(PICTURED AT LEFT)

I copied this recipe out of a magazine years ago…and am I ever glad I did! Whenever I take this salad to potlucks, I get many compliments and come home with an empty bowl.

    8 cups torn fresh spinach
    1 cup sliced fresh mushrooms
1/4 cup sliced green onions
    1 medium tomato, chopped
    5 bacon strips, cooked and crumbled
    1 hard-cooked egg, chopped
    1 cup shredded Parmesan cheese
HONEY-BACON DRESSING:
    2 bacon strips, cooked and crumbled
1/2 cup honey
1/2 cup vinegar
1/3 cup vegetable oil
    1 teaspoon yellow *or* spicy brown mustard
    1 teaspoon lemon juice

Combine the first seven ingredients in a large bowl. In a small bowl, whisk together dressing ingredients; pour over salad. Serve immediately. **Yield:** 8-10 servings.

Fire-and-Ice Salad

Anne daCosta, Sapphire, North Carolina
(PICTURED AT LEFT)

This recipe gets its unique name from the combination of cool crisp vegetables and the spicy jalapeno and dressing. Folks I serve it to agree this is the best cucumber salad that they've ever tasted.

    4 medium tomatoes, cut into eighths
    1 medium green pepper, julienned
    1 small jalapeno, minced
    1 medium onion, thinly sliced
3/4 cup cider vinegar
1/4 cup sugar
1-1/2 teaspoons mustard seed

1-1/2 teaspoons celery seed
1-1/2 teaspoons prepared horseradish
    1 teaspoon salt
    7 drops hot pepper sauce, optional
    2 medium cucumbers, peeled and thinly sliced

In a large bowl, combine tomatoes, green pepper, jalapeno and onion; set aside. Combine the next seven ingredients in a saucepan; bring to a boil and boil for 1 minute. Pour over vegetables. Let stand until mixture comes to room temperature. Stir in cucumbers. Refrigerate for 2 hours. Drain before serving. **Yield:** 8-10 servings.

Church Coleslaw

Marjorie Force, Boonton, New Jersey

After enjoying this coleslaw for years at many church functions, I finally asked for the recipe. It can be put together in no time, so it's perfect for last-minute guests.

    1 cup mayonnaise *or* salad dressing
1/2 cup sugar
1/3 cup cider vinegar
    1 teaspoon salt
1/8 teaspoon pepper
1/8 teaspoon paprika
1/2 medium head cabbage, shredded
    2 medium carrots, shredded
    1 celery rib, shredded

Place the first six ingredients in a blender or food processor; process until the sugar is dissolved, about 30 seconds. In a large bowl, combine cabbage, carrots, celery and dressing; toss to coat. Serve immediately. **Yield:** 8-10 servings.

Milly's Salad Dressing

Milly Heaton, Richmond, Indiana

I've found this flavorful dressing is perfect on green salads as well as potato salad, coleslaw and fruit salad. You'll also like the fact that it's quick and easy to prepare.

    1 bottle (8 ounces) sweet-sour celery seed salad dressing
    1 cup mayonnaise
    2 tablespoons sweet pickle relish
    2 tablespoons water
    4 teaspoons Dijon-mayonnaise blend
3/4 teaspoon prepared horseradish

In a small bowl, combine all ingredients; stir until well blended. Store in the refrigerator. **Yield:** 2 cups.

GARDEN-FRESH GOODNESS. *Pictured at left, top to bottom: Spinach Salad with Honey-Bacon Dressing and Fire-and-Ice Salad (both recipes on this page).*

Chunky Mushroom and Tomato Salad

Marion Kowalski, Wauwatosa, Wisconsin

We have family get-togethers frequently throughout the year, and I'm always looking for a new dish to take along. This super salad has become my trademark.

- 6 tablespoons olive *or* vegetable oil
- 2 tablespoons lemon juice
- 1/2 teaspoon salt
- 1/4 teaspoon pepper
- 1 pound fresh mushrooms, quartered
- 16 cherry tomatoes, halved
- 3 tablespoons minced chives
- 2 tablespoons sesame seeds, toasted

In a large bowl, whisk together oil, lemon juice, salt and pepper. Add mushrooms; toss to coat. Chill for at least 1 hour. Just before serving, stir in tomatoes and chives; sprinkle with sesame seeds. **Yield:** 6-8 servings.

Dijon Vinaigrette

Beth Philson, Lincoln, Nebraska

In this recipe, Dijon mustard adds a new twist to a traditional vinaigrette dressing. Olive oil gives it great flavor, but I have used vegetable oil in a pinch.

- 2/3 cup olive *or* vegetable oil
- 1/3 cup red wine vinegar
- 2 tablespoons Dijon mustard
- 1/2 teaspoon salt
- 1/4 teaspoon pepper
- 1/4 teaspoon sugar

Combine all ingredients in a jar with tight-fitting lid; shake until blended. Store in the refrigerator **Yield:** about 1 cup.

Mixed Greens with Mushrooms

Sue Walker, Greentown, Indiana

This is a great year-round salad because you can use whatever greens are in season. The tarragon in the dressing is subtle but really adds to the flavor.

✓ This tasty dish uses less sugar, salt and fat. Recipe includes *Diabetic Exchanges*.

- 6 cups mixed salad greens
- 1 cup halved cherry tomatoes
- 1/2 pound fresh mushrooms, sliced

DRESSING:
- 1 tablespoon red wine vinegar
- 1 tablespoon lemon juice
- 1 tablespoon thinly sliced green onion
- 1 tablespoon Dijon mustard
- 1 tablespoon minced fresh parsley
- 1/4 teaspoon salt, optional

- 1/4 teaspoon sugar
- 1/8 teaspoon dried tarragon
- Dash pepper

Toss greens, tomatoes and mushrooms in a large bowl. In a small bowl, whisk together dressing ingredients; pour over salad and serve immediately **Yield:** 8 servings. **Diabetic Exchanges:** One 1-cup serving (prepared without salt) equals 1 vegetable; also, 30 calories, 60 mg sodium, 0 cholesterol, 5 gm carbohydrate, 3 gm protein, trace fat.

Sour Cream Cucumber Salad

Ann Folmar, Erie, Pennsylvania

I serve this refreshing and simple salad year-round because it perks up everyday meals. I think what makes it so special is the addition of dill.

- 1/2 cup sour cream
- 2 teaspoons sugar
- 1 teaspoon vinegar
- 1 teaspoon salt
- 1/2 teaspoon dill weed
- 4 medium cucumbers, sliced

In a large bowl, combine sour cream, sugar, vinegar, salt and dill. Add cucumbers; toss to coat. Chill for at least 30 minutes. **Yield:** 8-10 servings.

Artichoke Potato Salad

Lori Gleason, Minneapolis, Minnesota

Featuring a light vinaigrette dressing, this salad is a nice change of pace from traditional potato salads. It's one of my husband's favorite side dishes for barbecued chicken.

- 2 pounds red potatoes, cooked and cubed
- 1 can (8-1/2 ounces) quartered artichoke hearts (in water), drained
- 1 small red onion, chopped
- 1 cup cubed brick *or* Monterey Jack cheese
- 1/2 cup crumbled blue cheese
- 3/4 cup vegetable oil
- 1/4 cup red wine *or* cider vinegar
- 2 garlic cloves, minced
- 1 teaspoon dried rosemary, crushed
- 1 teaspoon dill weed
- 1/2 teaspoon salt
- 1/4 teaspoon pepper

In a large bowl, combine potatoes, artichokes, onion and cheeses. In a jar with tight-fitting lid, combine oil, vinegar, garlic, rosemary, dill, salt and pepper; shake well. Pour over potato mixture; toss to coat. **Yield:** 10-12 servings.

> **SALAD SECRETS.** It's important to wash lettuce leaves thoroughly to avoid any gritty taste. Then dry thoroughly so they'll be crisp. Most green salads should be served immediately after the dressing is added.

Tangy Cabbage Salad

Sue Little, Prince Frederick, Maryland

Apples, marshmallows and pineapple add a new twist to coleslaw in this recipe. Everyone who samples this dish raves about the fresh, sweet flavor.

   1 can (8 ounces) pineapple chunks
2/3 cup mayonnaise
1/2 cup sugar
   4 cups chopped cabbage
   2 large tart apples, chopped
2/3 cup miniature marshmallows
1/2 cup chopped walnuts

Drain pineapple, reserving 2 tablespoons juice in a small bowl. Set pineapple aside. Stir mayonnaise and sugar into juice. In a large bowl, combine cabbage, apples, marshmallows, walnuts and pineapple. Just before serving, add dressing and toss to coat. **Yield:** 8-10 servings.

Pea Salad with Creamy Dressing

Martha Wilson, Kezar Falls, Maine

I found this recipe many years ago when I was planning a Father's Day party. My dad loved this refreshing crunchy salad so much he's requested it each year since.

   1 package (10 ounces) frozen peas, thawed
   6 bacon strips, cooked and crumbled
   1 can (8 ounces) sliced water chestnuts, drained
1/4 cup thinly sliced green onions
DRESSING:
1/4 cup sour cream
   4 teaspoons red wine vinegar
   1 garlic clove, minced
1/2 teaspoon sugar
1/8 teaspoon salt

In a bowl, combine peas, bacon, water chestnuts and onions; set aside. Combine all dressing ingredients until smooth; pour over salad and toss to coat. Refrigerate for at least 1 hour. **Yield:** 6 servings.

Spinach Salad with Orange Dressing

Judith McQuoid, Fort Jones, California

I reached for this special recipe one night when planning a dinner for friends. With it's slightly sweet dressing, this salad turned out to be the best part of the meal!

   1 bag (10 ounces) fresh spinach, torn
   1 can (11 ounces) mandarin oranges, drained
   3 hard-cooked eggs, chopped
   6 bacon strips, cooked and crumbled
   3 green onions, sliced

1/2 cup chopped pecans, toasted
DRESSING:
   1 cup mayonnaise
1/4 cup honey
1/4 cup orange juice
   2 ounces cream cheese, softened
1/2 teaspoon prepared mustard

In a large bowl, combine spinach, oranges, eggs, bacon, onions and pecans. In a blender, process all dressing ingredients until smooth. Pour over salad; toss to coat. Serve immediately. **Yield:** 14 servings.

Colorful Cauliflower Salad

Dorothy Newyear, Harrison, Arkansas

My husband and I are both retired and attend many potlucks for the various clubs we're involved with. This colorful salad serves as a nice side dish for any main meal.

   1 large head cauliflower, broken into florets and thinly sliced
   1 can (2-1/4 ounces) sliced ripe olives, drained
   1 medium green pepper, chopped
1/2 cup chopped onion
1/4 cup chopped pimientos
DRESSING:
1/2 cup vegetable oil
   3 tablespoons lemon juice
   3 tablespoons white wine vinegar
   1 teaspoon salt
1/2 teaspoon sugar
1/4 teaspoon pepper

In a large bowl, combine cauliflower, olives, green pepper, onion and pimientos. Combine all dressing ingredients in a jar with tight-fitting lid; shake well. Pour over vegetables; toss to coat. Refrigerate overnight. **Yield:** 8-10 servings.

Sweet-and-Sour Dressing

Marcia Orlando, Boyertown, Pennsylvania

When I was growing up, Dad made this so much it became our "house" dressing. This recipe makes a nice big batch that you can conveniently keep in your refrigerator.

1-1/2 cups sugar
   2 teaspoons dried minced onion
1/2 teaspoon salt
1/2 teaspoon chili powder
1/2 teaspoon ground mustard
1/4 teaspoon crushed red pepper flakes
   1 cup vinegar
   1 cup vegetable oil
1/4 to 1/2 cup light corn syrup

In a bowl, combine sugar and seasonings. Add vinegar; stir until sugar is dissolved. Whisk in oil and corn syrup until well blended. Store in the refrigerator. **Yield:** 3 cups.

A REFRESHING ROUNDUP OF NATURE'S BOUNTY.
Clockwise from top left: Harvest Layered Salad, Home-Style French Dressing, Marinated Vegetable Salad, Irish Potato Salad and Calico Tomato Salad (recipes on pages 64 and 65).

Marinated Vegetable Salad

Colleen Wachal, Richland, Nebraska
(PICTURED ON PAGE 63)

This beautiful salad has gone to many dinners with family and friends. It's one of my favorites because it can be prepared the night before, allowing the fabulous flavors to blend.

DRESSING:
- 1 cup vinegar
- 1 cup sugar
- 1/2 cup water
- 2 tablespoons vegetable oil
- 2 teaspoons salt
- 1 teaspoon celery seed
- 1 teaspoon dill seed

SALAD:
- 1 medium head cauliflower
- 1 pound carrots, sliced
- 2 medium cucumbers, sliced
- 1 medium green pepper, julienned
- 1 small onion, sliced into rings
- 1 jar (4-1/2 ounces) whole mushrooms, drained
- 1 can (2-1/4 ounces) sliced ripe olives, drained

In a saucepan, bring dressing ingredients to a boil, stirring occasionally. Remove from the heat; cool to room temperature. Break cauliflower into florets and blanch. Place in a large bowl; add remaining salad ingredients. Add dressing; toss to coat. Cover and refrigerate for several hours or overnight, stirring occasionally. Serve with a slotted spoon. **Yield:** 16-20 servings.

Harvest Layered Salad

Vera Ambroselli, Fort Meyers, Florida
(PICTURED ON PAGE 62)

Unlike most layered salads that have a mayonnaise topping, this version features a tasty vinegar-and-oil dressing. I often double it to serve for special occasions.

- 2-1/2 cups shredded carrots
- 2-1/2 cups sliced fresh mushrooms
- 2-1/2 cups shredded cabbage
- 2-1/2 cups sliced zucchini
- 1 small red onion, thinly sliced
- 1 cup (4 ounces) shredded Colby *or* cheddar cheese

DRESSING:
- 1/4 cup vegetable oil
- 2 tablespoons red wine vinegar
- 1/8 teaspoon ground mustard
- 1/8 teaspoon sugar
- 1/8 teaspoon garlic salt
- 1/8 teaspoon pepper

In a 3-1/2-qt. bowl, layer the first six ingredients in order listed. Combine all dressing ingredients in a jar with tight-

fitting lid; shake well. Pour over salad and serve immediately. **Yield:** 10-14 servings.

Home-Style French Dressing

Mary Paysinger, Salem, Arizona
(PICTURED ON PAGE 62)

This was the house dressing in a local restaurant several years ago and has long been a family favorite. We like it over salad greens and fresh vegetables.

- 1/2 medium onion, quartered
- 2 tablespoons lemon juice
- 3/4 cup ketchup
- 3/4 cup vegetable oil
- 1/2 cup vinegar
- 1/2 cup sugar
- 1-1/2 teaspoons salt

In a food processor or blender, puree onion and lemon juice until smooth. Add ketchup, oil, vinegar, sugar and salt; blend until smooth. Store in the refrigerator. **Yield:** 2-1/2 cups.

Irish Potato Salad

Nancy Martin, Martelle, Iowa
(PICTURED ON PAGE 63)

By combining potatoes, corned beef and cabbage, this hearty salad is a perfect dish for St. Patrick's Day. Everyone in my family favors the one-of-a-kind flavor.

- 3 large potatoes
- 2 tablespoons vinegar
- 2 teaspoons sugar
- 1 teaspoon mustard seed
- 1/2 teaspoon celery seed
- 3/4 teaspoon salt, *divided*
- 3 cups cubed cooked corned beef
- 3 cups chopped cabbage
- 1/2 cup chopped radishes, optional
- 3/4 cup mayonnaise
- 1/3 cup dill pickle relish
- 1/4 cup sliced green onions
- 4 teaspoons milk
- 3/4 teaspoon Dijon mustard, optional

Cook potatoes in boiling salted water until tender; drain. Peel and cube; place in a large bowl. Combine vinegar, sugar, mustard seed, celery seed and 1/2 teaspoon salt; pour over warm potatoes and toss to coat. Cover and chill. Just before serving, add corned beef, cabbage and radishes if desired. In a small bowl, combine mayonnaise, relish, onions, milk, mustard if desired and remaining salt; pour over salad and toss to coat. **Yield:** 8 servings.

> **GET 'EM "RED"Y.** Before boiling red potatoes for potato salad, cut in a circle around each potato, just piercing the skin. Once boiled, the potatoes are much easier to peel.

Calico Tomato Salad

Donna Cline, Pensacola, Florida
(PICTURED ON PAGE 62)

This recipe has been in our family for years. We always appreciate this wonderful, eye-catching salad because it's so easy to prepare and delicious to eat.

✓ **This tasty dish uses less sugar, salt and fat. Recipe includes *Diabetic Exchanges*.**

        5 medium tomatoes
        1 small zucchini
        1 small sweet yellow pepper
    1/4 cup cider vinegar
        2 tablespoons olive *or* vegetable oil
        2 tablespoons minced fresh parsley
        2 teaspoons sugar
    1/2 teaspoon salt, optional
    1/2 teaspoon dried basil
    1/4 teaspoon dried marjoram
    1/8 teaspoon pepper

Cut tomatoes, zucchini and yellow pepper into 1/2-in. pieces; place in a large bowl. In a jar with tight-fitting lid, combine remaining ingredients; shake well. Pour over vegetables and toss. Serve immediately. **Yield:** about 8 servings.
Diabetic Exchanges: One 3/4-cup serving (prepared without salt) equals 1 vegetable, 1/2 fat; also, 49 calories, 4 mg sodium, 0 cholesterol, 5 gm carbohydrate, 1 gm protein, 3 gm fat.

Shrimp Salad with Creamy Pepper Dressing

Mary Johnston, Valencia, Pennsylvania

When a local restaurant was closing, a friend of mine obtained this recipe from the chef. It didn't take long for her to share this wonderful recipe with everyone she knew.

DRESSING:
        1 cup mayonnaise
        1 cup (8 ounces) sour cream
    1/4 cup grated Parmesan cheese
    1/4 cup milk
        2 tablespoons lemon juice
        1 tablespoon vinegar
        1 teaspoon onion powder
        1 teaspoon pepper
    1/2 teaspoon garlic powder
    1/4 to 1/2 teaspoon Worcestershire sauce
        6 drops hot pepper sauce
SALAD:
        6 cups torn salad greens
        1 can (11 ounces) mandarin oranges, drained
        1 bag (5 ounces) frozen cooked salad shrimp,
            thawed and drained
        1 pint cherry tomatoes, halved

        2 tablespoons coconut, toasted
    Salad croutons

In a medium bowl, combine dressing ingredients. Cover and chill for least 8 hours. Just before serving, combine salad ingredients in a large bowl. Serve with dressing. Store remaining dressing in the refrigerator. **Yield:** 6 servings (2-1/2 cups dressing).

Blue Cheese-Bacon Dressing

Colleen Arthur, Indianapolis, Indiana
(PICTURED ON FRONT COVER)

Years ago, I went through my mom's recipe box and found this classic recipe. Everyone I know loves the rich and creamy blue cheese dressing with a hint of bacon.

        1 cup mayonnaise
    3/4 to 1 cup (3 to 4 ounces) crumbled blue cheese
        6 bacon strips, cooked and crumbled
        1 tablespoon lemon juice
        1 tablespoon white wine vinegar
        2 teaspoons sugar
    1-1/2 teaspoons Worcestershire sauce
    1/4 teaspoon seasoned salt
    1/8 teaspoon pepper

In a small bowl, combine all ingredients; mix well to blend. Cover and chill for at least 3 hours. Store in the refrigerator. **Yield:** 1-1/4 cups.

Mary's Caesar Salad

Mary Stepanian, North Tonawanda, New York

Whenever I entertain, this appears on my table...it never fails to win me rave reviews. Most folks seem to prefer this sweeter version to traditional Caesar salad.

        1 hard-cooked egg
        2 to 4 tablespoons mayonnaise
        2 tablespoons lemon juice
        1 garlic clove, minced
        3 tablespoons red wine vinegar
        1 to 3 teaspoons sugar
        1 teaspoon Worcestershire sauce
    1/2 teaspoon salt
    1/4 teaspoon ground mustard
    1/4 teaspoon pepper
    1/2 cup olive *or* vegetable oil
        1 large bunch romaine, torn
    3/4 cup Caesar-flavored salad croutons
    1/4 cup grated Parmesan cheese
        1 can (2 ounces) anchovy fillets, optional

Place the first 10 ingredients in a blender or food processor; process until egg is chopped. Add oil and blend until smooth. In a large bowl, toss romaine, croutons and Parmesan cheese. Add dressing; toss to coat. Top with anchovies if desired. **Yield:** 10 servings.

Low-Fat Ranch Dressing

Ruth Shugart, Plainview, Texas

Once I sampled this homemade ranch dressing, I quit buying the bottled variety. It can be easily doubled when you are serving a larger group.

✓ **This tasty dish uses less sugar, salt and fat. Recipe includes *Diabetic Exchanges*.**

    1 cup mayonnaise
    1 tablespoon dried parsley flakes
    1 tablespoon dried minced onion
1/4 to 1/2 teaspoon salt, optional
1/8 teaspoon garlic powder
3/4 cup buttermilk

In a small bowl, combine the first five ingredients. Stir in buttermilk. Cover and chill for at least 8 hours before serving. Store any leftovers in the refrigerator. **Yield:** 1-1/4 cups.
Diabetic Exchanges: One 2-tablespoon serving (prepared with fat-free mayonnaise and without salt) equals a free food; also, 25 calories, 189 mg sodium, 0 cholesterol, 5 gm carbohydrate, 1 gm protein, trace fat.

Italian Broccoli Salad

Patricia Free, Baton Rouge, Louisiana

I received this recipe from my cousin several years ago, and it remains a family favorite. It's also a real crowd-pleaser whenever I take it to a potluck.

2-1/2 pounds fresh broccoli
    1 pound sliced bacon, cooked and crumbled
    1 jar (5-1/4 ounces) stuffed olives, drained and sliced
    1 cup sliced green onions
    1 bottle (16 ounces) Italian salad dressing
    1 cup mayonnaise
3/4 cup shredded Parmesan cheese

Parboil broccoli; cool and cut into bite-size pieces. Place in a large bowl; add bacon, olives and onions. In a small bowl, combine salad dressing, mayonnaise and Parmesan cheese; mix well. Pour over vegetables and toss. Serve immediately. **Yield:** 10-12 servings.

Sour Cream Potato Salad

Marilyn Lamp, Davenport, Iowa

I'm a big fan of potato salad but don't really care for heavy mayonnaise dressings. A sour cream dressing turns a classic recipe into a dish my family and I really enjoy.

    6 cups diced cooked potatoes
    1 cup chopped celery
1/2 cup chopped seeded peeled cucumber
1/2 cup chopped green pepper
1/4 cup sliced green onions
    6 hard-cooked eggs
    1 cup (8 ounces) sour cream
1/2 cup mayonnaise
    1 tablespoon prepared mustard
    4 teaspoons vinegar
1-1/2 teaspoons salt
1/2 teaspoon pepper
    1 teaspoon celery seed, optional

In a large bowl, combine the first five ingredients. Remove egg yolks from whites. Chop whites and add to potato mixture; toss lightly. Mash yolks with sour cream, mayonnaise, mustard, vinegar, salt, pepper and celery seed if desired. Fold into potato mixture. Refrigerate for at least 6 hours. **Yield:** 8-10 servings.

Cauliflower Lettuce Salad

Denise Goedeken, Platte Center, Nebraska

This crispy crunchy salad captures the flavor of seven-layer salad with a few less layers and fuss. This is one of my family's most-requested recipes.

    1 head iceberg lettuce, torn
    1 small head cauliflower, broken into florets
3/4 pound sliced bacon, cooked and crumbled
1/4 cup finely chopped red onion
1/4 cup sugar
1/4 cup grated Parmesan cheese
    1 cup mayonnaise *or* salad dressing

In a large bowl, layer lettuce, cauliflower, bacon, onion, sugar and cheese. Spread mayonnaise over the top; do not toss. Cover and chill for 2 hours or overnight. Toss just before serving. **Yield:** 8 servings.

Cranberry Cabbage Salad

Connie Johnson, Litchfield, Minnesota

Fresh cranberries are abundant here during the holidays, so my family always expects to see this colorful salad on the Christmas table.

3/4 cup fresh *or* frozen cranberries, halved
1/4 cup sugar
    6 cups shredded cabbage
    1 cup seedless green grapes, halved
1/2 cup thinly sliced celery
1/4 cup orange juice
    3 tablespoons mayonnaise
1/2 teaspoon salt

Toss cranberries with sugar and set aside. In a large bowl, combine the cabbage, grapes and celery. Add cranberries and toss. Combine orange juice, mayonnaise and salt; pour over salad and toss to coat. Serve immediately. **Yield:** 6-8 servings.

Tangy Salad Dressing

Karen Krause, Newton, Wisconsin

This is one salad dressing that I know my family will eat. It's easy to make and better tasting than store-bought dressings.

1/2 cup vinegar
1/2 cup sugar
3 tablespoons olive *or* vegetable oil
1 teaspoon celery seed
1/4 teaspoon salt
1/8 teaspoon pepper

In a jar with tight-fitting lid, combine all ingredients; shake well. Store in the refrigerator. **Yield:** 3/4 cup.

Ginger French Dressing

Ann Marie Glaser, Independence, Ohio

This simple-to-prepare recipe begins with bottled dressing. Add just a few ingredients, and you'll have a zesty dressing that really perks up ordinary lettuce salads.

1 bottle (8 ounces) olive oil Italian dressing
1/3 cup peanut *or* vegetable oil
1/4 cup ketchup
3 tablespoons honey
2 tablespoons soy sauce
3/4 teaspoon ground ginger
1/8 teaspoon cayenne pepper

In a small bowl, whisk together all ingredients until well blended. Store in the refrigerator. **Yield:** 1-3/4 cups.

Succotash Salad

Martha Fehl, Brookville, Indiana

At the end of the summer, we search our garden for the last few remaining vegetables and add them to this salad. This dish nicely pairs corn, beans and seasonings.

1 small onion, chopped
2 tablespoons vegetable oil
1 small green pepper, julienned
1 small sweet red pepper, julienned
1/2 cup thinly sliced carrots
2 tablespoons all-purpose flour
2 tablespoons sugar
3/4 teaspoon salt
1/2 cup water
1/3 cup cider vinegar
3 cups fresh *or* frozen corn
1 cup fresh *or* frozen lima beans
1 cup cubed fully cooked ham

1 teaspoon minced chives
1/2 teaspoon lemon-pepper seasoning

In a saucepan, saute onion in oil until tender. Add peppers and carrots; cook for 2 minutes. Blend in flour, sugar and salt. Gradually add water and vinegar, stirring constantly. Bring to a boil; boil for 1 minute. Add corn and beans. Reduce heat; cover and simmer for 5-7 minutes or until vegetables are tender. Remove from the heat. Add ham, chives and lemon pepper; toss. Serve warm or chilled. **Yield:** 4-6 servings.

Garbanzo Avocado Salad

Eileen McConnell, Annapolis, Maryland

This salad is so hearty I've often served it as the main course with soup and bread. If you're looking for a deliciously different salad, this recipe's for you!

3 medium tomatoes, diced
2 medium avocados, diced
1 can (15 ounces) garbanzo beans, rinsed and drained
1 cup cubed Monterey Jack cheese
1/4 cup chopped onion
6 tablespoons olive *or* vegetable oil
1/4 cup lemon juice
1 garlic clove, minced
2 teaspoons Worcestershire sauce
3/4 teaspoon salt
1/2 teaspoon hot pepper sauce
1/4 teaspoon pepper
5 bacon strips, cooked and crumbled

In a large bowl, combine the first five ingredients. In a small bowl, combine the oil, lemon juice, garlic, Worcestershire sauce, salt, hot pepper sauce and pepper; pour over vegetables and toss. Refrigerate for at least 1 hour. Just before serving, add bacon and toss. **Yield:** 8-10 servings.

Creamy Cauliflower Salad

Mrs. Floyd Farmer, Grants Pass, Oregon

When summer rolls around, we look forward to inviting family and friends over for a barbecue in our backyard. This salad often seems to accompany whatever meal we serve.

1 cup (8 ounces) sour cream
1/2 cup French salad dressing
2 teaspoons caraway seed
1/2 teaspoon salt
1 large head cauliflower, broken into florets and thinly sliced
1/2 cup minced celery leaves
1/4 cup thinly sliced green onions

In a large bowl, combine sour cream, salad dressing, caraway seed and salt. Add cauliflower, celery leaves and onions; toss. Refrigerate for 2-3 hours before serving. **Yield:** 10-12 servings.

Fruit & Molded Salads

Add an attractive appeal to your menus with a colorful collection of sweet side salads. Or serve them as delightfully different desserts!

Three-Ring Mold

Anne Maurer, Chicago, Illinois
(PICTURED AT LEFT)

A dear friend shared this recipe with me some 30 years ago. My family never seems to tire of seeing this salad on the table.

FIRST LAYER:
   2 cans (29 ounces *each*) pear halves
   1 package (3 ounces) cherry gelatin
3/4 cup boiling water
SECOND LAYER:
   1 package (8 ounces) cream cheese, softened
   1 package (3 ounces) lemon gelatin
3/4 cup boiling water
3/4 cup cold water
   1 cup whipping cream, whipped
THIRD LAYER:
   1 can (20 ounces) crushed pineapple
   1 package (3 ounces) lime gelatin
3/4 cup boiling water

Drain pears, reserving 3/4 cup juice. Arrange pears in a 4-qt. glass bowl or trifle dish. Dissolve cherry gelatin in boiling water; add reserved juice. Pour over pears. Chill until firm. For second layer, beat cream cheese in a mixing bowl until smooth and creamy. Dissolve lemon gelatin in boiling water; gradually add to cream cheese. Beat until smooth. Stir in cold water. Add cream and blend until smooth. Pour over first layer. Chill until firm. For third layer, drain pineapple, reserving 3/4 cup juice. Dissolve lime gelatin in boiling water; add pineapple and reserved juice. Pour over second layer. Chill until firm. **Yield:** 16-18 servings. **Editor's Note:** This salad takes time to prepare since each layer must be set before the next layer is added.

Poppy Seed Dressing

Elizabeth Hibbs, Brooksville, Florida
(PICTURED AT LEFT)

I like to serve this tangy dressing over fruit but have found it also adds a subtle sweet flavor to salad greens and chicken.

3/4 cup olive *or* vegetable oil

PALATE PLEASERS. *Pictured at left, top to bottom: Three-Ring Mold, Poppy Seed Dressing and Special Fruit Salad (all recipes on this page).*

1/3 cup honey
1/4 cup red wine vinegar
   2 tablespoons poppy seeds
   1 tablespoon finely chopped onion
   1 tablespoon Dijon mustard
1/2 teaspoon salt

Combine all ingredients in a blender; process for 30 seconds. Chill. Stir before using. **Yield:** 1-1/3 cups.

Special Fruit Salad

Alice Orton, Big Bear Lake, California
(PICTURED AT LEFT)

The combination of juices in the dressing brings out the fabulous flavors of all the fruits featured in this salad.

   1 can (20 ounces) pineapple chunks
   2 cups diced red apples
   2 cups cubed cantaloupe
   1 cup seedless green grapes, halved
   1 cup halved fresh strawberries
   3 ripe kiwifruit, peeled and sliced
DRESSING:
1/2 cup mayonnaise
1/2 cup sour cream
   2 tablespoons sugar
   1 tablespoon orange juice
1-1/2 teaspoons lemon juice
1/2 teaspoon grated lemon peel
1/2 teaspoon grated orange peel

Drain pineapple, reserving 1 tablespoon juice. Combine all fruit in a large bowl; cover and chill. In a small bowl, combine reserved pineapple juice and dressing ingredients; mix well. Cover and chill. Spoon dressing over fruit or toss just before serving. **Yield:** 8-10 servings.

Surprise Fruit Salad

Julie Sterchi, Flora, Illinois

With only four ingredients—including the "surprise" of candy—this makes a fast and delicious salad as well as a delightful dessert. Watch it disappear quickly from your bowl!

   1 carton (12 ounces) frozen whipped topping, thawed
   2 red apples, cubed
   2 green apples, cubed
   4 Snickers candy bars (2.07 ounces *each*), cut into 1/2-inch chunks

Combine all ingredients in a large bowl; cover and chill. Store in the refrigerator. **Yield:** 12-14 servings.

Tropical Turkey Salad

Penny Gillard, San Antonio, Texas

When my husband brought home a lunch guest unexpectedly one day, I created this salad on the spot using leftover holiday turkey. It's such a family favorite I make it year-round.

✓ **This tasty dish uses less sugar, salt and fat. Recipe includes *Diabetic Exchanges*.**

- 1 can (20 ounces) pineapple tidbits
- 3 cups cubed cooked turkey
- 1 can (8 ounces) sliced water chestnuts, drained and halved
- 1 cup thinly sliced fresh mushrooms
- 1 cup thinly sliced celery
- 1/2 cup thinly sliced green onions
- 3/4 cup ranch salad dressing
- 1/8 teaspoon garlic powder
- 1/8 teaspoon onion powder
- 7 cups torn mixed greens, *divided*
- 2 tablespoons slivered almonds, toasted, optional

Drain pineapple, reserving 3 tablespoons juice. In a large bowl, combine pineapple, turkey, water chestnuts, mushrooms, celery and onions. In a small bowl, combine reserved juice, dressing, garlic powder and onion powder. Add to turkey mixture; toss to coat. Divide greens among nine plates; top each with 1 cup turkey mixture. Sprinkle with almonds if desired. **Yield:** 9 servings. **Diabetic Exchanges:** One serving (prepared with pineapple in natural juices, turkey breast and fat-free salad dressing and without almonds) equals 1 very lean meat, 1 vegetable, 1 fruit; also, 120 calories, 252 mg sodium, 11 mg cholesterol, 23 gm carbohydrate, 6 gm protein, 1 gm fat.

Spinach Salad Ring

Mrs. W.M. Jacobs, Perrysburg, Ohio

I've been serving this salad on special occasions for more than 20 years. It's a new and interesting way to eat spinach.

- 2 envelopes unflavored gelatin
- 1 can (10-1/2 ounces) condensed beef broth
- 1/4 cup water
- 2 tablespoons lemon juice
- 1/2 teaspoon salt
- 1 cup mayonnaise *or* salad dressing
- 1 package (10 ounces) frozen chopped spinach, thawed and squeezed dry
- 4 hard-cooked eggs, chopped
- 1/4 pound sliced bacon, cooked and crumbled
- 1/4 cup thinly sliced green onions

Cherry tomatoes, optional

In a saucepan, sprinkle gelatin over broth; let stand for 5 minutes. Cook over low heat until gelatin is dissolved. Add water, lemon juice and salt; mix well. Place mayonnaise in a bowl. Gradually add broth mixture, stirring constantly un-

til smooth. Chill until slightly thickened, about 40 minutes. Fold in spinach, eggs, bacon and onions. Pour into an oiled 6-cup mold. Chill until firm. When ready to serve, unmold onto a platter; garnish with tomatoes if desired. **Yield:** 10-12 servings.

Apple Cider Salad

Laverne Campbell, LaConner, Washington

I especially like to present this salad at holiday potlucks. By adding food coloring to the bottom layer, I can easily create a fun, festive look.

- 1-3/4 cups apple cider *or* juice, *divided*
- 1 package (3 ounces) cherry gelatin
- 1 cup chopped peeled apple
- 1 envelope unflavored gelatin
- 1/4 cup cold water
- 1 cup applesauce
- 1 package (3 ounces) cream cheese, softened
- 1 can (5 ounces) evaporated milk

Red *or* green food coloring, optional

In a small saucepan, bring 1 cup apple cider to a boil. Remove from the heat; stir in cherry gelatin until dissolved. Stir in remaining cider. Chill until mixture begins to thicken. Stir in apples. Pour into an oiled 6-cup mold; chill until set. Meanwhile, soften unflavored gelatin in cold water. In a saucepan, whisk applesauce and cream cheese until smooth. Add milk and unflavored gelatin; cook and stir over low heat for 4 minutes or until gelatin completely dissolves. Add food coloring if desired. Chill until mixture begins to thicken. Pour over first layer. Chill until set. Unmold onto a serving platter. **Yield:** 6-8 servings.

Mini Molded Salads

Delores Baumhofer, Montevideo, Minnesota

My homemaker club is proud to say we've never served a dish more than once at our monthly meetings. That's quite an accomplishment—considering we've been together 43 years! They're still talking about this one-of-a-kind salad.

- 1 package (6 ounces) lemon gelatin
- 2 cups boiling water
- 1 package (3 ounces) cream cheese, softened
- 1 cup whipping cream, *divided*
- 1 cup thinly sliced celery
- 1 cup sliced stuffed olives

SHRIMP SAUCE:
- 2 hard-cooked eggs, chopped
- 1 cup mayonnaise
- 1 can (4-1/4 ounces) tiny shrimp, rinsed and drained
- 1 jar (2 ounces) chopped pimientos, drained
- 1/4 cup minced fresh parsley
- 2 tablespoons minced onion
- 1 tablespoon lemon juice

1/2 teaspoon salt
1/4 teaspoon pepper

In a bowl, dissolve gelatin in boiling water. Chill until syrupy, about 30-45 minutes. Meanwhile, beat cream cheese and 1 tablespoon cream in a mixing bowl until smooth. In another bowl, beat remaining cream until soft peaks form; fold into cream cheese mixture. Fold in celery, olives and gelatin. Pour into seven oiled 6-oz. custard cups or molds; chill until firm. Combine sauce ingredients; mix well. Chill. Unmold salads onto individual plates. Serve with sauce. **Yield:** 7 servings.

Fluffy Fruit Salad

Darcy Taylor, Merrill, Wisconsin

When fresh fruits aren't readily available, this recipe comes in handy because it calls for the canned variety. It's a nice way to offer folks fruit while appeasing their sweet tooth.

  1 can (20 ounces) pineapple chunks, drained
  1 can (17 ounces) fruit cocktail, drained
  1 can (16 ounces) sliced pears, drained and cut into chunks
  1 can (15 ounces) mandarin oranges, drained
  1 jar (10 ounces) maraschino cherries, drained
  1 carton (12 ounces) frozen whipped topping, thawed
  2 cups (16 ounces) sour cream
1/2 cup sugar
  1 tablespoon fresh lemon juice
Dash salt
1/2 cup chopped walnuts

Combine all the fruit in a large bowl. In another bowl, combine whipped topping, sour cream, sugar, lemon juice and salt; fold into fruit mixture. Chill. Just before serving, stir in nuts. **Yield:** 12-16 servings.

Luncheon Mold

Judith Reed, Jackson, Michigan

My mother served this many times at her bridge club when I was a child. It's now a favorite of my family on those hot summer days when a lighter meal is more appealing.

  1 package (3 ounces) lemon gelatin
1-1/3 cups boiling water
1/2 cup mayonnaise *or* salad dressing
  2 tablespoons prepared horseradish
  1 teaspoon prepared mustard
  2 cups chopped cooked corned beef
  1 cup chopped celery
1/4 cup chopped green pepper
  3 hard-cooked eggs, chopped
  2 tablespoons finely chopped onion
Lettuce leaves, optional

In a mixing bowl, dissolve gelatin in boiling water; stir in mayonnaise, horseradish and mustard. Chill until partially set; beat until foamy. Fold in corned beef, celery, green

pepper, eggs and onion. Spoon into an oiled 4-cup mold. Chill until firm. Unmold onto a lettuce-lined platter if desired. **Yield:** 6-8 servings.

Ambrosia Salad

Judi Brinegar, Liberty, North Carolina

During last-minute menu planning, I often include this recipe because I keep the ingredients on hand.

  1 can (11 ounces) mandarin oranges, drained
  1 can (8 ounces) pineapple chunks, drained
  1 cup miniature marshmallows
  1 cup flaked coconut
  1 cup (8 ounces) sour cream

In a bowl, combine oranges, pineapple, marshmallows and coconut. Add sour cream and toss to mix. Chill for several hours. **Yield:** 4-6 servings.

Apple-Cinnamon Coleslaw

Sharon Leno, Bricktown, New Jersey

When the weather starts turning warmer, this coleslaw is often a welcome change from ordinary pasta or potato salads. I often double the batch…much to everyone's delight.

  2 cups shredded cabbage
1-1/2 cups chopped apple
1/2 cup raisins
1/2 cup chopped walnuts, optional
  1 carton (8 ounces) vanilla yogurt
  2 tablespoons apple juice
1/4 teaspoon ground cinnamon

In a medium bowl, toss cabbage, apple, raisins and walnuts if desired. Combine yogurt, apple juice and cinnamon; mix well. Pour over cabbage mixture and toss to coat. Chill until ready to serve. **Yield:** 4-6 servings.

Raspberry Vinaigrette

Valerie Jordan, Kingmont, West Virginia

My family loves this light fruity dressing anytime of year. I especially like to make it in the summer as an alternative to heavy cream-based dressings.

1/2 cup raspberry vinegar
1/3 cup sugar
3/4 cup olive *or* vegetable oil
1/2 teaspoon Dijon mustard
1/8 teaspoon pepper

In a small saucepan, cook vinegar and sugar over low heat until sugar is dissolved. Pour into a jar with tight-fitting lid. Add remaining ingredients; cover and shake well. Chill. Shake before using. **Yield:** 1-1/4 cups.

FRESH AND FRUITY. *Clockwise from top left: Favorite Fruit Salad, Special Strawberry Salad, Anise Fruit Salad, Turkey Salad with Raspberries and Apricot Aspic (all recipes on pages 74 and 75).*

Favorite Fruit Salad

Doris Dion, Lake Ozark, Missouri
(PICTURED ON PAGE 72)

I spend a lot of time in the kitchen, especially when our four children and nine grandchildren come to visit. This salad is always requested when they're here for dinner.

1/4 cup *each* grapefruit, orange and pineapple juice
2 teaspoons cornstarch
1/4 cup vinegar
2 tablespoons vegetable oil
1 garlic clove, minced
2 to 3 teaspoons sugar
1 teaspoon prepared mustard
1/2 teaspoon salt
1/2 teaspoon paprika
1/2 teaspoon ground nutmeg
8 cups torn iceberg lettuce
6 cups torn Bibb lettuce
3 cups orange sections
3 cups fresh pineapple chunks
3 cups sliced fresh strawberries

In a saucepan, stir juices and cornstarch until smooth. Bring to a boil over medium heat; cook and stir for 2 minutes. Cool to room temperature. Add vinegar, oil, garlic, sugar, mustard, salt, paprika and nutmeg; stir to mix. Cover and chill. In a salad bowl, toss lettuces, oranges, pineapple and strawberries. Pour dressing over salad and toss; serve immediately. **Yield:** 12-14 servings.

Special Strawberry Salad

Linda Goulet, Hadley, Massachusetts
(PICTURED ON PAGE 73)

This superb-looking salad may take some time to prepare, but one taste and you'll agree it's worth the extra effort. I treat family and friends to this dish on special occasions.

1 envelope unflavored gelatin
1/4 cup cold water
1 cup half-and-half cream
2/3 cup sugar
2 cups (16 ounces) sour cream
1 teaspoon vanilla extract
1 package (6 ounces) strawberry gelatin
2 cups boiling water
1 package (16 ounces) unsweetened frozen
   strawberries
1 can (11 ounces) mandarin oranges

Dissolve unflavored gelatin in cold water. In a medium saucepan over low heat, heat cream and sugar until sugar dissolves. Stir in gelatin mixture until dissolved. Remove from the heat; stir in sour cream and vanilla. Pour into a 2-qt. glass bowl; chill until firm. Dissolve strawberry gelatin in boiling water. Drain orange liquid into strawberry gelatin;

blend well. Gently stir in strawberries until thawed. Pour over cream layer; arrange oranges on top (allow to settle) and chill until firm. **Yield:** 10-12 servings.

Anise Fruit Salad

Jean Clause, Lago Vista, Texas
(PICTURED ON PAGE 73)

The thing I like best about fruit salads is you can change the ingredients based on what fruits are in season. Here, a subtle anise flavor highlights a bounty of fresh fruit.

2 cups water
1-1/2 cups sugar
3 tablespoons lemon juice
1 tablespoon aniseed
6 cups cubed honeydew
4 cups cubed fresh pineapple
2-1/2 cups cubed cantaloupe
2 cups seedless green grapes
2 cups seedless red grapes
2 cups cubed orange sections
1 cup sliced fresh strawberries
1 medium firm banana, sliced
2 kiwifruit, peeled and sliced

In a saucepan over medium-high heat, combine water, sugar, lemon juice and aniseed; bring to a boil. Reduce heat to medium; cook, uncovered, for 40 minutes or until mixture is slightly thickened and reduced by one-third (about 1-1/2 cups). Remove from the heat; cover and cool to room temperature, about 30 minutes. Meanwhile, in a large bowl, combine honeydew, pineapple, cantaloupe, grapes and oranges. Pour anise mixture over fruit; toss to coat. Cover and chill for at least 1 hour. Just before serving, add strawberries and banana; gently toss. Garnish with kiwi. **Yield:** 12-14 servings.

Turkey Salad with Raspberries

Carla Radewahn, Milwaukee, Wisconsin
(PICTURED ON PAGE 73)

I originally developed this recipe as a way to use leftover turkey. Now I find myself preparing turkey with this recipe specifically in mind!

6 cups torn romaine
6 cups torn Bibb *or* Boston lettuce
1 can (15 ounces) mandarin oranges, drained
1 can (8 ounces) sliced water chestnuts, drained
1 cup fresh raspberries
1/3 cup salted sunflower seeds
2 tablespoons chopped chives
3/4 pound turkey tenderloin, cooked and sliced
DRESSING:
1/2 cup raspberry *or* red wine vinegar
1/2 cup honey
2 tablespoons soy sauce
2 teaspoons Dijon mustard

In a large bowl, toss lettuces, oranges, water chestnuts, raspberries, sunflower seeds and chives. Divide among six salad plates; arrange turkey on top. Combine dressing ingredients in a jar with tight-fitting lid; shake well. Pour over salads. Serve immediately. **Yield:** 6 servings.

Apricot Aspic

Neva Jane Upp, Hutchinson, Kansas
(PICTURED ON PAGE 72)

A family who usually passes up molded salads will hunt for this fruity version at our covered dish buffet. Not only is it delicious, it adds color to any meal.

✓ This tasty dish uses less sugar, salt and fat. Recipe includes *Diabetic Exchanges*.

> **2 cans (16 ounces *each*) apricot halves**
> **Pinch salt**
> **2 packages (3 ounces *each*) orange gelatin**
> **1 can (6 ounces) frozen orange juice concentrate, thawed**
> **1 tablespoon lemon juice**
> **1 cup lemon-lime soda**

Drain apricots, reserving 1-1/2 cups juice; set apricots aside. In a small saucepan over medium heat, bring apricot juice and salt to a boil. Remove from the heat; add gelatin and stir until dissolved. In a blender, process apricots, orange juice concentrate and lemon juice until smooth. Add to gelatin mixture along with soda; mix well. Pour into a 6-cup mold that has been sprayed with nonstick cooking spray. Chill until firm. **Yield:** 10 servings. **Diabetic Exchanges:** One 1/2- cup serving (prepared with unsweetened apricots, sugar-free gelatin and diet soda) equals 1-1/2 fruit; also, 93 calories, 55 mg sodium, 0 cholesterol, 21 gm carbohydrate, 1 gm protein, 0 fat.

Cinnamon Fruit Compote

Lynn Jahn, Elma, New York
(PICTURED ON FRONT COVER)

I've been asked to make this fruity salad for countless potlucks, picnics and parties. In a clear glass bowl, this wonderfully refreshing dish adds color to any table.

> **1-1/2 cups white grape juice**
> **1 cinnamon stick (4 inches)**
> **2 tablespoons sugar**
> **1 teaspoon grated orange peel**
> **1/4 teaspoon ground nutmeg**
> **2 cups fresh strawberries, halved**
> **3 medium nectarines, peeled and sliced**
> **2 cups seedless green grapes**
> **1 can (15 ounces) mandarin oranges, drained**
> **3 kiwifruit, peeled and sliced**

In a saucepan, bring the first five ingredients to a boil. Reduce heat; cover and simmer for 5 minutes. Remove from the heat; let stand for 15 minutes. Discard cinnamon stick; chill. Meanwhile, in a glass bowl, layer half of the strawberries and all of the nectarines, grapes and oranges. Top with kiwi and remaining strawberries. Stir juice mixture and pour over fruit; do not mix. Chill for 30 minutes. **Yield:** 8-10 servings.

Apple-Strawberry Peanut Salad

Mardi DesJardins, Winnipeg, Manitoba

This recipe originally called just for apples, but I added the strawberries for extra color. Folks who try this salad agree the salty nuts contrast nicely with the sweet fruit.

> **3 medium apples, cubed**
> **1 to 2 cups sliced strawberries**
> **1 cup thinly sliced celery**
> **1/2 cup mayonnaise**
> **3 tablespoons honey**
> **3/4 teaspoon celery seed**
> **3/4 cup salted peanuts**

In a large bowl, combine apples, strawberries and celery. In a small bowl, combine mayonnaise, honey and celery seed; mix well. Just before serving, add peanuts to fruit mixture and drizzle with dressing. **Yield:** 6-8 servings.

Nutty Mandarin Salad

Trina Boice, Alpharetta, Georgia

Sugar-coated almonds give this lettuce salad just the right amount of crunch. Whenever I make this for luncheons, it's always a success.

TOASTED ALMONDS:
> **2 tablespoons sugar**
> **1 tablespoon butter *or* margarine**
> **1 tablespoon water**
> **1/2 cup sliced almonds**

DRESSING:
> **1/2 cup vegetable oil**
> **1/2 cup tarragon *or* white wine vinegar**
> **2-1/2 teaspoons sugar**
> **2 teaspoons minced fresh parsley**
> **1/2 teaspoon dried tarragon**
> **1/2 teaspoon Dijon mustard**
> **1/2 teaspoon salt**
> **1/4 teaspoon pepper**

SALAD:
> **8 cups torn romaine**
> **6 cups torn Bibb lettuce**
> **1 can (15 ounces) mandarin oranges, drained**
> **1 cup thinly sliced green onions**

In a skillet over medium heat, cook sugar, butter and water, stirring constantly, until a syrup is formed. Add almonds; cook and stir for 4-6 minutes or until almonds are coated and browned. Set aside. In a jar with tight-fitting lid, combine dressing ingredients; shake well. In a large bowl, combine greens, oranges and onions. Break almonds apart and add to salad. Add dressing and toss. Serve immediately. **Yield:** 12-14 servings.

Guacamole Mousse with Salsa

Pat Cronin, Laredo, Texas

People who try this comment on the beautiful color and great combination of cool creamy guacamole topped with zesty salsa. This unique dish really captures the flavor of the Southwest.

- 3 ripe avocados, peeled and pitted
- 4 teaspoons lemon juice
- 3/4 teaspoon chili powder
- 1/4 teaspoon salt
- Pinch white pepper
- 3 plum tomatoes, peeled, seeded and chopped
- 1 cup (8 ounces) sour cream
- 1 cup whipping cream
- 1/3 cup mayonnaise
- 4 teaspoons finely chopped onion
- 2 envelopes unflavored gelatin
- 1/4 cup cold water
- 3 tablespoons minced fresh cilantro *or* parsley

SALSA:
- 5 plum tomatoes, seeded and diced
- 2 medium sweet red peppers, diced
- 1 to 2 medium jalapeno peppers, seeded and minced
- 1/4 cup finely chopped onion
- 4 teaspoons lime juice
- 4 teaspoons olive *or* vegetable oil
- 1/8 to 1/4 teaspoon salt

In a food processor or blender, process avocados, lemon juice, chili powder, salt and pepper until smooth. Place in a bowl; add tomatoes, sour cream, whipping cream, mayonnaise and onion. In a small saucepan, sprinkle gelatin over cold water; let stand 1 minute. Cook and stir over low heat until gelatin dissolves. Stir into avocado mixture. Pour into an oiled 6-cup mold; sprinkle with cilantro. Chill until set. Meanwhile, combine all salsa ingredients; chill. To serve, unmold mousse onto a platter; pass the salsa. **Yield:** 18-24 servings.

Refresing Turkey Salad

Carolyn Lough, Medley, Alberta

When the heat of summer hits, I want to spend time with my family, not with my oven! So I'll often cook a turkey, then dice and freeze leftovers for fast hearty dishes like this.

✓ This tasty dish uses less sugar, salt and fat. Recipe includes *Diabetic Exchanges.*

- 3 cups cooked wild rice
- 2 cups cubed cooked turkey
- 2 cups thinly sliced celery
- 1/2 cup seedless green grapes, halved
- 1/2 cup seedless red grapes, halved
- 1/4 cup chopped green pepper
- 1/4 cup chopped sweet red pepper
- 1 jar (2 ounces) chopped pimientos, drained
- 1/2 cup mayonnaise
- 1/2 cup sour cream
- 1 tablespoon honey
- 1 teaspoon Dijon mustard
- 1 teaspoon celery seed
- 1/2 teaspoon poppy seeds
- 1/2 teaspoon salt, optional
- 1/4 teaspoon pepper
- 1 tablespoon slivered almonds, toasted, optional

In a bowl, combine rice, turkey, celery, grapes, peppers and pimientos; set aside. In a small bowl, combine mayonnaise, sour cream, honey, mustard, celery seed, poppy seeds, salt if desired and pepper; mix well. Pour over rice mixture; toss to coat. Cover and chill at least 1 hour. If desired, garnish with almonds just before serving. **Yield:** 8 servings. **Diabetic Exchanges:** One 1-cup serving (prepared with turkey breast, unsweetened pineapple and fat-free mayonnaise and sour cream, and without salt and almonds) equals 1 starch, 1 very lean meat, 1 vegetable, 1/2 fruit; also, 160 calories, 340 mg sodium, 13 mg cholesterol, 27 gm carbohydrate, 9 gm protein, 1 gm fat.

Creamy Citrus Salad

Mary Prior, St. Paul, Minnesota

This crowd-pleasing salad frequently appeared on the table while I was growing up. But with my four brothers, it never lasted long! The flavors are a nice addition to any meal.

- 1 package (6 ounces) orange gelatin
- 2 cups boiling water
- 1 can (6 ounces) frozen orange juice concentrate, thawed
- 2 cans (11 ounces *each*) mandarin oranges, drained
- 1 can (20 ounces) crushed pineapple, undrained
- 1 cup cold milk
- 1 package (3.4 ounces) instant lemon pudding mix
- 1 cup whipping cream, whipped

In a large bowl, dissolve gelatin in boiling water; stir in orange juice concentrate. Cool until partially set. Fold in oranges and pineapple. Pour into an oiled 13-in. x 9-in. x 2-in. dish. Chill until firm. In a small bowl, beat milk and pudding mix for 2 minutes; fold in cream. Spread over gelatin. Chill for 30 minutes. **Yield:** 12-14 servings.

Grandma's Apple Salad

Robin Ford, New Haven, Indiana

I can still remember my grandmother preparing this succulent salad...it was her trademark. So I was thrilled when she passed this precious recipe on to me.

- 1 cup mayonnaise *or* salad dressing
- 1/2 cup milk
- 2 tablespoons sugar
- 5 tart apples, diced

1-1/2 cups sliced celery
1-1/2 cups miniature marshmallows
1 cup salted peanuts

In a bowl, stir mayonnaise, milk and sugar until smooth. Add apples, celery and marshmallows. Just before serving, stir in peanuts. **Yield:** 10-12 servings.

Rosy Raspberry Salad

Jane Vanderground, Macedonia, Ohio

Whenever I make this salad, people comment on its attractive appearance and wonderful flavor. It's a festive side dish that works well for celebrations throughout the year.

3 packages (3 ounces *each*) raspberry gelatin
3 cups boiling water
3 cups raspberry sherbet
1 package (12 ounces) unsweetened frozen raspberries

In a large bowl, dissolve gelatin in boiling water. Add sherbet and stir until melted. Chill until syrupy. Add raspberries. Pour into an oiled 8-cup mold. Chill until firm. **Yield:** 12-14 servings.

Lime Pear Salad

Carol Wattles, Little Marsh, Pennsylvania

Through my years of working in the food service industry, I've collected a bounty of salad recipes. This pleasantly colored side dish is cool, creamy and comforting.

1 package (3 ounces) cream cheese, softened
1 package (3 ounces) lime gelatin
1 can (16 ounces) pear halves
2 cups vanilla ice cream, softened

In a mixing bowl, beat cream cheese and gelatin until smooth. Drain pears, reserving syrup; set pears aside. If necessary, add enough water to syrup to equal 1 cup. In a small saucepan, bring syrup to a boil. Gradually add to gelatin mixture, beating until smooth. Stir in ice cream until dissolved. Mash pears and fold into gelatin mixture. Pour into an oiled 6-cup mold. Chill until firm. **Yield:** 6-8 servings.

Cranberry Gelatin Salad

Marguerite Dixon, Carthage, Missouri

I got this recipe from a magazine and made some changes to suit my family's tastes. This salad is especially nice during the holidays, but it's good with any main meal.

2 packages (3 ounces *each*) cherry *or* cranberry gelatin
2 cups boiling water
1 package (12 ounces) fresh *or* frozen cranberries

1-1/2 medium seedless oranges, quartered
1-3/4 cups sugar
2 cans (8 ounces *each*) crushed pineapple, undrained
1 cup chopped celery
1/2 cup chopped walnuts

In a large bowl, dissolve gelatin in boiling water. In a food processor, finely chop cranberries and oranges. Transfer to a bowl; stir in sugar until dissolved. Add pineapple, celery and nuts. Stir in gelatin. Chill for at least 6 hours. **Yield:** 16-20 servings.

Fruit Bowl with Mandarin Dressing

Judy Brinegar, Liberty, North Carolina

In this recipe, fresh fruit is refreshingly cool, while the dressing adds just the right amount of sweetness. This colorful salad makes a nice addition to any buffet table.

2 cups cubed watermelon
2 cups cubed cantaloupe
2 cups seedless grapes, halved
2 cups halved fresh strawberries
2 cups fresh blueberries
1 cup mayonnaise
1 cup marshmallow creme
2 teaspoons grated gingerroot *or* 1/2 teaspoon ground ginger
1 teaspoon grated orange peel

Combine fruit in a large bowl. Cover and chill. In a small bowl, combine mayonnaise, marshmallow creme, ginger and orange peel; gently mix until smooth. Serve over fruit. **Yield:** 8-10 servings (1-1/2 cups dressing).

Molded Cherry-Pineapple Salad

Deanna Richter, Elmore, Minnesota

I found this recipe in an area newspaper years ago. When this festive salad appears at a potluck, folks always come back for seconds…and sometimes thirds! I sometimes tint it with food coloring for the holidays.

2 envelopes unflavored gelatin
1/4 cup cold water
1 can (20 ounces) crushed pineapple, undrained
1 package (8 ounces) cream cheese
1/2 cup sugar
2 tablespoons lemon juice
2 tablespoons maraschino cherry juice
1/2 pint whipping cream, whipped
12 maraschino cherries, halved

In a medium saucepan, dissolve gelatin in cold water. Add pineapple, cream cheese, sugar and juices; cook over medium heat, stirring often, until cream cheese is melted and gelatin is dissolved. Chill until syrupy. Fold in cream and cherries. Pour into an oiled 6-cup mold. Chill until firm. **Yield:** 8-10 servings.

Hot Sandwich Specialties

When you serve these oven-baked, pan-fried or grilled sandwiches to family and friends, some mighty good eating is sure to follow!

Turkey Gobble-Up

Elly Senior, Vancouver, British Columbia
(PICTURED AT LEFT)

Whenever I roast a turkey, my family never grumbles about the leftovers because they know I'll be making these delicious sandwiches. I've been serving them for 25 years now, and they still look forward to them!

    1 large ripe avocado, peeled and pitted
    1 tablespoon lemon juice
    2 tablespoons mayonnaise
    2 tablespoons sour cream
 1/4 teaspoon hot pepper sauce
    6 English muffins, split and toasted
   12 slices cooked turkey breast
   12 slices tomato
   12 slices American *or* cheddar cheese
   12 bacon strips, halved, cooked and drained

In a small bowl, mash the avocado; add lemon juice, mayonnaise, sour cream and hot pepper sauce. Spread over muffin halves; top with turkey, tomato, cheese and bacon. Broil 6 in. from the heat for 3-4 minutes or until cheese begins to melt. **Yield:** 6 servings.

Open-Faced Mozzarella Sandwiches

Valerie Hart, Mt. Dora, Florida
(PICTURED AT LEFT)

These zesty sandwiches are a family favorite at our house. They have a distinctly Italian flavor, plus a fresh-from-the-garden taste that can't be beat.

    1 cup seeded chopped plum tomatoes
    3 tablespoons olive *or* vegetable oil
    1 garlic clove, minced
    1 teaspoon thinly sliced green onion
    1 teaspoon chopped fresh basil *or* 1/4 teaspoon
      dried basil
 1/4 teaspoon salt
 1/8 teaspoon pepper

GOOD IN BETWEEN. *Pictured at left, top to bottom: Turkey Gobble-Up, Open-Faced Mozzarella Sandwiches and Oriental Chicken Grill (all recipes on this page).*

Dash cayenne pepper
    4 slices Italian bread (3/4 inch thick)
 1/2 cup shredded mozzarella cheese

In a small bowl, combine the first eight ingredients. Cover and refrigerate for at least 1 hour. Drain 2 teaspoons liquid from the tomato mixture; brush onto one side of each slice of bread. Broil 5 in. from the heat until crisp, about 1-2 minutes. Spoon 1/4 cup tomato mixture on each piece of bread; sprinkle with cheese. Broil 1-2 minutes longer or until bubbly. **Yield:** 2 servings.

BETTER THAN BUTTER. Add a new twist to traditional grilled sandwiches by spreading the side of the bread to be grilled with mayonnaise instead of butter.

Oriental Chicken Grill

Rosemary Splittgerber, Mesa, Arizona
(PICTURED AT LEFT)

Since my husband and I are empty nesters, this recipe is great for just the two of us, although it could be increased. We both love these tasty sandwiches—especially my husband, who "lives to eat" rather than "eats to live"!

 1/2 cup orange juice
    2 tablespoons honey
    2 tablespoons soy sauce
    1 teaspoon lemon-pepper seasoning
    1 teaspoon ground ginger
 1/2 teaspoon garlic powder
    2 boneless skinless chicken breast halves
    2 hamburger buns, split
Lettuce leaves and tomato slices, optional

In a small bowl, combine the first six ingredients; mix well. Set aside 1/4 cup for basting chicken; cover and refrigerate. Pound chicken breasts to 3/8-in. thickness. Place in a resealable plastic bag or glass bowl; pour remaining marinade over chicken. Close bag or cover and refrigerate overnight. Drain, discarding marinade. Grill chicken, uncovered, over medium coals for 6-8 minutes per side or until juices run clear. Baste several times with reserved marinade while grilling. Serve on buns with lettuce and tomato if desired. **Yield:** 2 servings.

Italian Beef Sandwiches

Susan Carter, American Fork, Utah

I like to prepare this recipe on the weekend so it has time to marinate. Then we can have hearty sandwiches all week long. It's also ideal for entertaining.

      1 boneless sirloin tip roast (4 to 5 pounds)
  1/2 teaspoon salt
      3 medium onions, thinly sliced
      3 beef bouillon cubes
      7 hot banana peppers, seeded and thinly sliced
      2 teaspoons Italian seasoning
      1 teaspoon dried basil
      1 teaspoon dried oregano
      1 teaspoon garlic salt
      1 teaspoon onion salt
  20 to 24 hard rolls, split

Place roast on a rack in a 13-in. x 9-in. x 2-in. baking pan. Sprinkle with salt; top with onions. Add 1/2 in. of water to pan. Cover with heavy-duty foil. Bake at 350° for 2 to 2-1/4 hours or until a meat thermometer reads 160°-170°. Remove meat; set aside until cool enough to handle. Slice thin; place in a large bowl. Pour pan juices into a saucepan; add bouillon, peppers and seasonings. Bring to a boil. Reduce heat; cover and simmer for 10 minutes. Pour over beef; cover and refrigerate at least 8 hours. Reheat before serving. Serve 1/2 cup on each roll. **Yield:** 20-24 servings.

Zesty Meatball Sandwiches

Cindy Renner, Geneva, Illinois

A close family friend always had a pot of these saucy meatballs simmering on the stove when I was growing up. Now my own kids—triplet sons!—like them as much as I do.

SAUCE:
1-1/2 cups chopped onion
      2 garlic cloves, minced
      2 tablespoons olive *or* vegetable oil
      2 cans (28 ounces *each*) diced tomatoes, undrained
      1 can (6 ounces) tomato paste
      1 cup water
      2 bay leaves
      1 tablespoon dried oregano
      2 tablespoons sugar
      1 teaspoon salt
  1/4 teaspoon pepper
MEATBALLS:
      8 slices white bread, crusts removed and cubed
  1/3 cup water
      4 eggs, lightly beaten
      2 pounds ground beef
      1 cup grated Parmesan cheese
  1/4 cup minced fresh parsley
      2 garlic cloves, minced

      1 teaspoon dried oregano
      1 teaspoon salt
Dash pepper
  10 to 12 Italian rolls, split

In a large saucepan or Dutch oven, saute onion and garlic in oil until tender. Add the remaining sauce ingredients; bring to a boil. Reduce heat; cover and simmer for 30 minutes. Remove bay leaves; set sauce aside. In a large bowl, toss bread cubes with water. Add eggs, beef, Parmesan, parsley, garlic, oregano, salt and pepper; mix well. Shape into 1-1/2-in. balls. Place on an ungreased shallow baking pan. Bake, uncovered, at 350° for 20-25 minutes. Add to sauce. Simmer, uncovered, for 30 minutes. Serve on rolls. **Yield:** 10-12 servings.

Hot 'n' Cheesy Chicken Sandwiches

Nancy Frederiksen, Springfield, Minnesota

Here's a nice change of pace from traditional chicken sandwiches. Cream of mushroom soup gives a rich homey flavor, and vegetables add just the right amount of crunch.

      6 cups cubed cooked chicken
1-1/2 cups chopped celery
      1 can (10-3/4 ounces) condensed cream of mushroom soup, undiluted
  3/4 cup mayonnaise
  3/4 cup chopped onion
  1/2 cup chopped green pepper
      1 teaspoon ground mustard
  1/2 teaspoon salt
  1/2 teaspoon pepper
      3 cups cubed process American cheese
  24 hamburger buns, split

In a large bowl, combine the first nine ingredients; mix well. Pour into an ungreased 2-1/2-qt. casserole; top with cheese. Cover and bake at 350° for 45 minutes or until bubbly. Let stand for 5 minutes; spoon 1/3 cup onto each bun. **Yield:** 24 servings.

Turkey BLT

Deborah Westbrook, York Springs, Pennsylvania

As much as my family loves them, leftover turkey sandwiches can get pretty boring. This recipe dresses them up and adds a nice twist to a traditional treat.

      2 tablespoons mayonnaise
      1 tablespoon spicy brown mustard
      1 tablespoon honey
      2 large pumpernickel rolls, split
      4 slices cooked turkey
      4 bacon strips, cooked and drained
      2 slices Swiss cheese
      4 slices tomato
Lettuce leaves

In a small bowl, combine mayonnaise, mustard and honey; spread on cut sides of rolls. On bottom halves of rolls, layer turkey, bacon and cheese. Broil 4 in. from the heat for 2-3 minutes or until cheese begins to melt. Top with tomato and lettuce; replace roll tops. **Yield:** 2 servings.

Beef 'n' Braised Onion Sandwiches

Lois McAtee, Oceanside, California

These easy sandwiches have been a favorite of my four grown children since they were teenagers. They're wonderfully delicious and perfect for any occasion.

✓ This tasty dish uses less sugar, salt and fat. Recipe includes *Diabetic Exchanges*.

  2 tablespoons water
  2 teaspoons prepared horseradish
  2 teaspoons cooking oil
  2 teaspoons red wine *or* cider vinegar
  1 cup thinly sliced onion rings
  4 onion rolls *or* hamburger buns, split
3/4 pound thinly sliced roast beef
  4 slices brick *or* Monterey Jack cheese (1 ounce *each*)

In a skillet over medium heat, combine water, horseradish, oil and vinegar. Add onions; cook and stir until liquid is absorbed and onions are golden, about 12-14 minutes. Place bottom halves of rolls on a baking sheet; top with beef, onion mixture and cheese. Broil 4 in. from the heat for 1-2 minutes or until cheese is melted. Replace roll tops. **Yield:** 4 servings. **Diabetic Exchanges:** One sandwich (prepared with lean roast beef and Monterey Jack cheese and served on a hamburger bun) equals 4 meat, 2 starch; also, 433 calories, 453 mg sodium, 103 mg cholesterol, 24 gm carbohydrate, 37 gm protein, 21 gm fat.

Ground Turkey Turnovers

Myrna Shirts, Idaho Falls, Idaho

I have a variety of turkey recipes that my family "gobbles" up, but this is one of their favorites. When they were young, our kids often requested these for Saturday night dinner.

1-1/2 pounds ground turkey
  1 can (10-3/4 ounces) condensed cream of chicken soup, undiluted
  1 egg, lightly beaten
  2 tablespoons all-purpose flour
1/2 teaspoon salt
1/4 teaspoon pepper
  1 can (8-1/4 ounces) mixed vegetables, drained
  1 jar (2 ounces) diced pimientos, drained
1/2 cup shredded mozzarella cheese
  2 tubes (17.3 ounces *each*) Southern-style biscuits

In a nonstick saucepan over medium heat, brown turkey; drain. Combine soup, egg, flour, salt and pepper; add to turkey. Cook, stirring occasionally, for 5 minutes. Add vegetables and pimientos; cook for 2 minutes. Remove from the heat; stir in cheese. On a floured board, pat eight of the biscuits into circles; top each with about 2/3 cup turkey mixture. Pat remaining biscuits into 5-in. circles and place on top of turkey mixture. Seal edges with water. Press edges

together with a fork dipped in flour. Place on an ungreased baking sheet. Bake at 375° for 12-14 minutes or until golden brown. **Yield:** 8 servings.

Ground Beef Bundles

Denise Goedeken, Platte Center, Nebraska

These little pockets are made in kitchens throughout Nebraska. With ground beef and cabbage, they truly capture the down-home country cooking we all enjoy.

1/2 pound ground beef
  2 cups shredded cabbage
1/2 cup chopped onion
  2 tablespoons butter *or* margarine
  1 teaspoon Worcestershire sauce
1/4 teaspoon salt
1/8 teaspoon pepper
  1 loaf (1 pound) frozen bread dough, thawed
1/2 cup shredded Swiss cheese
Melted butter *or* margarine

In a skillet, brown beef; drain. Add cabbage, onion, butter, Worcestershire sauce, salt and pepper. Cook and stir until cabbage is crisp-tender. Meanwhile, cut bread dough into eight equal pieces; roll each into a 5-in. square. Place 1/4 cup meat mixture in the center of each square; sprinkle with about 1 tablespoon cheese. Bring corners together in the center; pinch edges to seal. Place on an ungreased baking sheet; brush tops with melted butter. Bake at 350° for 16-18 minutes. Serve warm. **Yield:** 8 servings.

Crescent Chicken Squares

Ruth Dyck, Forest, Ontario

Through many years living on a farm, I've collected quite a few recipes using chicken. Family and friends tell me this is one of my best dishes featuring this versatile, tasty meat.

  1 package (3 ounces) cream cheese, softened
  3 tablespoons butter *or* margarine, melted, *divided*
1/4 teaspoon salt
1/8 teaspoon pepper
  2 cups cubed cooked chicken
  2 tablespoons milk
  1 tablespoon chopped onion
  1 tablespoon diced pimientos
  1 tube (8 ounces) refrigerated crescent rolls
1/4 cup seasoned bread crumbs

In a mixing bowl, beat cream cheese, 2 tablespoons butter, salt and pepper until smooth. Stir in chicken, milk, onion and pimientos. Unroll crescent roll dough and separate into four rectangles; place on an ungreased baking sheet and press perforations together. Spoon 1/2 cup chicken mixture into the center of each rectangle. Bring edges up to the center and pinch to seal. Brush with remaining butter; sprinkle with crumbs. Bake at 350° for 20-25 minutes or until golden. **Yield:** 2-4 servings.

Reuben Deli Sandwiches

Gigi LaFave Ryan, Longmont, Colorado
(PICTURED AT LEFT)

Here's a new twist on the classic Reuben sandwich. The filling is easy to prepare and keeps well in the fridge. Add a salad and dessert, and you have a delicious brunch.

3/4 cup mayonnaise
1 tablespoon chili sauce
1-1/2 teaspoons mustard
1/4 teaspoon prepared horseradish
1 can (14 ounces) sauerkraut, rinsed and well drained
3/4 pound finely chopped corned beef (about 3 cups)
2 cups (8 ounces) shredded Swiss cheese
30 slices rye bread
1/2 cup butter *or* margarine, softened

In a large bowl, combine mayonnaise, chili sauce, mustard and horseradish. Stir in sauerkraut, corned beef and Swiss cheese. Spread 1/3 cup on 15 slices of bread; top with remaining bread. Lightly butter the outsides of bread. Toast sandwiches on a hot griddle for 4-5 minutes per side or until golden brown. **Yield:** 15 servings.

French Onion-Beef Strudel

Sherry Keethler, Lake St. Louis, Missouri
(PICTURED AT LEFT)

I prepared this flavorful strudel for my craft club meeting, and everyone asked me for the recipe. It makes such a nice presentation, so it's great to serve at gatherings.

1 loaf (1 pound) frozen bread dough, thawed
2 cups thinly sliced onion
1/4 cup butter *or* margarine
6 ounces beef tenderloin *or* sirloin steak (1 inch thick)
1 teaspoon all-purpose flour
1 teaspoon brown sugar
1/2 teaspoon ground cumin
1/4 teaspoon salt
1/4 teaspoon pepper
1/2 cup beef broth
3/4 cup shredded Monterey Jack cheese
6 tablespoons grated Parmesan cheese, *divided*
1 can (10 ounces) beef au jus gravy

Allow dough to rise until nearly doubled. Meanwhile, in a skillet, saute onion in butter over low heat for 15-20 minutes or until golden brown. With a slotted spoon, remove onion from skillet; set aside. Cut beef into 1/8-in. slices; add to skillet. Increase heat to medium; cook and stir for 3 min-

utes or until browned. Return onion to skillet. Stir in flour, brown sugar, cumin, salt and pepper. Add broth; cook and stir for 6-8 minutes or until liquid has evaporated. Remove from the heat. Punch dough down; roll on a floured board to a 16-in. x 12-in. rectangle. Place on a greased baking sheet. Place beef mixture down the center of the long side of the dough. Sprinkle with Monterey Jack cheese and 4 tablespoons Parmesan cheese. With a sharp knife, cut dough on each side of beef filling into 1-3/4-in.-wide strips. Fold strips alternately across filling. Sprinkle with remaining Parmesan. Cover and let rise until nearly doubled, about 30 minutes. Bake at 375° for 20-25 minutes or until golden brown. Heat gravy; serve as a dipping sauce. **Yield:** 6 servings.

Barbecued Ham Sandwiches

Mary Lou Amoroso, Marion, Illinois

This meaty mixture is ideal for company because it can be made in advance. When you're ready to eat, just spoon a heaping helping onto each bun for a tasty meal.

1/4 cup chopped onion
1/4 cup butter *or* margarine
1 cup chili sauce
3/4 cup water
2 tablespoons vinegar
2 tablespoons brown sugar
1 teaspoon ground mustard
1 pound shaved fully cooked ham
8 hamburger buns, split

In a large saucepan or Dutch oven, saute onion in butter. Add chili sauce, water, vinegar, brown sugar and mustard; bring to a boil. Reduce heat; cover and simmer for 20 minutes. Add ham; return to a boil. Reduce heat; cover and simmer for 10 minutes or until heated through. Spoon about 1/2 cup onto each bun. **Yield:** 8 servings.

Three Cheese Tomato Melt

Shirlee Medema, Grandville, Michigan

I love to make this open-faced sandwich for myself or unexpected guests…especially when homegrown tomatoes are ripe on the vine. Try it for lunch or a snack.

1/4 cup shredded cheddar cheese
2 tablespoons shredded mozzarella cheese
1 tablespoon grated Parmesan cheese
2 tablespoons mayonnaise
1/8 teaspoon garlic powder
4 slices tomato
2 bagels *or* English muffins, split and toasted

Combine cheeses, mayonnaise and garlic powder; set aside. Place a tomato slice on each bagel half; broil 5 in. from the heat for 1-2 minutes or until tomato is warm. Spread about 1 tablespoon cheese mixture over each tomato; broil 2-3 minutes longer or until cheese is melted. **Yield:** 2 servings.

PERFECT FOR PARTIES. *Pictured at left, top to bottom: Reuben Deli Sandwiches and French Onion-Beef Strudel (both recipes on this page).*

Beef Barbecue Biscuits

Gail Schreiter, Gordon, Nebraska

These little meat-filled cups are simple to prepare and make great finger food for meals and snacks. My husband and I enjoy them almost as much as our kids do!

    3/4 pound ground beef
    1/2 cup barbecue sauce
      1 tablespoon dried minced onion
      4 teaspoons brown sugar
      1 tube (12 ounces) refrigerated buttermilk biscuits
    3/4 cup shredded cheddar cheese

In a skillet, brown beef; drain. Add barbecue sauce, onion and brown sugar; set aside. Separate dough into 10 biscuits; flatten into 5-in. circles. Press firmly into the bottom and up the sides of greased muffin cups. Spoon 2 tablespoons of beef mixture into each cup; sprinkle with cheese. Bake at 400° for 10-15 minutes or until biscuits are golden and cheese is melted. **Yield:** 10 servings.

Chili Sandwiches

Kerry Haglund, Wyoming, Minnesota

No one will be able to resist these special sandwiches stuffed with spicy chili. Of course, the chili also makes a wonderfully filling meal by itself.

      1 pound dry navy beans
      2 pounds beef stew meat
      2 cups water
      1 pound sliced bacon, diced
      1 cup chopped onion
      1 cup shredded carrots
      1 cup chopped celery
    1/3 cup chopped green pepper
    1/3 cup chopped sweet red pepper
      4 garlic cloves, minced
      3 cans (14-1/2 ounces *each*) diced tomatoes, undrained
      1 cup barbecue sauce
      1 cup chili sauce
    1/2 cup honey
    1/4 cup hot pepper sauce
      1 tablespoon chili powder
      1 tablespoon baking cocoa
      1 tablespoon Dijon mustard
      1 tablespoon Worcestershire sauce
      1 bay leaf
      4 teaspoons beef bouillon granules
     30 hamburger buns, split

Place beans and enough water to cover in a saucepan. Bring to a boil; boil for 2 minutes. Remove from the heat and let stand for 1 hour; drain and rinse. In a large kettle or Dutch oven, simmer beans and beef in water for 2 hours or until very tender; drain. Shred beef and place it and the beans in

a slow cooker. In a large skillet, cook bacon until crisp. With a slotted spoon, remove bacon to the slow cooker. Discard all but 3 tablespoons drippings. Saute onion, carrots, celery, peppers and garlic in drippings until tender. Transfer to the slow cooker. Add remaining ingredients except buns. Cover and cook on high for 3-4 hours, stirring often. Remove bay leaf. Spoon 1/2 cup onto each bun. **Yield:** 30 servings.

Mustard Turkey Sandwiches

Monica Wilcott, Sturgis, Saskatchewan

This recipe is perfect for casual dinners with friends. The turkey can be marinating while you visit with guests, then popped onto the grill for a mouth-watering meal in no time.

    1/2 cup olive *or* vegetable oil
    1/2 cup honey
    1/4 cup Dijon mustard
      1 tablespoon curry powder
Pinch cayenne pepper
1-1/4 pounds uncooked turkey breast slices
      6 onion *or* kaiser rolls, split
Lettuce leaves

In a small saucepan, combine the first five ingredients. Cook over medium heat until honey is melted, stirring constantly; set 1/4 cup aside. Pour remaining mixture into a shallow glass dish or resealable plastic bag; add turkey. Cover or close bag and refrigerate for at least 2 hours. Drain, discarding marinade. Broil or grill turkey for 4 minutes per side or until no longer pink. Spread reserved honey mixture on cut sides of rolls. Add lettuce and turkey. **Yield:** 6 servings.

Sausage-Stuffed French Loaf

Mary Petit, Lindenhurst, Illinois

When my family first tried this sandwich loaf, they suggested I include it as part of our annual New Year's Day celebration. It tastes great with homemade soup.

      1 loaf (1 pound) French bread
    1/2 pound ground beef
    1/2 pound bulk pork sausage
      1 medium onion, chopped
      1 cup (4 ounces) shredded mozzarella cheese
      1 egg, beaten
    1/4 cup chopped fresh parsley
      1 teaspoon Dijon mustard
    1/4 teaspoon pepper
    1/4 teaspoon salt
    1/8 teaspoon fennel seed
      2 tablespoons butter *or* margarine
      1 garlic clove, minced

Cut a thin slice off the top of the bread. Hollow out bottom half, leaving a 1/4-in. shell. In a food processor or blender, process bread crumbs until coarse; set aside 1 cup. (Discard remaining crumbs or save for another use.) In a skillet, brown beef, sausage and onion; drain. Stir in reserved crumbs, cheese, egg, parsley, mustard, pepper, salt and fennel; mix well. Spoon into bread shell; replace bread top. Place on a large sheet of heavy-duty foil. In a small saucepan, melt butter; add garlic and cook for 1 minute. Brush over tops and sides of loaf. Seal the foil. Bake at 400° for 20 minutes or until cheese is melted. **Yield:** 6-8 servings.

Spinach Bacon Sandwiches

Jeanette Hios, Brooklyn, New York

My cousin introduced me to this sandwich years ago. Not only is it quick and easy, it's a guaranteed crowd-pleaser. Try it at your next potluck and see for yourself.

    3 garlic cloves, minced
    3 tablespoons olive *or* vegetable oil
    2 packages (10 ounces *each*) frozen chopped spinach, thawed and squeezed dry
  3/4 teaspoon salt
  1/4 teaspoon pepper
    6 bacon strips, cooked and crumbled
1-1/2 cups (6 ounces) shredded mozzarella cheese
    1 loaf (1 pound) Italian bread
  1/4 cup shredded Parmesan cheese, optional

In a large skillet over medium heat, saute garlic in oil. Add spinach, salt and pepper; cook, stirring occasionally, until heated through. Remove from the heat; cool for 5 minutes. Add bacon and mozzarella; mix well. Slice bread horizontally. Spread about 2-1/4 cups spinach mixture on each half. Sprinkle with Parmesan if desired. Bake at 450° for 6-8 minutes or until cheese is melted. **Yield:** 8-10 servings.

Turkey Muffins with Cheese Sauce

Mary Jane Freymuth, Troy, Missouri

My cooking days began as a child when my mom let me assist her in the kitchen by grating, chopping…and, of course, washing dishes! We continue to have many wonderful times cooking together.

    2 tablespoons butter *or* margarine
    2 tablespoons all-purpose flour
  1/2 teaspoon salt
  1/8 teaspoon pepper
    1 cup milk
    1 cup (4 ounces) shredded cheddar cheese
  1/4 teaspoon Worcestershire sauce
    3 English muffins, split and toasted
    6 slices Canadian bacon
    6 slices cooked turkey
Chopped fresh parsley

In a saucepan over low heat, melt butter; stir in flour, salt and pepper until smooth. Gradually add milk. Bring to a boil; boil for 2 minutes, stirring constantly. Reduce heat to low. Add cheese and Worcestershire sauce; cook and stir until cheese melts. Place muffins in a shallow baking pan. Top each half with a slice of bacon and turkey. Top with 2-

3 tablespoons cheese sauce. Broil 5 in. from the heat for about 5 minutes. Sprinkle with parsley. **Yield:** 6 servings.

Turkey Burritos

Chris Bakewell, Glendale, Arizona

When my husband and I were married almost 30 years ago, my biggest challenge was learning to cook. Now I struggle to find filling lunches for our son. He loves these burritos.

      1 pound ground turkey
    1/2 cup chopped onion
      1 can (14-1/2 ounces) diced tomatoes, undrained
      1 can (16 ounces) refried beans with green chilies
      1 can (4 ounces) chopped green chilies
      1 can (2-1/4 ounces) sliced ripe olives, drained
      1 envelope taco seasoning mix
    1/4 cup frozen corn
    1/4 cup uncooked instant rice
     10 to 12 flour tortillas (7 to 8 inches)
Shredded cheddar *or* Monterey Jack cheese, optional

In a large nonstick saucepan, brown turkey and onion; drain. Add tomatoes, beans, chilies, olives, taco seasoning and corn; bring to a boil. Reduce heat; cover and simmer for 15 minutes. Return to a boil. Stir in rice; remove from the heat. Cover; let stand for 5 minutes. Place about 1/2 cup filling down the center of each tortilla; sprinkle with cheese if desired. Fold in sides of tortilla. **Yield:** 10-12 servings.

Grilled Blue Cheese Sandwiches

Linda Zweifel, Beresford, South Dakota

Once they try these rich tasty sandwiches, the blue cheese lovers in your family will never request a traditional grilled cheese sandwich again!

1-1/2 cups sliced fresh mushrooms
    2 tablespoons chopped onion
  1/2 cup mayonnaise, *divided*
    2 cups (8 ounces) shredded cheddar cheese
  1/4 cup crumbled blue cheese
    1 teaspoon yellow *or* Dijon mustard
    1 teaspoon Worcestershire sauce
  1/4 teaspoon salt
  1/8 teaspoon cayenne pepper
   12 slices white *or* wheat bread
    2 to 4 tablespoons butter *or* margarine

In a large skillet over medium heat, saute mushrooms and onion in 3 tablespoons mayonnaise for 5 minutes or until mushrooms are tender; cool. In a bowl, combine cheeses, mustard, Worcestershire sauce, salt, cayenne, mushroom mixture and remaining mayonnaise; mix well. Spread 1/3 cup on six slices of bread; top with remaining bread. Melt 2 tablespoons butter in a large skillet. Add sandwiches and cook until each side is golden brown and cheese is melted, adding additional butter if necessary. **Yield:** 6 servings.

Dorothy's Barbecue

Virginia Bowser, Palm Springs, California
(PICTURED AT LEFT)

A friend shared this recipe with me, and my son loves it! It's a bit sweeter than most barbecue recipes. It also freezes well, so it's convenient for a meal on a moment's notice.

- 1 boneless rump roast (5 to 6 pounds)
- 3 quarts water
- 1 bottle (14 ounces) ketchup
- 1 cup packed brown sugar
- 1 cup hot coffee
- 3 tablespoons vinegar
- 2 tablespoons Worcestershire sauce
- 1 tablespoon ground mustard
- 1 tablespoon horseradish
- 1/2 teaspoon celery seed
- 1/2 teaspoon garlic powder
- 1/2 teaspoon salt
- 1/4 teaspoon pepper
- 1/8 teaspoon ground allspice
- 18 to 20 hamburger buns, split

Place roast and water in a Dutch oven; bring to a boil. Reduce heat; cover and simmer for 3 to 3-1/2 hours or until meat is tender. Remove meat; cool. Strain broth; set aside 1-1/2 cups. In a large saucepan or Dutch oven, combine ketchup, brown sugar, coffee, vinegar, Worcestershire sauce, mustard, horseradish, seasonings and reserved broth; bring to a boil. Reduce heat; simmer, uncovered, for 30 minutes. Thinly slice or shred roast; add to sauce and heat through. Serve on buns. **Yield:** 18-20 servings.

Grilled "PBJ" Sandwiches

Barb Trautmann, Ham Lake, Minnesota
(PICTURED AT LEFT)

I was going to make grilled cheese sandwiches one day and had already buttered several slices of bread when I found I was out of cheese. So I pulled out some peanut butter and jelly, and the result was this tasty variation of a popular classic.

- 4 tablespoons peanut butter
- 2 tablespoons strawberry jam
- 4 slices English muffin *or* white toasting bread
- 2 tablespoons butter *or* margarine, softened
Confectioners' sugar, optional

Spread peanut butter and jam on two slices of bread; top with remaining bread. Butter the outsides of sandwiches; cook in a large skillet over medium heat until golden brown on each side. Dust with confectioners' sugar if desired. **Yield:** 2 servings.

Hot Dogs with Chili Beans

Joella Bachicha, Pflugerville, Texas
(PICTURED AT LEFT)

This was a recipe my mom used often when I was growing up. These hot dogs were a favorite summertime meal with potato salad and chips.

- 1 pound ground beef
- 2 garlic cloves, minced
- 1 cup chopped onion, *divided*
- 1 can (15 ounces) pinto beans, rinsed and drained
- 1 cup water
- 4 teaspoons chili powder
- 1/2 teaspoon salt
- 1/4 teaspoon pepper
- 12 hot dogs, heated
- 12 hot dog buns, split
Shredded Colby *or* cheddar cheese

In a saucepan over medium heat, brown beef, garlic and 1/2 cup onion; drain. Add beans, water, chili powder, salt and pepper; bring to a boil. Reduce heat; simmer, uncovered, for 30 minutes. Place hot dogs in buns. Top each with about 1/4 cup chili bean mixture. Sprinkle with cheese and remaining onion. **Yield:** 12 servings.

Wonderburgers for Two

Cathy Zadel, Hanalei, Hawaii

I often cook for just my husband and myself, so this perfectly portioned recipe really comes in handy. The "homemade" hamburger buns make these sandwiches extra special.

BUNS:
- 1 tube (11 ounces) refrigerated breadsticks
- 1 egg
- 1 tablespoon water
Sesame seeds
HAMBURGERS:
- 2/3 to 3/4 pound ground beef
- 1/4 cup chopped onion
- 1 egg
- 1 to 2 tablespoons soy sauce
- 1/2 to 1 teaspoon dried thyme
- 1/4 teaspoon salt
- 1/4 teaspoon pepper

Separate breadsticks into eight strips; connect two strips by pinching ends together. Roll strips into four coils; flatten by hand to 1/2-in. thickness. Layer two coils together on an ungreased baking sheet. Beat egg and water; brush over dough. Sprinkle with sesame seeds. Bake at 350° for 15-18 minutes or until golden brown; cool. Combine all hamburger ingredients; shape into two patties. Grill over medium-hot coals, turning once, until no longer pink. Cut buns in half; add burgers. **Yield:** 2 servings.

KIDS'LL LOVE 'EM. *Pictured at left, top to bottom: Hot Dogs with Chili Beans, Grilled "PBJ" Sandwiches and Dorothy's Barbecue (all recipes on this page).*

Turkey Mornay

Shirley Nowicki, Temperance, Michigan

This recipe proves that leftover holiday turkey doesn't have to be lifeless! Liven up your extra turkey with a creamy Swiss cheese sauce and tender asparagus over toasted bread.

- 3 tablespoons butter *or* margarine
- 3 tablespoons all-purpose flour
- 1/2 teaspoon salt
- 1/8 teaspoon pepper
- 2 cups milk
- 3/4 cup shredded Swiss cheese
- 4 slices white bread, toasted
- 4 slices cooked turkey breast
- 1 can (15 ounces) asparagus spears, drained
- 2 tablespoons shredded Parmesan cheese

In a saucepan over medium heat, cook butter, flour, salt and pepper until smooth. Gradually add milk. Bring to a boil; cook and stir for 2 minutes or until thickened. Add Swiss cheese; stir until melted. Place bread in a shallow baking pan; top with turkey, asparagus and 1/2 cup sauce. Sprinkle with Parmesan cheese. Broil 5 in. from the heat for 4-6 minutes or until browned and bubbly. **Yield:** 4 servings.

Open-Faced Chicken Benedict

Cathy Tyrrell, Colorado Springs, Colorado

My husband enjoyed this recipe when he was growing up, so my mother-in-law passed it on to me when I wanted to surprise him with a special Valentine's Day dinner.

- 6 boneless skinless chicken breast halves
- 1/2 cup all-purpose flour
- 1 teaspoon paprika
- 1/2 teaspoon salt
- 1/4 teaspoon pepper
- 2 tablespoons cooking oil
- 6 slices Canadian bacon

SAUCE:
- 1/2 cup sour cream
- 1/2 cup mayonnaise
- 1 tablespoon lemon juice
- 1 teaspoon yellow mustard
- 1/8 teaspoon pepper
- 3 English muffins, split and toasted

Pound chicken to 1/4-in. thickness. In a large resealable plastic bag, combine flour, paprika, salt and pepper. Add chicken, one piece at a time, and shake to coat. In a large skillet, cook chicken in oil until browned and juices run clear. Transfer to a platter and keep warm. Brown bacon in the same skillet, turning once; remove and keep warm. For sauce, combine sour cream, mayonnaise, lemon juice, mustard and pepper in a small saucepan. Cook, stirring constantly, until heated through; hold over low heat (do not boil). Place English muffin halves on a baking sheet. Top

each with a slice of bacon, one chicken breast half and 2 tablespoons sauce. Broil until bubbly. **Yield:** 6 servings.
Editor's Note: One envelope of Hollandaise sauce mix prepared according to package directions may be substituted for the homemade sauce.

Veggie Delights

Barb Trautmann, Ham Lake, Minnesota

I started making these sandwiches after sampling a similar version in a local restaurant. They're especially tempting as a quick summer meal using the season's freshest produce.

- 1/2 cup thinly sliced onion rings
- 2 cups sliced fresh mushrooms
- 3 tablespoons butter *or* margarine, *divided*
- 1/4 teaspoon salt
- 1/4 teaspoon pepper
- 1/4 teaspoon garlic powder
- 1/8 teaspoon onion powder
- 1/8 teaspoon celery seed
- 4 French rolls, split
- 8 thin green pepper rings
- 8 thin slices Co-Jack *or* cheddar cheese, halved
- 8 thin slices tomato
- 20 thin slices zucchini
- 8 thin sweet red pepper rings
- 1/4 cup sliced stuffed olives

In a skillet over medium heat, saute onion rings and mushrooms in 1 tablespoon butter until tender. Sprinkle with salt and pepper; set aside. Combine remaining butter with garlic powder, onion powder and celery seed; spread over cut sides of rolls. Broil 4-5 in. from the heat for 1-2 minutes or until lightly browned. Place about 1/4 cup mushroom mixture on the bottom of each roll. Layer with green pepper rings and two cheese slices. On top halves, layer tomato and zucchini slices, red pepper rings, olives and remaining cheese. Broil 4 in. from the heat for 3-4 minutes or until cheese is bubbly. Put tops and bottoms of sandwiches together. **Yield:** 4 servings.

Spicy Barbecued Beef Sandwiches

Sandra Longcor, Shingle Springs, California

I work full-time outside of the home, so I look for economical meals like this that can be served for a couple of days. I like to serve these sandwiches with baked beans and coleslaw.

- 1 large onion, chopped
- 4 garlic cloves, minced
- 1 tablespoon olive *or* vegetable oil
- 1 boneless sirloin tip roast (3 pounds)
- 4 cups water
- 2 cups ketchup
- 1 cup salsa
- 2 fresh jalapeno peppers, seeded and minced
- 2 tablespoons brown sugar

- **1 tablespoon Worcestershire sauce**
- **1 to 2 tablespoons minced fresh rosemary *or* 1 to 2 teaspoons dried rosemary, crushed**
- **1 teaspoon pepper**
- **1/2 teaspoon salt**
- **1/4 teaspoon liquid smoke, optional**
- **12 to 14 hard rolls, split and toasted**

In a Dutch oven over medium heat, saute onion and garlic in oil until lightly browned. Add roast and brown on all sides. Add the next 10 ingredients; bring to a boil. Reduce heat; cover and simmer for 3-1/2 to 4 hours or until meat is tender. Remove meat; cool. Simmer sauce, uncovered, for 30 minutes. Shred meat; return to sauce and heat through. Serve about 1/2 cup on each roll. **Yield:** 12-14 servings.

Curried Tuna Melt

Rose Maldet, Johnstown, Pennsylvania

An old-fashioned favorite is updated with curry powder and raisins. Your family will be delighted to see these open-faced sandwiches make an appearance on your table.

- **1 can (6 ounces) tuna, drained and flaked**
- **1/4 cup thinly sliced celery**
- **1/4 cup mayonnaise**
- **2 tablespoons thinly sliced green onions**
- **2 tablespoons raisins**
- **2 teaspoons lemon juice**
- **1/4 teaspoon salt**
- **1/4 teaspoon curry powder**
- **2 English muffins, split and toasted**
- **4 slices cheddar cheese**

In a small bowl, combine tuna, celery, mayonnaise, onions, raisins, lemon juice, salt and curry powder. Spread about 1/4 cup on each muffin half; top with cheese. Broil 4 in. from the heat for 1-2 minutes or until cheese is melted. **Yield:** 4 servings.

Elegant Omelet Loaf

Mary Shinholt, Catonsville, Maryland

I first tried this one-of-a-kind sandwich loaf at a party and asked for the recipe. Now I make it both for special brunches and everyday meals.

- **1 unsliced round loaf (1 pound) French bread**
- **8 bacon strips, diced**
- **1 can (4 ounces) sliced mushrooms, drained**
- **1 small sweet red pepper, julienned**
- **5 eggs**
- **1/4 cup milk**
- **2 tablespoons chopped chives**
- **1/4 teaspoon pepper**
- **1-1/2 cups (6 ounces) shredded mozzarella cheese**

Cut a thin slice off the top of the bread; set aside. Hollow out bottom half, leaving a 1/2-in. shell. (Discard removed bread or save for another use.) In a large skillet, cook bacon and mushrooms until bacon is crisp. Remove with a slotted spoon; set aside. Discard all but 1 tablespoon drippings. Saute red pepper in drippings until crisp-tender. Remove with a slotted spoon; set aside. Lightly beat eggs with milk, chives and pepper; add to skillet along with reserved bacon mixture. Cook and stir gently until eggs are set; remove from the heat. Place bread shell on a large sheet of heavy-duty foil. Spoon half of egg mixture into shell; sprinkle with half of the red pepper and half of the cheese. Repeat layers. Replace bread top and wrap bread tightly with foil. Bake at 400° for 20-25 minutes or until filling is heated through. Let stand for 5 minutes; cut into wedges. **Yield:** 6 servings.

Chalupa Joes

Nancy Means, Moline, Illinois

Ordinary sloppy joes get a lift from extra seasonings and picante sauce. Try serving them with refried beans and tortilla chips for a mouth-watering Mexican meal.

- **1 pound ground beef**
- **1 cup picante sauce**
- **2 tablespoons soy sauce**
- **1 tablespoon olive *or* vegetable oil**
- **1 teaspoon Dijon mustard**
- **1/2 teaspoon lemon-pepper seasoning**
- **1/4 teaspoon garlic powder**
- **1/8 teaspoon ground nutmeg**
- **1/8 teaspoon ground cardamom**
- **1 cup (4 ounces) shredded Monterey Jack cheese**
- **6 Italian-style buns, split**
- **1/4 cup sliced green onions**

In a skillet, brown beef; drain. Add picante sauce, soy sauce, oil, mustard, lemon pepper, garlic powder, nutmeg and cardamom; simmer for 3-4 minutes. Remove from the heat. Stir in cheese. Spoon onto buns and sprinkle with onions. **Yield:** 6 servings.

Hot Turkey Sandwiches

Elaine Cooley, Louisville, Kentucky

My mom made these turkey sandwiches as far back as I can remember...and I still make them often today. You'll love their fast-to-fix convenience.

- **4 slices bread, toasted and buttered**
- **4 slices cooked turkey**
- **1/2 cup shredded cheddar *or* process American cheese**
- **8 bacon strips, cooked and drained**
- **4 slices tomato, optional**
- **1/4 cup grated Parmesan cheese**

Place toast in a shallow baking pan. Top with turkey, cheddar cheese, two bacon strips and tomato if desired. Sprinkle with Parmesan cheese. Broil 5 in. from the heat for 3-4 minutes or until cheddar cheese is melted. **Yield:** 4 servings.

Satisfying Cold Sandwiches

With succulent spreads and fabulous fillings, these delicacies deliciously prove that cold sandwiches are anything but boring.

Terrific Sub Sandwich

Becky Ledford, Wilmington, Ohio
(PICTURED AT LEFT)

This sandwich is an all-time family favorite around our house. We love the leftovers—if we're lucky enough to have any!—for brown-bag lunches the next day.

    1 loaf (1 pound) French bread
    1/2 cup mayonnaise *or* salad dressing
    2 tablespoons Italian salad dressing
    1/2 pound sliced fully cooked ham
    1/4 pound sliced Genoa salami
    1/4 pound sliced Canadian bacon
    1/4 pound sliced Swiss cheese
Shredded lettuce
Tomato slices, optional

Cut bread in half lengthwise. Combine mayonnaise and Italian dressing until smooth; spread on cut sides of bread. On bottom half, layer ham, salami, bacon, cheese, lettuce and tomatoes if desired; replace top half. **Yield:** 6 servings.

Ham and Double Cheese Sandwiches

B.J. DeWitt, Lakeview, Oregon
(PICTURED AT LEFT)

This original recipe won me first prize in a local sandwich contest. Sometimes I'll use hazelnut bread instead of whole wheat to add to the nutty flavor.

    1 package (3 ounces) cream cheese, softened
    2 tablespoons chopped green chilies
    1 tablespoon dry onion soup mix
    1 cup (4 ounces) shredded cheddar cheese
    1/4 cup chopped hazelnuts, toasted, optional
    8 slices whole wheat bread
    16 slices fully cooked ham
    4 lettuce leaves

In a mixing bowl, beat cream cheese, chilies and soup mix until smooth. Add cheese and nuts if desired; mix well. Evenly spread on four slices of bread; layer each with four

---

FRESH AND FILLING. *Pictured at left, top to bottom: Terrific Sub Sandwich, Ham and Double Cheese Sandwiches and Thanksgiving Sandwiches (all recipes on this page).*

---

slices of ham and one lettuce leaf. Top with remaining bread. **Yield:** 4 servings.

Thanksgiving Sandwiches

Rose Bralowas, New Port Richey, Florida
(PICTURED AT LEFT)

When I first tried this recipe for leftover turkey, I knew it would be an instant hit with my family. These sandwiches really capture the flavor of the holidays.

    2 cups cubed cooked turkey breast
    1/2 cup mayonnaise
    1/2 cup finely chopped fresh *or* frozen cranberries
    1 orange, peeled and chopped
    1 teaspoon sugar
    1 teaspoon prepared mustard
    1/2 teaspoon salt
    1/4 cup chopped pecans
Lettuce leaves
    6 rolls *or* croissants, split

In a medium bowl, combine turkey, mayonnaise, cranberries, orange, sugar, mustard and salt. Just before serving, stir in pecans. Place lettuce and 1/2 cup turkey mixture on each roll. **Yield:** 6 servings.

Tarragon Chicken Salad Sandwiches

Caroleah Johnson, Berry Creek, California

I became tired of traditional chicken sandwiches, so I came up with this recipe. Tarragon provides a nice subtle seasoning, while sunflower seeds add extra crunch.

    1/2 cup mayonnaise
    1 tablespoon lemon juice
    1 teaspoon Dijon mustard
    3 cups cubed cooked chicken
    3/4 cup chopped celery
    1 tablespoon minced fresh tarragon *or* 1 teaspoon dried tarragon
    1/3 cup salted sunflower seeds
    8 croissants *or* rolls, split
Lettuce leaves

In a bowl, combine the first three ingredients. Stir in chicken, celery and tarragon. Just before serving, add sunflower seeds. Line croissants with lettuce; top with 1/2 cup chicken salad. **Yield:** 8 servings.

Pork Salad Rolls

Katie Koziolek, Hartland, Minnesota

Our teenage boys request these sandwiches so much I often prepare extra pork roast with this recipe in mind. They especially like them served on tortillas.

    1/2 cup mayonnaise
      1 teaspoon Dijon mustard
    1/2 teaspoon lemon juice
    1/2 teaspoon seasoned salt
    1/4 teaspoon pepper
      3 cups shredded cooked pork
    1/2 cup thinly sliced celery
    1/2 cup halved seedless green grapes
      6 flour tortillas (6-1/2 inches) *or* rolls
Lettuce leaves, optional

In a medium bowl, combine the mayonnaise, mustard, lemon juice, seasoned salt and pepper. Add pork, celery and grapes; mix well. Refrigerate for at least 1 hour. Spoon 1/2 cup onto each tortilla; add lettuce if desired. Roll up. **Yield:** 6 servings.

Arkansas Travelers

Robi Kastner, Springfield, Missouri

I came across this club-style sandwich in a tearoom in Arkansas. I brought the "secret" recipe back home, much to the delight of my husband and our two sons.

      1 pound turkey breast
      1 block (5 ounces) Swiss cheese
      1 avocado, peeled and pitted
      1 large tomato
    10 bacon strips, cooked and crumbled
    1/3 to 1/2 cup ranch salad dressing
    10 slices whole wheat bread, toasted

Chop turkey, cheese, avocado and tomato into 1/4-in. cubes; place in a large bowl. Add bacon and dressing. Spoon 1/2 cup between two slices of toast. **Yield:** 6 servings.

Seafood Salad Sandwiches

Saundra Woods, Woodbury, Tennessee

I've enjoyed cooking for many years…luckily my husband and two sons were always ready to try new recipes. Now I have three grandsons who love to come and eat at Grandma's house.

✓ **This tasty dish uses less sugar, salt and fat. Recipe includes** *Diabetic Exchanges.*

      8 ounces cooked salad shrimp *or* flaked cooked crab
    3/4 cup chopped celery
    2/3 cup mayonnaise *or* salad dressing
      1 teaspoon dried minced onion

    1/2 teaspoon dried tarragon, crushed
    1/2 teaspoon hot pepper sauce
      4 sandwich buns, split
Fresh spinach leaves

In a medium bowl, combine the first six ingredients; mix well. Chill for at least 1 hour. Spoon 1/2 cup onto each bun; top with spinach leaves. **Yield:** 4 servings. **Diabetic Exchanges:** One serving (prepared with shrimp and fat-free mayonnaise) equals 2 starch, 1-1/2 very lean meat; also, 201 calories, 673 mg sodium, 111 mg cholesterol, 26 gm carbohydrate, 15 gm protein, 3 gm fat.

Curried Chicken Pita Pockets

Vicky Whitehead, Norman, Oklahoma

I like to prepare these sandwiches for special luncheons. Everyone who tries them raves about the refreshing combination of tender chicken, flavorful curry and cool grapes.

    3/4 cup mayonnaise
      1 teaspoon soy sauce
      1 teaspoon lemon juice
    1/2 teaspoon curry powder
      1 small onion, finely chopped
  2-1/2 cups cubed cooked chicken
  1-1/2 cups halved seedless green grapes
    3/4 cup chopped celery
    1/2 cup sliced almonds
    10 pita breads, halved

In a large bowl, combine the first five ingredients. Stir in chicken, grapes and celery; refrigerate. Just before serving, add almonds. Stuff about 1/4 cup into each pita half. **Yield:** 10 servings.

Hearty Muffaleta Loaf

Myra Innes, Auburn, Kansas

In the summer, we love to picnic outdoors as much as possible. Loaded with meat and flavor, this sandwich always satisfies the heartiest of appetites.

      1 loaf (1 pound) French bread
    1/2 cup olive *or* vegetable oil
    1/3 cup red wine vinegar
      1 teaspoon dried oregano
      2 garlic cloves, minced
      1 cup (4 ounces) shredded mozzarella cheese
      1 jar (6-1/2 ounces) marinated artichoke hearts, drained and chopped
    1/2 cup sliced stuffed olives
      1 can (2-1/4 ounces) sliced ripe olives, drained
    1/2 cup sliced fresh banana peppers
    1/4 cup chopped red onion
    1/4 pound sliced Genoa salami
    1/4 pound sliced Cotto salami
    1/4 pound sliced pepperoni
    1/4 pound sliced provolone cheese

Cut bread in half lengthwise; hollow out top and bottom, leaving a 1-in. shell. (Discard removed bread or save for another use.) Combine oil, vinegar, oregano and garlic; brush half on the inside of shell. Add the next six ingredients to the remaining oil mixture. Spoon into bottom of bread shell; layer with meats and cheese. Replace bread top. Wrap tightly in plastic wrap; refrigerate until ready to serve. **Yield:** 6-8 servings.

Italian Submarine Sandwich

Susan Brown, Richland, Washington

I first sampled this at a dinner where it was served as an appetizer, and I almost didn't have room for the main course! Since then, it's become our family's standard sandwich.

  2 jars (2 ounces *each*) diced pimientos, drained
  1 can (4-1/4 ounces) chopped ripe olives
2/3 cup chopped stuffed olives
1/2 cup olive *or* vegetable oil
1/2 cup minced fresh parsley
  3 garlic cloves, minced
  1 teaspoon dried oregano
1/4 teaspoon pepper
  1 loaf (1 pound) Italian bread
1/3 pound thinly sliced fully cooked ham
1/3 pound thinly sliced Genoa salami
1/3 pound thinly sliced provolone *or* mozzarella cheese

In a jar with tight-fitting lid, combine the first eight ingredients; refrigerate for at least 12 hours. Cut bread in half lengthwise; hollow out top and bottom, leaving a 1-in. shell. (Discard removed bread or save for another use.) Drain 2 tablespoons liquid from olive mixture; spread on the inside of bread top. Spoon 1 cup olive mixture evenly into bottom of bread shell. Layer with ham, salami and cheese; spread with remaining olive mixture. Replace bread top. Slice into serving-size pieces. **Yield:** 4-6 servings.

Chicken Avocado Sandwiches

Dorothy LaCombe, Hamburg, New York

My love of cooking stems from my grandfather, who was a professional chef. He left his legacy behind in the marginal notes of all his cookbooks. They're my greatest treasure.

  1 medium avocado, peeled and cubed
  2 teaspoons lemon juice
  2 cups cubed cooked chicken
  1 cup alfalfa sprouts
1/2 teaspoon salt
1/4 teaspoon lemon-pepper seasoning
  2 packages (3 ounces *each*) cream cheese, softened
  1 can (2-1/4 ounces) sliced ripe olives
1/4 cup chopped walnuts
  16 slices of bread

In a medium bowl, toss avocado with lemon juice. Add chicken, alfalfa sprouts, salt and lemon pepper; mix gently.

In a mixing bowl, beat cream cheese until smooth. Stir in olives and walnuts; spread on eight slices of bread. Spoon about 1/2 cup chicken mixture onto each slice; top with remaining bread. **Yield:** 8 servings.

Creamy Egg Salad Sandwiches

Edie DeSpain, Logan, Utah

My family looks forward to these sandwiches year-round. But I reach for this recipe most often after Easter, when I have lots of leftover hard-cooked eggs.

  1 package (3 ounces) cream cheese, softened
  2 tablespoons butter *or* margarine, softened
  1 tablespoon mayonnaise
  1 teaspoon finely chopped onion
  1 teaspoon sugar
1/2 teaspoon prepared horseradish
1/2 teaspoon lemon juice
1/4 teaspoon salt
1/8 teaspoon pepper
Dash garlic powder
  6 hard-cooked eggs, chopped
  8 slices rye bread
Alfalfa sprouts, optional

In a medium bowl, combine the first 10 ingredients until smooth. Stir in eggs. Chill for 1 hour. Spread 1/2 cup onto four slices of bread; top with alfalfa sprouts if desired. Cover with remaining bread. **Yield:** 4 servings.

Vegetable Tuna Sandwiches

Mrs. Allan Miller, St. John, New Brunswick

I packed lunches for a husband and seven children for years and tried many different recipes to keep things new and exciting. I hope you enjoy these fun sandwiches.

  2 packages (3 ounces *each*) cream cheese, softened, *divided*
  6 tablespoons mayonnaise, *divided*
1/4 teaspoon salt
1/8 teaspoon pepper
  1 can (6 ounces) tuna, drained and flaked
  3 tablespoons finely chopped celery
  3 tablespoons finely chopped green pepper
  1 cup shredded carrots
  2 tablespoons finely chopped onion
  8 slices white bread
  4 slices whole wheat bread

In a bowl, combine one package of cream cheese, 3 tablespoons mayonnaise, salt and pepper until smooth. Add tuna, celery and green pepper; mix well. In another bowl, combine carrots, onion and remaining cream cheese and mayonnaise; mix well. Spread 1/3 cup tuna mixture on four slices of white bread; top with a slice of whole wheat bread. Spread 1/4 cup carrot mixture on the whole wheat bread; top with a slice of white bread. **Yield:** 4 servings.

Fiesta Loaf

Kathleen Hooker, Toledo, Ohio
(PICTURED AT LEFT)

When planning a camping trip a few years back, I looked for recipes that could be made ahead of time for quick eating later. This filling sandwich was the perfect solution.

    1 round loaf (1 pound) sourdough bread
    1/2 cup refried beans
    4 ounces sliced Colby cheese
    1 small sweet red pepper, sliced
    4 ounces sliced Monterey Jack cheese
    1 can (4 ounces) chopped green chilies
    1 can (2-1/4 ounces) sliced ripe olives, drained
    1 small tomato, seeded and diced
    1 cup (4 ounces) shredded taco cheese
    2 tablespoons ranch salad dressing
    1 avocado, peeled and sliced
    4 ounces sliced cheddar cheese

Cut the top fourth off loaf of bread. Carefully hollow out top and bottom of loaf, leaving a 1/2-in. shell. (Discard removed bread or save for another use.) Set top aside. Spread refried beans inside bottom of shell. Layer with Colby cheese, red pepper, Monterey Jack cheese, chilies, olives and tomato. Gently press layers together to flatten as needed. Combine taco cheese and ranch dressing; spoon over tomato. Top with avocado and cheddar cheese. Replace bread top and wrap tightly in plastic wrap. Chill. **Yield:** 6 servings.

Beef 'n' Cheese Tortillas

Myra Innes, Auburn, Kansas
(PICTURED AT LEFT)

I like to take these sandwiches along on our many outings. They can be made in advance and don't get soggy. You'll appreciate the convenience...your family and friends will love the great taste!

    1/2 cup garlic-herb cheese spread
      4 flour tortillas (10 inches)
    3/4 pound thinly sliced cooked roast beef
     20 to 25 whole spinach leaves
     11 to 12 sweet banana peppers

Spread about 2 tablespoons cheese spread over each tortilla. Layer with roast beef and spinach. Remove seeds from peppers and slice into thin strips; arrange over spinach. Roll up each tortilla tightly; wrap in plastic wrap. Refrigerate until ready to serve. **Yield:** 4 servings.

MEXICAN MEDLEY. *Pictured at left, top to bottom: Fiesta Loaf, Beef 'n' Cheese Tortillas and Egg Salad Tacos (all recipes on this page).*

Egg Salad Tacos

Janet Smith, Smithton, Missouri
(PICTURED AT LEFT)

Our card parties just wouldn't be the same without these fun-filled egg salad sandwiches. The taco shells are a nice alternative to bread.

    2 tablespoons mayonnaise
    2 tablespoons salsa
    1 tablespoon sour cream
    1/8 teaspoon salt
    1/8 teaspoon pepper
    4 hard-cooked eggs, chopped
    1/4 cup shredded sharp cheddar cheese
    1 tablespoon sliced green onion
    4 to 6 taco shells *or* 4 to 6 slices of bread
Shredded lettuce
Additional salsa *or* taco sauce, optional

In a bowl, combine the first five ingredients. Stir in eggs, cheese and onion. Line each taco shell or slice of bread with lettuce; fill with egg salad. Top with additional salsa or taco sauce if desired. **Yield:** 2-3 servings.

Giant Picnic Sandwich

Rosie Fager, Idaho Falls, Idaho
(PICTURED ON FRONT COVER)

I'm always looking for fun foods to prepare for company in the summer. This delicious sandwich travels well for a picnic or get-together held the same day it is made...plus it looks as good as it tastes.

    1 package (16 ounces) hot roll mix
    1 teaspoon milk
    2 teaspoons sesame seeds
    1/2 cup creamy Italian salad dressing
    6 to 8 lettuce leaves
    6 ounces thinly sliced fully cooked ham
    6 ounces thinly sliced Genoa salami
    1 medium cucumber, sliced
    4 slices red onion, separated into rings
    6 ounces sliced Swiss cheese
    1 medium green pepper, sliced
    2 medium tomatoes, thinly sliced

Prepare hot roll mix according to package instructions. Pat or roll into a 12-in. circle; place on a greased 12-in. pizza pan. Cover and let rise in a warm place until doubled, about 30 minutes. Brush with milk; sprinkle with sesame seeds. Bake at 375° for 20-25 minutes or until golden brown. Cool on a wire rack. Cut in half horizontally; spread salad dressing on cut sides. On bottom half, layer lettuce, ham, salami, cucumber, onion, cheese, green pepper and tomatoes. Replace top half. Refrigerate until ready to serve. Cut into wedges. **Yield:** 6-8 servings.

Ham and Spinach Loaf

Elizabeth Petryk, Edmonton, Alberta

My adventures in cooking started some 30 years ago as a stay-at-home mom. Now retired, I'm once again an "at-home" person. This is perfect when entertaining at lunch.

    1 pound fully cooked ham
    1/3 cup mayonnaise
    1 tablespoon Dijon mustard
    1/4 cup chopped pistachios, toasted
    2 cups packed fresh spinach
    1 package (3 ounces) cream cheese, softened
    1 tablespoon milk
    2 teaspoons dill weed
    1 loaf (1 pound) French bread

In a food processor, process ham until minced or ground. Transfer to a medium bowl; add mayonnaise, mustard and pistachios. Mix well; set aside. Rinse spinach in cold water. Cook in a large skillet with only water clinging to the leaves until limp; drain. In a food processor, process spinach, cream cheese, milk and dill until smooth; set aside. Cut bread in half lengthwise; hollow out top and bottom, leaving a 1/2-in. shell. (Discard removed bread or save for another use.) Spread spinach mixture inside top and bottom halves of bread. Pack ham mixture into bottom half, mounding slightly. Replace bread top and wrap tightly with foil. Chill for at least 2 hours. **Yield:** 6 servings.

NO MORE SOGGY SANDWICHES. When making sandwiches to be eaten later, pack toppings like tomatoes, lettuce and pickle spears in separate plastic bags. Add them to the sandwiches just before serving.

Turkey Tomato Club

Lisa Klicker, Walla Walla, Washington

This sandwich gets its irresistible crunch and flavor from a quick-and-easy coleslaw...what a nice change of pace from lettuce! You'll never make an ordinary club again.

    1/2 cup mayonnaise
    1 tablespoon cider vinegar
    2 teaspoons sugar
    1/4 teaspoon salt
    1/8 teaspoon pepper
    4 cups thinly sliced cabbage
    1 round loaf (1 pound) sourdough bread
    10 bacon strips, cooked and drained
    6 tomato slices
    1 cup thinly sliced cucumber
    1/2 pound thinly sliced smoked turkey

Combine the first five ingredients in a bowl. Add cabbage; toss. Set aside for 30 minutes. Cut a thin slice off the top of the bread; hollow out bottom half, leaving a 1-in. shell.

(Discard removed bread or save for another use.) Place half of the cabbage mixture in bottom of loaf. Layer with bacon, tomato, cucumber and turkey; top with remaining cabbage mixture. Replace bread top. Cut into wedges. **Yield:** 6-8 servings.

Special Ham 'n' Cheese Sandwiches

Shirley Fredricks, Orchard Park, New York

When I tire of ordinary meat and cheese sandwiches for my brown-bag lunch, I try creative alternatives like this creamy ham spread. You'll appreciate its ease of preparation.

    1 package (3 ounces) cream cheese, softened
    2 tablespoons sweet pickle relish
    1 tablespoon Dijon mustard
    1/2 cup shredded cheddar cheese
    2 ounces fully cooked ham, finely chopped
    4 slices of bread *or* 2 buns

In a small bowl, combine cream cheese, pickle relish and mustard. Stir in cheese and ham. Spread 1/2 cup between slices of bread or in buns. **Yield:** 2 servings.

Chocolate Peanut Butter

Opal Wagoner, Northwood, Ohio

While growing up, I looked forward to this special sandwich treat in my lunches. I still make this recipe today and keep some in the refrigerator...but it never lasts too long!

    1/2 cup butter *or* margarine
    1/2 cup honey
    1/4 cup baking cocoa
    1-1/3 cups creamy peanut butter
    1/4 teaspoon vanilla extract

Melt butter in a small saucepan. Stir in honey and cocoa until smooth. Remove from the heat; stir in peanut butter and vanilla. Refrigerate. **Yield:** 2-1/4 cups. **Editor's Note:** Mixture solidifies as it cools.

Spicy Summer Sub

Barb McMahan, Fenton, Missouri

A few years back, I served this sandwich to friends and family who came to help with our garage sale. Everyone was impressed with the presentation and combination of flavors.

    1 round loaf (1-1/2 pounds) rye bread
    1 cup mayonnaise
    2 tablespoons Dijon mustard
    1 jar (2 ounces) diced pimientos, drained
    1/4 to 1/2 teaspoon hot pepper sauce
    1/2 pound sliced provolone cheese
    1/4 pound sliced fully cooked ham

1/4 pound sliced Genoa salami
1/4 pound sliced cooked turkey
1/4 pound sliced mozzarella cheese

Cut bread in half horizontally; hollow out top and bottom, leaving a 3/4-in. shell. (Discard removed bread or save for another use.) In a small bowl, combine mayonnaise, mustard, pimientos and hot pepper sauce; spread 1/4 cup in the bottom bread shell. Layer with a fourth of the provolone, ham, salami, turkey and mozzarella. Spread with more of the mayonnaise mixture. Repeat layers three times (you may not use up all of the mayonnaise mixture). Replace bread top and wrap tightly with plastic wrap. Chill for at least 3 hours. Remove from the refrigerator 30 minutes before serving. Cut into wedges; serve with remaining mayonnaise mixture if desired. **Yield:** 6-8 servings.

Nutty Shrimp Salad Sandwiches

Delores Hicks, Kernersville, North Carolina

My daughter is a terrific cook and likes to come up with original adaptations of old favorites. As a matter of fact, she created this tropical-tasting shrimp salad.

    2 cups cooked salad shrimp
    3 kiwifruit, peeled, sliced and quartered
  3/4 cup shredded carrots
  1/2 cup mayonnaise
  1/2 cup chopped pecans
  1/8 teaspoon ground nutmeg
Lettuce leaves
    3 pita breads (6 inches), halved

In a medium bowl, combine the first six ingredients. Line pita halves with lettuce; spoon about 1/2 cup shrimp mixture into each. **Yield:** 6 servings.

Oregon Muffaleta

Marilou Robinson, Portland, Oregon

Traditional muffaleta is made extra special with the addition of apples, blueberries and cranberries. This is a meaty make-ahead meal that's perfect for picnics and potlucks.

    1 small tart apple, chopped
  1/2 cup fresh blueberries
  1/2 cup thinly sliced celery
  1/2 cup dried cranberries
  1/2 cup thinly sliced green onions
  1/2 cup orange juice
    3 tablespoons vegetable oil
    3 tablespoons cider vinegar
  1/2 teaspoon pepper
  1/8 teaspoon salt
    1 round loaf (2 pounds) Italian bread
  3/4 pound thinly sliced fully cooked ham, *divided*
  1/2 pound thinly sliced cheddar cheese

In a large bowl, combine the first 10 ingredients; chill for at least 8 hours, stirring occasionally. Cut a thin slice off the top

of the bread; hollow out the bottom half, leaving a 1-in. shell. (Discard removed bread or save for another use.) Drain 1/4 cup liquid from the fruit mixture; brush on inside of bread shell. In bottom of bread shell, layer half of the ham, 1-1/4 cups fruit mixture, cheese, remaining fruit mixture and remaining ham. Replace bread top and wrap tightly with plastic wrap. Chill for at least 2 hours. Remove from the refrigerator 30 minutes before serving. Cut into wedges. **Yield:** 8-10 servings.

Triple Tasty Sandwich Spread

Mickey Schnell, Myrtle Beach, South Carolina

An assortment of ham, salami and eggs makes this specially seasoned sandwich spread delicious. I'm sure your family will love the old-fashioned flavor as much as mine does.

  1/2 to 2/3 cup mayonnaise
    1 tablespoon Dijon mustard
    1 tablespoon finely chopped onion
    1 tablespoon minced jalapeno pepper
    1 teaspoon Worcestershire sauce
  1/2 pound fully cooked ham, ground
  1/2 pound Genoa salami, ground
  1/4 cup finely chopped sweet pickle
    3 hard-cooked eggs, chopped
   12 slices whole wheat bread, toasted

Combine the first five ingredients in a medium bowl. Stir in ham, salami, pickle and eggs. Spoon about 1/2 cup between slices of whole wheat toast. **Yield:** 6 servings.

Pepper Lovers' BLT

Carol Reaves, San Antonio, Texas

One of my family's favorite sandwiches is a BLT, and they especially love this one because it combines the tantalizing tastes of bacon, fresh tomatoes and hot peppers.

  1/4 cup mayonnaise
    1 tablespoon diced pimientos
  1/8 teaspoon coarsely ground pepper
  1/4 teaspoon hot pepper sauce
    8 slices sourdough bread, toasted
    4 teaspoons Dijon-mayonnaise blend
    6 tablespoons shredded sharp cheddar cheese
    4 pickled jalapeno peppers *or* green chilies, thinly sliced
   12 bacon strips, cooked and drained
    8 tomato slices
    4 lettuce leaves
    8 thin slices cooked turkey

In a small bowl, combine mayonnaise, pimientos, pepper and hot pepper sauce; mix well. Chill for at least 1 hour. Spread four slices of toast with Dijon-mayonnaise blend. Sprinkle with cheese; top with jalapenos, bacon, tomato, lettuce and turkey. Spread mayonnaise mixture on remaining slices of toast; place over turkey. **Yield:** 4 servings.

Quick & Easy Favorites

When your hungry clan has a hankering for a savory meal in a snap, nothing can top these timeless treasures. Just watch as they quickly disappear!

Deli Club Sandwich

Louise Strunk, Auburn, Pennsylvania
(PICTURED AT LEFT)

This fresh-tasting club is a family favorite. The flavorful blend of ingredients makes it stand out in a crowd.

   2 tablespoons Dijon mustard
Dash dried basil
Dash dill weed
   2 sandwich buns, split *or* 4 slices sourdough bread
   4 slices smoked turkey
 10 slices pepperoni
   4 to 6 slices tomato
   4 slices Swiss cheese
Alfalfa sprouts

Combine mustard, basil and dill; spread on buns or two pieces of bread. Layer with turkey, pepperoni, tomato, cheese and alfalfa sprouts. Cover with bun tops or remaining bread. **Yield:** 2 servings.

Crunchy Pea Salad

Phyllis Barkey, Warren, Michigan
(PICTURED AT LEFT)

After I had this salad in two different restaurants—one here in Michigan and one in Florida—I finally decided to try my hand at duplicating the recipe. My family thinks I succeeded!

1/3 cup ranch salad dressing
1/3 cup mayonnaise
   1 tablespoon lemon juice
1/4 teaspoon celery seed
1/4 teaspoon salt
1/8 teaspoon pepper
   2 packages (10 ounces *each*) frozen peas, thawed
   3 tablespoons finely chopped onion
3/4 cup salted peanuts

In a large bowl, combine salad dressing, mayonnaise, lemon juice, celery seed, salt and pepper. Add peas and onion; toss. Just before serving, stir in peanuts. **Yield:** 6 servings.

FAST AND FLAVORFUL. *Pictured at left: Deli Club Sandwich and Crunchy Pea Salad (both recipes on this page).*

Tomato Mushroom Consomme

Kris Countryman, Joliet, Illinois

A family friend gave me this recipe. Fresh mushrooms and seasonings really dress up canned consomme. I like to serve it alongside a sandwich for a complete meal.

   2 cups sliced fresh mushrooms
1/4 cup snipped fresh dill
   1 tablespoon butter *or* margarine
   1 can (10-1/2 ounces) condensed beef consomme, undiluted
   1 can (10-3/4 ounces) condensed tomato soup, undiluted
   2 cups water
1/4 cup sliced green onions
1/4 cup chopped fresh parsley
   1 teaspoon lemon juice

In a saucepan, saute mushrooms and dill in butter for 5 minutes or until mushrooms are tender. Add remaining ingredients; bring to a boil. Reduce heat; cover and simmer for 5 minutes. **Yield:** 4 servings.

Spaghetti Soup

Laura Braun, Appleton, Wisconsin

With spaghetti sauce, noodles and Italian seasonings, this soup tastes like spaghetti! It's so easy, even our preteen daughter can make it by herself.

   2 pounds bulk Italian sausage
   1 cup chopped onion
   1 garlic clove, minced
   2 cans (14-1/2 ounces *each*) beef broth
   1 jar (30 ounces) spaghetti sauce
   1 can (15 ounces) sliced carrots, drained
   1 can (14-1/2 ounces) Italian flat beans, drained
   1 cup water
   1 teaspoon Italian seasoning
   1 teaspoon dried basil
3-1/2 cups cooked macaroni
Grated Parmesan *or* shredded mozzarella cheese, optional

In a large saucepan or Dutch oven over medium heat, brown the sausage, onion and garlic; drain. Add broth, spaghetti sauce, carrots, beans, water, Italian seasoning and basil; bring to a boil. Reduce heat; cover and simmer for 10-15 minutes. Just before serving, add the macaroni and heat through. Garnish with cheese if desired. **Yield:** 12-14 servings (3 quarts).

Salsa Sloppy Joes

Mary Banninga, Austin, Minnesota

I was looking for a way to spice up my already quick-and-easy sloppy joe recipe. So I decided to add a little salsa. Everyone who's tried this recipe really likes the results.

- 3 pounds ground beef
- 1 cup chopped onion
- 1 jar (16 ounces) salsa
- 1 can (15 ounces) sloppy joe sauce
- 16 to 20 hamburger buns, split

In a large skillet, brown beef and onion; drain. Stir in salsa and sloppy joe sauce; bring to a boil. Reduce heat; cover and simmer for 20 minutes. Spoon about 1/2 cup onto each bun. **Yield:** 16-20 servings.

Chicken Tortellini Salad

Mary Bilke, Eagle River, Wisconsin

This is one of the many dishes we offer at the salad bar in the restaurant where I work—it seems to disappear before our eyes!

- 8 ounces tortellini, cooked, drained and cooled
- 1 cup cubed cooked chicken
- 3/4 cup frozen peas, thawed
- 1/2 cup mayonnaise
- 1/2 cup diced mozzarella cheese
- 1/2 cup Parmesan ranch salad dressing
- 2 tablespoons minced green onions
- 2 tablespoons finely chopped sweet red pepper
- 1 tablespoon minced fresh parsley

Combine all ingredients in a large bowl. Refrigerate until ready to serve. **Yield:** 6 servings.

Easy Chicken Chili

Nancy Maxey, Rogue River, Oregon

We have lots of visitors on our 10-acre farm, so I like to make down-home dishes. Whenever I serve this chili, I'm asked for the recipe, which I'm happy to share.

- 1/2 cup chopped onion
- 1 tablespoon cooking oil
- 2 cans (14-1/2 ounces *each*) chicken broth
- 2 cans (16 ounces *each*) great northern beans, rinsed and drained
- 1 can (4 ounces) chopped green chilies
- 2 cups cubed cooked chicken
- 2 garlic cloves, minced
- 2 tablespoons minced fresh cilantro *or* parsley
- 1 teaspoon salt
- 1 teaspoon dried oregano

- 1 teaspoon ground cumin
- 1/8 to 1/4 teaspoon cayenne pepper

In a 3-qt. saucepan over medium heat, saute onion in oil until tender. Add remaining ingredients; bring to a boil. Reduce heat; cover and simmer for 10-15 minutes or until heated through. **Yield:** 6-8 servings.

Quick Turkey-Bean Soup

Debbie Schermerhorn, Colorado Springs, Colorado

This recipe calls for canned beans, so cooking time is minimal. I make this soup mild and allow guests to add as much "heat" as they want with hot pepper sauce.

- 1 pound ground turkey
- 2 garlic cloves, minced
- 1 medium onion, chopped
- 1 tablespoon cooking oil
- 1-1/2 cups chopped celery
- 1 medium green pepper, chopped
- 1 medium sweet red pepper, chopped
- 2 cans (14-1/2 ounces *each*) beef broth
- 1 can (28 ounces) stewed tomatoes
- 3 tablespoons tomato paste
- 1/2 teaspoon cayenne pepper
- 1/4 teaspoon dried basil
- 1/4 teaspoon dried oregano
- 2 cans (15 to 16 ounces *each*) kidney beans, rinsed and drained
- 1 can (15 ounces) black beans, rinsed and drained
- 1 can (15 ounces) pinto beans, rinsed and drained
- 1 can (15-1/4 ounces) whole kernel corn, drained

In a soup kettle or Dutch oven over medium heat, brown turkey, garlic and onion in oil; drain. Add celery and peppers; cook and stir for 2 minutes. Add broth, tomatoes, tomato paste, cayenne, basil and oregano; mix well. Bring to a boil. Add beans and corn. Reduce heat; cover and simmer for 15 minutes. **Yield:** 14-16 servings (4 quarts).

Creamy Turkey Melt

DeAnn Alleva, Columbus, Ohio

Cream cheese and sour cream make these sandwiches rich and irresistible. Using rye bread gives extra flavor and adds a nice contrast to the creamy white filling.

- 1/2 cup chopped red onion
- 5 tablespoons butter *or* margarine, softened, *divided*
- 1 package (3 ounces) cream cheese, cubed
- 1/3 cup sour cream
- 2 cups cubed cooked turkey
- 8 slices dark rye *or* pumpernickel bread
- 4 slices Swiss cheese

In a saucepan over medium heat, saute onion in 1 tablespoon butter until tender. Reduce heat to low. Add cream cheese and sour cream; cook and stir until smooth. Add turkey; cook until heated through (do not boil). Spoon 1/2 cup filling onto four slices of bread; top with a slice of cheese. Spread outside of bread with remaining butter. In a skillet over medium heat, cook sandwiches until lightly browned on both sides. **Yield:** 4 servings.

Polish Sausage Soup

Kristie Franklin, Powell, Wyoming

I had this recipe in my files for years before I tried it. Now this soup appears on my menus often. It's a quick and hearty meal that warms us up after doing farm chores.

> 1/2 pound smoked Polish sausage, cubed
> 1 can (14-1/2 ounces) Cajun-style stewed tomatoes
> 1 can (11-1/2 ounces) condensed bean with bacon soup, undiluted
> 1 can (10-3/4 ounces) condensed cream of potato soup, undiluted
> 2 cups water
> 1/2 teaspoon dried basil

In a 3-qt. saucepan over medium heat, brown sausage; drain. Stir in remaining ingredients; bring to a boil. Reduce heat; cover and simmer for 10 minutes. **Yield:** 4-6 servings.

Fluffy Fruit Delight

Margaret Naylor, Salt Lake City, Utah

I came up with this dish by combining several different recipes. It's light and refreshing…just perfect for picnics and potlucks on hot summer days.

> 1 carton (8 ounces) frozen whipped topping, thawed
> 1/2 of a 3-ounce package of raspberry gelatin
> 1 can (20 ounces) pineapple tidbits, drained
> 1 can (16 ounces) fruit cocktail, drained
> 2 large apples, diced
> 2 large firm bananas, sliced

In a large bowl, combine whipped topping and gelatin. Stir in fruit. Chill until ready to serve. **Yield:** 12-16 servings.

Minestrone in Minutes

Susan Herman-Havens, Beggs, Oklahoma

I found this recipe in a magazine years ago and adapted it to suit my family's taste. It tastes especially good accompanied by oven-fresh garlic bread.

> 1 can (14-1/2 ounces) beef broth
> 1 can (14-1/2 ounces) diced tomatoes, undrained
> 1 tablespoon chopped fresh parsley
> 1 teaspoon dried basil
> 1 garlic clove, minced
> Pinch sugar

> 1/4 cup uncooked macaroni
> 2 cups frozen peas, thawed
> 1/2 cup frozen green beans, thawed
> Grated Parmesan cheese, optional

In a 2-qt. saucepan, combine the first six ingredients; bring to a boil. Add macaroni; cover and cook for 10 minutes or until macaroni is tender. Stir in peas and beans. Cook for 3 minutes. Garnish with Parmesan cheese if desired. **Yield:** 4 servings.

Hearty Hamburger Soup

Guynell Boyd, Jayess, Mississippi

We work up big appetites here on our farm, where we raise beef cattle, so I depend on recipes like this that are flavorful and fast. This soup is great served with corn bread.

> 1-1/2 pounds ground beef
> 1 medium onion, chopped
> 2 cans (15 ounces *each*) mixed vegetables
> 1 can (14-3/4 ounces) cream-style corn
> 1 can (14-1/2 ounces) stewed tomatoes
> 1 can (14-1/2 ounces) chicken broth
> 1 can (11-1/2 ounces) tomato juice
> 1 teaspoon salt
> 1/2 teaspoon pepper

In a Dutch oven or soup kettle over medium heat, brown beef and onion; drain. Add remaining ingredients; bring to a boil. Reduce heat; cover and simmer for 10 minutes. **Yield:** 10 servings (about 2-1/2 quarts).

Salmon Salad

Diane Benskin, Lewisville, Texas

I'm an avid herb gardener and can't wait to use the products of my labor in dishes like this salad. For a different twist, I include chopped apple…it adds some natural sweetness.

✓ This tasty dish uses less sugar, salt and fat. Recipe includes *Diabetic Exchanges*.

> 2 cans (14-3/4 ounces *each*) salmon, drained and bones removed
> 2 celery ribs, sliced
> 1 large apple, peeled and chopped
> 5 green onions, sliced
> 1/2 cup mayonnaise *or* salad dressing
> 2 teaspoons snipped fresh dill *or* 3/4 teaspoon dill weed
> 3/4 teaspoon minced fresh basil *or* pinch dried basil
> 1/4 teaspoon garlic salt
> 1/4 teaspoon minced fresh tarragon *or* pinch dried tarragon

Flake salmon into a bowl. Add remaining ingredients; stir gently. Chill until ready to serve. **Yield:** 8 servings. **Diabetic Exchanges:** One 1/2-cup serving (prepared with fat-free mayonnaise) equals 2 lean meat, 1 vegetable; also, 147 calories, 626 mg sodium, 37 mg cholesterol, 6 gm carbohydrate, 17 gm protein, 5 gm fat.

PICNIC PLEASERS. *Clockwise from bottom left: Hot Antipasto Poor Boys, Fresh Fruit Salad, Honey-Pecan Kiwi Salad, Favorite Sloppy Joes and 30-Minute Chili (recipes on pages 104 and 105).*

Hot Antipasto Poor Boys

Robyn Thompson, Culver City, California
(PICTURED ON PAGE 102)

I like a simple sandwich recipe that eats like a meal, and these zesty Italian sandwiches really hit the spot.

- 1/4 cup creamy Italian *or* Parmesan salad dressing
- 2 tablespoons grated Parmesan cheese
- 1 can (14 ounces) artichoke hearts in water, drained and quartered
- 1 cup quartered cherry tomatoes
- 1 package (5 ounces) thinly sliced pepperoni
- 1 can (2-1/4 ounces) sliced ripe olives, drained
- 2 submarine sandwich buns (about 10 inches)
- 1/2 cup shredded mozzarella cheese

In a medium bowl, combine dressing and Parmesan cheese. Add the artichokes, tomatoes, pepperoni and olives; toss to coat. Cut each bun in half horizontally; place with cut side up on an ungreased baking sheet. Broil 5 in. from the heat for 3-4 minutes or until golden brown. Spread filling over buns; sprinkle with mozzarella. Broil 3-4 minutes more or until filling is hot and cheese is bubbly. **Yield:** 4 servings.

Fresh Fruit Salad

Dianna Shimizu, Issaquah, Washington
(PICTURED ON PAGE 102)

We enjoy picking our own raspberries for this scrumptious salad. Sometimes I'll add cold cubed chicken and serve it in cantaloupe shells. It's flavorful and refreshing!

- 2 large cantaloupe, peeled, seeded and cubed
- 1 cup seedless green grapes
- 1 cup fresh raspberries
- 2 kiwifruit, peeled and sliced

DRESSING:
- 1/3 cup lime juice
- 1/2 cup honey
- 1/4 teaspoon ground coriander
- 1/4 teaspoon ground nutmeg

Toss fruit in a large bowl. In a small bowl, mix dressing ingredients; pour over fruit and toss to coat. **Yield:** 6-8 servings.

30-Minute Chili

Janice Westmoreland, Brooksville, Florida
(PICTURED ON PAGE 102)

A dear neighbor gave me a pot of this delicious chili, and I asked for the recipe. The pork sausage is a nice change from the ground beef many chili recipes call for.

- 1 pound bulk pork sausage
- 1 large onion, chopped

- 1 can (28 ounces) crushed tomatoes
- 2 cans (15-1/2 ounces *each*) chili beans
- 3 cups water
- 1 can (4 ounces) chopped green chilies
- 1 envelope chili seasoning mix
- 2 tablespoons sugar

In a Dutch oven or soup kettle, brown sausage and onion; drain. Add remaining ingredients; cover and simmer for 20 minutes, stirring often. **Yield:** 12 servings (3 quarts).

Honey-Pecan Kiwi Salad

Marla Arbet, Kenosha, Wisconsin
(PICTURED ON PAGE 103)

This dish won second place in a summer salad recipe feature published in our local newspaper. But it takes first place with my family, who loves to try all my new creations.

- 5 cups torn Boston lettuce
- 3 kiwifruit, peeled and sliced
- 1/4 cup chopped pecans, toasted
- 2 tablespoons vanilla yogurt
- 2 tablespoons lemon juice
- 1 tablespoon olive *or* vegetable oil
- 1 tablespoon honey

In a large bowl, combine lettuce, kiwis and pecans. In a small bowl, mix yogurt, lemon juice, oil and honey until smooth. Pour over salad and toss. Serve immediately. **Yield:** 4-6 servings.

Favorite Sloppy Joes

Eleanor Mielke, Snohomish, Washington
(PICTURED ON PAGE 103)

I've prepared these sandwiches for years. I've tried many sloppy joe recipes, but this one is the best by far. It also travels well for picnics or potlucks.

- 2 pounds ground beef
- 1/2 cup chopped onion
- 3/4 cup chili sauce
- 1/2 cup water
- 1/4 cup prepared mustard
- 2 teaspoons chili powder
- 12 hamburger buns, split
- 12 slices cheddar cheese

In a skillet, cook beef and onion until beef is browned; drain. Add chili sauce, water, mustard and chili powder. Simmer, uncovered, for 20 minutes, stirring occasionally. Spoon 1/2 cup onto each bun; top with a cheese slice. **Yield:** 12 servings.

> **ZIPPY JOES.** Next time you make sloppy joes, add 2 teaspoons of sweet pickle relish for every 1 to 2 pounds of ground beef. Folks will never guess your secret ingredient!

Cheeseburger Soup

Janne Rowe, Wichita, Kansas

I don't have a lot of extra time to spend in the kitchen. That's why I appreciate this robust soup. You can cook the ground beef and rice ahead of time for fast assembly.

>   1 cup shredded carrot
>   1 cup chopped onion
> 1/2 cup chopped celery
>   2 cans (14-1/2 ounces *each*) chicken broth
>   1 pound ground beef, browned and crumbled
>   2 cups cooked rice
>   3 cups milk
>   1 pound process American cheese, cubed
>   1 cup (8 ounces) sour cream

In a large saucepan, bring carrot, onion, celery and broth to a boil; reduce heat and simmer for 15 minutes or until vegetables are tender. Add beef, rice, milk and cheese; simmer until cheese is melted (do not boil). Just before serving, whisk in the sour cream; heat through. **Yield:** 10 servings (about 2-1/2 quarts).

Quick Mulligatawny

Ernie Soderlund, Elgin, Illinois

When I was a boy, my father frequently traveled to India on business. He brought back many curry recipes, but mulligatawny was the family favorite...and still is!

>   1 can (19 ounces) lentil soup
>   1 can (11 ounces) condensed tomato rice soup,
>   undiluted
> 1-1/2 cups water
>   1 cup cubed cooked chicken
>   1 medium onion, chopped
>   2 teaspoons curry powder
>   2 bay leaves
> 1/2 to 1 teaspoon hot pepper sauce
> 1/4 teaspoon coarsely ground pepper

In a 3-qt. saucepan, combine all ingredients; bring to a boil. Reduce heat; cover and simmer for 30 minutes. Remove bay leaves before serving. **Yield:** 6 servings.

Apple Cottage Cheese Salad

Diane Sparrow, Osage, Iowa

This refreshing salad is a welcome addition to any potluck or buffet. I always receive recipe requests and come home with an empty bowl...two great compliments for any cook!

✓ **This tasty dish uses less sugar, salt and fat. Recipe includes *Diabetic Exchanges*.**

>   3 cups cottage cheese
>   2 small apples, chopped

> 1/4 cup raisins
>   2 teaspoons poppy seeds
>   2 tablespoons lemon juice
>   2 tablespoons honey
> 1/2 cup salted sunflower seeds

In a bowl, combine cottage cheese, apples, raisins and poppy seeds. Combine lemon juice and honey; add to apple mixture. Chill. Just before serving, stir in sunflower seeds if desired. **Yield:** 10 servings. **Diabetic Exchanges:** One 1/2-cup serving (prepared with fat-free cottage cheese) equals 1-1/2 lean meat, 1 fruit; also, 128 calories, 323 mg sodium, 3 mg cholesterol, 19 gm carbohydrate, 10 gm protein, 4 gm fat.

Artichoke 'n' Olive Salad

Marilou Robinson, Portland, Oregon

When unexpected company showed up for dinner, I quickly scanned my pantry for items I could put together for a side dish. After some digging, this was the delicious result.

>   2 jars (6 ounces *each*) marinated artichokes,
>   undrained
>   1 can (6 ounces) pitted ripe olives, drained
>   1 jar (5 ounces) stuffed olives, drained
>   1 jar (3-1/4 ounces) cocktail onions, drained
>   1 cup banana pepper rings, drained
>   1 can (8 ounces) tomato sauce

In a large bowl, combine artichokes, olives, onions and pepper rings. Add tomato sauce; mix well. Let stand at room temperature for 15 minutes. Serve with a slotted spoon. **Yield:** 8-10 servings.

Tortellini Soup

Karen Shiveley, Springfield, Minnesota

This rich and spicy soup brings a little Italian flair to your table. It's a recipe I invented after trying a similar version in a local restaurant.

>   2 packages (7 ounces *each*) pork breakfast sausage
>   links
>   2 cans (14-1/2 ounces *each*) Italian-style stewed
>   tomatoes
>   2 cups water
>   1 cup chopped onion
> 1/2 cup chopped celery
>   1 garlic clove, minced
>   1 teaspoon dried oregano
> 1/8 to 1/4 teaspoon cayenne pepper
> 1/8 to 1/4 teaspoon hot pepper sauce
>   1 bay leaf
> 3/4 cup refrigerated tortellini

In a 3-qt. saucepan, brown sausage; drain and cut into bite-size pieces. Return to pan; add the next nine ingredients. Bring to a boil; reduce heat and simmer for 15 minutes. Add tortellini; simmer for 5 minutes or until tender. Discard bay leaf. **Yield:** 8 servings.

Chopped Salad

Ann Buege, Winona, Minnesota

This dish has traveled with me to many potlucks and picnics, where it's always met with rave reviews. It's one of my favorite salads because it's so simple to prepare.

- 1 can (6 ounces) pitted ripe olives, drained and chopped
- 1 jar (5 ounces) stuffed olives, drained and chopped
- 1 large cucumber, seeded and chopped
- 1 large green pepper, chopped
- 1 large tomato, chopped
- 1 small onion, chopped
- 1 bottle (8 ounces) Catalina salad dressing

Combine all ingredients in a large bowl. Serve immediately or refrigerate. **Yield:** 8-10 servings.

Southwestern Vegetable Soup

Nancy Chumbley, Argyle, Texas

In addition to being a teacher, I'm a graduate student and mother of three. So this quick and easy soup is perfect for my busy schedule. A real plus is that my family loves it!

- 2 pounds ground beef
- 1 medium onion, chopped
- 2 cans (15 ounces *each*) chili beans, undrained
- 2 cans (14-1/2 ounces *each*) beef broth
- 1 can (15-1/2 ounces) hominy, rinsed and drained
- 1 can (15-1/4 ounces) whole kernel corn, drained
- 1 can (14-1/2 ounces) Mexican-style stewed tomatoes
- 1 can (10 ounces) diced tomatoes and green chilies, undrained
- 1 can (4 ounces) chopped green chilies

In a Dutch oven or soup kettle, brown beef and onion; drain. Add remaining ingredients; bring to a boil. Reduce heat; cover and simmer for 15 minutes. **Yield:** 12-14 servings (3-1/2 quarts).

Stuffed Pizza Sandwiches

Mary Clare, Dodge City, Kansas

I work outside the home, so time spent with my family is precious. I make these sandwiches often...they take just minutes to put together before popping into the oven.

- 6 French sandwich rolls (6 inches)
- 2 cups spaghetti sauce

- 1 pound smoked sausage, cubed
- 2 cups cubed mozzarella cheese

Cut 1 in. off the end of each roll; set ends aside. Hollow out the center of each roll, leaving a 1/2-in. shell. (Discard removed bread or save for another use.) In a saucepan over medium heat, combine spaghetti sauce and sausage; heat through. Remove from the heat; stir in cheese. Spoon about 3/4 cup filling into each roll. Replace ends of rolls; wrap each tightly in foil. Bake at 350° for 20 minutes or until heated through. **Yield:** 6 servings.

Broccoli Cheese Soup

Gladys Schuler, Bismarck, North Dakota

This simple homemade soup gets a head start from canned potato soup and frozen broccoli. People will be surprised to hear that it takes less than 30 minutes to prepare (if you tell them!).

- 1/2 cup shredded carrot
- 2 tablespoons finely chopped onion
- 2 tablespoons butter *or* margarine
- 2 cups milk
- 1 cup water
- 1 package (10 ounces) frozen chopped broccoli
- 1/8 teaspoon pepper
- 2 cans (10-3/4 ounces *each*) condensed cream of potato soup, undiluted
- 1 cup (4 ounces) shredded cheddar cheese

In a 3-qt. saucepan, saute carrot and onion in butter until carrot is tender. Add milk, water, broccoli and pepper; simmer, uncovered, for 10 minutes or until broccoli is tender, stirring occasionally. Add soup and cheese; cook over low heat until soup is heated through and cheese is melted. **Yield:** 6 servings.

From-the-Garden Soup

Eleanor Sweet, Eiberon, Iowa

I love eating and making soup all year long but don't always have the time needed to prepare it. This tasty soup is cooked in the microwave for added convenience.

✓ This tasty dish uses less sugar, salt and fat. Recipe includes *Diabetic Exchanges*.

- 3 cups chicken broth
- 1 teaspoon soy sauce
- 1/2 teaspoon sugar
- 1/8 teaspoon dried thyme
- 1/8 teaspoon dried basil
- 1/8 teaspoon onion powder
- 1/4 cup water
- 1 tablespoon cornstarch
- 1-1/2 cups chopped fresh broccoli
- 1 medium carrot, thinly sliced
- 1 cup shredded lettuce *or* spinach

In a 2-qt. microwave-safe bowl, combine broth, soy sauce, sugar, thyme, basil and onion powder. In a small bowl, combine water and cornstarch; stir until smooth. Add to the broth. Cover and microwave on high for 8 minutes or until broth comes to a boil. Add broccoli and carrot; cover and microwave on high for 5 minutes. Stir in lettuce; cover and let stand for 5 minutes. **Yield:** 4 servings. **Editor's Note:** This recipe was tested in a 700-watt microwave. **Diabetic Exchanges:** One 1-cup serving (prepared with low-sodium chicken broth and soy sauce) equals 2 vegetable; also, 48 calories, 94 mg sodium, 0 cholesterol, 8 gm carbohydrate, 4 gm protein, 1 gm fat.

Hot Tuna Buns

Mrs. Bob Keeley, Otter, Montana

You can mix the ingredients for these comforting sandwiches ahead of time and then bake them later. They're perfect for lunch or a snack.

    1 block (4 ounces) cheddar cheese, cut into 1/4-inch
      cubes
    1 can (6 ounces) tuna, drained and flaked
    3 hard-cooked eggs, chopped
  1/3 cup mayonnaise
    3 tablespoons sweet pickle relish
    2 tablespoons finely chopped onion
  1/4 teaspoon salt
    6 hot dog buns, split

In a medium bowl, combine the first seven ingredients. Spread about 1/3 cup on bottoms of buns; replace tops. Wrap in foil. Bake at 400° for 10 minutes or until cheese is melted. **Yield:** 6 servings.

Simple Fruit Salad

Debbie Zimmerman, East Alton, Illinois

This recipe is delicious with canned fruit, but fresh fruit can easily be substituted or added. It's also very versatile—you can use whatever fruit happens to be in season.

    1 can (20 ounces) pineapple chunks, drained
    1 can (15 ounces) mandarin oranges, drained
    1 can (29 ounces) sliced peaches, drained
    1 large firm banana, sliced, optional
  1/4 cup maraschino cherries, halved
    1 cup sugar
    2 tablespoons cornstarch
  1/8 to 1/4 teaspoon ground nutmeg
    1 cup water
  1/2 of a 3-ounce package of peach *or* apricot gelatin

Toss fruit in a large bowl; chill. In a saucepan, combine sugar, cornstarch and nutmeg; stir in water until smooth. Bring to a boil over medium heat; boil and stir for 2 minutes. Remove from the heat; stir in gelatin until dissolved.

Pour over fruit and toss to coat. Refrigerate until serving. **Yield:** 8-10 servings. **Editor's Note:** Sauce will thicken upon standing.

Easy Seafood Bisque

Cindy Rogowski, Lancaster, New York

I've always enjoyed seafood bisque at restaurants and one day decided to try my hand at a homemade version. Everyone says this is one of the better recipes they've tasted.

  1/2 cup chopped onion
    1 tablespoon butter *or* margarine
    1 can (10-3/4 ounces) condensed cream of celery
      soup, undiluted
    1 can (10-3/4 ounces) condensed cream of shrimp
      soup, undiluted
    1 package (8 ounces) imitation crabmeat, chopped
2-1/4 cups milk
    1 teaspoon chicken bouillon granules
  1/2 teaspoon dried parsley flakes
  1/4 teaspoon garlic powder
  1/4 teaspoon dried marjoram
  1/4 teaspoon pepper

In a 3-qt. saucepan, saute onion in butter until tender. Stir in remaining ingredients. Cover and cook over medium-low heat for 20 minutes or until heated through, stirring occasionally. **Yield:** 4-5 servings.

Turkey-Blue Cheese Pasta Salad

Angela Leinenbach, Newport News, Virginia

The blue cheese dressing makes this pasta salad unique and delicious. I've served it many times, and it's always a hit.

✓ This tasty dish uses less sugar, salt and fat. Recipe includes *Diabetic Exchanges*.

    1 box (16 ounces) pasta shells, cooked, drained and
      cooled
    3 cups cubed cooked turkey *or* chicken
    1 cup diced green pepper
  1/4 cup chopped onion
    1 cup blue cheese salad dressing
  1/4 cup sour cream
    2 teaspoons celery seed
  1/4 teaspoon pepper
  1/2 teaspoon salt, optional

Combine pasta, turkey, green pepper and onion in a large bowl. In a small bowl, combine dressing, sour cream, celery seed, pepper and salt if desired; pour over salad and toss. Serve immediately. **Yield:** 12 servings. **Diabetic Exchanges:** One 1-cup serving (prepared with turkey breast and fat-free salad dressing and sour cream and without salt) equals 2 starch, 1 very lean meat, 1 vegetable; also, 213 calories, 240 mg sodium, 22 mg cholesterol, 38 gm carbohydrate, 11 gm protein, 2 gm fat.

Spicy Corn Salad

Diane Mason, Eddy, Texas
(PICTURED AT LEFT)

This is my mother's recipe. With just the right amount of zip, it's one of my favorite dishes to serve at a good old-fashioned Texas barbecue.

    2 cans (15-1/4 ounces *each*) whole kernel corn,
      drained
    1 can (15 ounces) black beans, rinsed and drained
    1 jar (4-1/2 ounces) sliced mushrooms, drained
    1 can (4 ounces) chopped green chilies
  1/2 cup vinegar
  1/4 cup vegetable oil
    2 garlic cloves, minced
    2 tablespoons minced fresh cilantro *or* parsley
  1/2 teaspoon salt
  1/4 teaspoon pepper
  1/4 teaspoon ground cumin

In a large bowl, combine corn, beans, mushrooms and chilies. Combine remaining ingredients in a small bowl; pour over salad and toss to coat. Chill until serving. **Yield:** 8-10 servings.

Hearty Hash Brown Soup

Frances Rector, Vinton, Iowa
(PICTURED AT LEFT)

Once they take a spoonful of this soup chock-full of potatoes and ham, folks will think you fussed. Since it uses frozen hash browns, it's really simple and fast to make.

    2 pounds frozen hash browns
    4 cups water
    1 large onion, chopped
  3/4 cup sliced celery
    4 chicken bouillon cubes
  1/2 teaspoon celery seed
  1/4 teaspoon pepper
    4 cans (10-3/4 ounces *each*) condensed cream of
      chicken soup, undiluted
    1 quart milk
    2 cups cubed fully cooked ham
    1 tablespoon dried parsley flakes
1-1/2 teaspoons garlic salt
    8 bacon strips, cooked and crumbled

In a Dutch oven or soup kettle, combine the first seven ingredients; bring to a boil. Reduce heat; cover and simmer

---

WINTER WARM-UP. *Pictured at left: Spicy Corn Salad, Champion Roast Beef Sandwiches and Hearty Hash Brown Soup (all recipes on this page).*

---

for 20 minutes or until vegetables are tender. Mash vegetables with cooking liquid. Add soup and milk; stir until smooth. Add ham, parsley and garlic salt; simmer for 10 minutes or until heated through. Garnish with bacon. **Yield:** 12-16 servings (4 quarts).

Champion Roast Beef Sandwiches

Ann Eastman, Greenville, California
(PICTURED AT LEFT)

When I have time, I like to prepare a roast with this much-requested recipe in mind. But when I need a quick meal in a hurry, I use deli roast beef with delicious results.

  1/2 cup sour cream
    1 tablespoon dry onion soup mix
    1 tablespoon prepared horseradish, drained
  1/8 teaspoon pepper
    8 slices rye *or* pumpernickel bread
  1/2 pound sliced roast beef
Lettuce leaves

In a small bowl, combine the first four ingredients; mix well. Spread 1 tablespoon on each slice of bread. Top four slices of bread with roast beef and lettuce; cover with remaining bread. **Yield:** 4 servings.

Mock Minestrone

Jorja Hutton, Sturgeon Bay, Wisconsin

Don't let the number of ingredients in this recipe fool you. The bulk of the items are combined all at once and simmered, making this a no-fuss favorite.

    2 pounds bulk Italian sausage
    1 large onion, chopped
    1 garlic clove, minced
    6 cups water
    1 jar (30 ounces) chunky spaghetti sauce
    2 cans (10-3/4 ounces *each*) condensed beef broth,
      undiluted
    1 can (15 ounces) garbanzo beans, rinsed and drained
    1 package (10 ounces) frozen chopped spinach,
      thawed and squeezed dry
    1 cup diced zucchini
    1 cup thinly sliced carrots
1-1/2 teaspoons dried basil
  1/2 teaspoon pepper
    4 cups cooked pasta
Grated Parmesan cheese, optional

In a Dutch oven or soup kettle, cook sausage, onion and garlic until sausage is browned and onion is tender; drain. Stir in all remaining ingredients except the pasta and cheese. Simmer for 20 minutes. Add pasta and heat through. Garnish with cheese if desired. **Yield:** 20-22 servings (5-1/2 quarts).

Index

APPLE
Apple Cider Salad, 70
Apple-Cinnamon Coleslaw, 71
Apple Cottage Cheese Salad, 105
Apple-Strawberry Peanut Salad, 75
Fluffy Fruit Delight, 101
Fruit 'n' Spice Salad, 44
Fruity Pasta Salad, 57
Grandma's Apple Salad, 76
Mulligatawny Soup, 22
Salmon Salad, 101
Special Fruit Salad, 69
Surprise Fruit Salad, 69
Tangy Cabbage Salad, 61
Turkey Chutney Salad, 49

APRICOTS
Apricot Aspic, 75
Sweet and Savory Turkey Salad, 48

ARTICHOKES
Artichoke 'n' Olive Salad, 105
Artichoke Potato Salad, 60
Garbanzo Bean Salad, 53
Hearty Muffaleta Loaf, 92
Hot Antipasto Poor Boys, 104

ASPARAGUS
Asparagus Soup, 27
Southern Garden Soup, 18
Turkey Mornay, 88

AVOCADO
Arkansas Travelers, 92
Chicken Avocado Sandwiches, 93
Fiesta Loaf, 95
Garbanzo Avocado Salad, 67
Guacamole Mousse with Salsa, 76
Shrimp Blitz, 41
Taco Soup, 25
Turkey Gobble-Up, 79

BACON & CANADIAN BACON
Arkansas Travelers, 92
Blue Cheese-Bacon Dressing, 65
Cauliflower Lettuce Salad, 66
Chicken and Bacon Chowder, 35
Chili Sandwiches, 84
Elbow Macaroni Medley, 52
Elegant Omelet Loaf, 89
Hearty Hash Brown Soup, 109
Hearty Luncheon Salad, 48
Hot Turkey Sandwiches, 89
Italian Broccoli Salad, 66

Mixed Legume Soup, 13
Open-Faced Chicken Benedict, 88
Pea Salad with Creamy Dressing, 61
Pepper Lovers' BLT, 97
Spinach Bacon Sandwiches, 85
Spinach Salad Ring, 70
Spinach Salad with Honey-Bacon
    Dressing, 59
Spinach Salad with Orange
    Dressing, 61
Terrific Sub Sandwich, 91
Turkey BLT, 80
Turkey Gobble-Up, 79
Turkey Muffins with Cheese
    Sauce, 85
Turkey Tomato Club, 96

BARLEY & OATS
Beef Barley Soup, 25
Dilly Beef Barley Soup, 14
Garlic Oatmeal Soup, 34
Swiss-Barley Mushroom Soup, 34
Turkey Barley Soup, 21

BEANS
(also see Green Beans)
Black-and-White Bean Salad, 55
Black Bean Soup, 15
Chicken Chili, 8
Chicken Lima Bean Soup, 7
Chili Sandwiches, 84
Citrus Black Bean and Rice Salad, 52
Country Bean Soup, 9
Country-Style Stew, 15
Country Vegetable Soup, 21
Easy Chicken Chili, 100
Dilly Beef Barley Soup, 14
Favorite Chili, 13
Fiesta Black Bean Salad, 55
Four-Bean Salad, 56
Garbanzo Avocado Salad, 67
Garbanzo Bean Salad, 53
Ham and Bean Soup, 13
Hearty Black Bean Chili, 8
Hot Dogs with Chili Beans, 87
Hunter's Chili, 7
Italian Macaroni Salad, 12
Mexican Bean Soup, 12
Minty Bean Salad, 53
Oven-Baked Bean Soup, 8
Quick Turkey-Bean Soup, 100
Sausage Bean Chowder, 15
Southwestern Vegetable Soup, 106
Spicy Corn Salad, 109
Succotash Salad, 67
Sweet Succotash Chili, 14
30-Minute Chili, 104
Three-Bean Garden Salad, 51
Tuscan Soup, 12
Two-Bean Tuna Salad, 52
Vegetarian Chili, 14
White Chili, 9
Winter Vegetable Soup, 8

BEEF
*(also see Corned Beef and
    Ground Beef)*
Beef 'n' Braised Onion Sandwiches, 81
Beef 'n' Cheese Tortillas, 95
Beef and Pasta Salad, 45
Beef Barley Soup, 25
Champion Roast Beef
    Sandwiches, 109
Chili Sandwiches, 84
Country Tomato-Rice Soup, 21
Dilly Beef Barley Soup, 14
Dorothy's Barbecue, 87
Favorite Chili, 13
French Onion-Beef Strudel, 83
Gingersnap Goulash, 27
Italian Beef Sandwiches, 80
Mexican Beef Soup, 22
Oriental Friendship Soup, 26
Roast Beef Soup, 27
Spicy Barbecued Beef Sandwiches, 88
Stroganoff Soup, 30
Zesty Tortilla Soup, 19

BEETS
Beet Borscht, 39
Russian Borscht, 25

BLUEBERRIES
Fresh Fruit Soup, 39
Fruit Bowl with Mandarin Dressing, 77
Oregon Muffaleta, 97

BROCCOLI
Broccoli-Cauliflower Cheese Soup, 35
Broccoli Cheese Soup, 106
From-the-Garden Soup, 106
Garden Chowder, 31
Italian Broccoli Salad, 66
Swiss 'n' Cheddar Broccoli Soup, 37
Turkey Pasta Salad, 55

CABBAGE
Apple-Cinnamon Coleslaw, 71
Beet Borscht, 39
Church Coleslaw, 59
Country-Style Stew, 15
Cranberry Cabbage Salad, 66
Grandma's Harvest Soup, 23
Ground Beef Bundles, 81
Harvest Layered Salad, 64
Irish Potato Salad, 64
Meatless Minestrone, 25
Rainy Day Soup, 19
Reuben Deli Sandwiches, 83
Russian Borscht, 25
Tangy Cabbage Salad, 61

Turkey Tomato Club, 96
Winter Vegetable Soup, 8

CANTALOUPE
Anise Fruit Salad, 74
Fresh Fruit Salad, 104
Fruit Bowl with Mandarin Dressing, 77
Pineapple Peach Soup, 40
Special Fruit Salad, 69

CARROTS
Carrot Soup, 33
Confetti Soup, 34
Hamburger Soup, 26
Harvest Layered Salad, 64
Golden Autumn Soup, 33
Marinated Vegetable Salad, 64
Shoestring Salad, 43
Vegetable Tuna Sandwiches, 93

CAULIFLOWER
Broccoli-Cauliflower Cheese Soup, 35
Cauliflower Lettuce Salad, 66
Colorful Cauliflower Salad, 61
Creamy Cauliflower Salad, 67
Marinated Vegetable Salad, 64
Southern Garden Soup, 18

CHEESE
Antipasto Pasta Salad, 51
Apple Cottage Cheese Salad, 105
Beef 'n' Cheese Tortillas, 95
Blue Cheese-Bacon Dressing, 65
Blue Cheese Tomato Soup, 41
Broccoli-Cauliflower Cheese Soup, 35
Broccoli Cheese Soup, 106
Cheeseburger Soup, 105
Cheesy Clam Chowder, 29
Creamy Turkey Melt, 100
Curried Tuna Melt, 89
Dilly Cheese Soup, 33
Elbow Macaroni Medley, 52
Favorite Sloppy Joes, 104
Fiesta Loaf, 95
French Onion-Beef Strudel, 83
Garlic Oatmeal Soup, 34
Giant Picnic Sandwich, 95
Grilled Blue Cheese Sandwiches, 85
Ham and Blue Cheese Pasta Salad, 53
Ham and Double Cheese
    Sandwiches, 91
Haystack Salad, 47
Hearty Muffaleta Loaf, 92
Hot 'n' Cheesy Chicken
    Sandwiches, 80
Hot Tuna Buns, 107
Italian Market Salad, 55
Macaroni and Cheese Soup, 37
Open-Faced Mozzarella
    Sandwiches, 79
Pesto Pasta Salad, 56
Special Ham 'n' Cheese
    Sandwiches, 96
Spicy Summer Sub, 96

Spinach Bacon Sandwiches, 85
Spinach Bisque, 35
Spinach Cheese Soup, 37
Stuffed Pizza Sandwiches, 106
Swiss 'n' Cheddar Broccoli Soup, 37
Swiss-Barley Mushroom Soup, 34
Taco Soup, 25
Terrific Sub Sandwich, 91
Three Cheese Tomato Melt, 83
Turkey Mornay, 88
Turkey Muffins with Cheese Sauce, 85
Zesty Chili-Cheese Soup, 31

CHERRIES
Cherry Dumpling Soup, 40
Christmas Soup, 40
Molded Cherry-Pineapple Salad, 77

CHICKEN
Chicken and Bacon Chowder, 35
Chicken and Dumpling Soup, 34
Chicken Avocado Sandwiches, 93
Chicken Bisque, 31
Chicken Chili, 8
Chicken Lima Bean Soup, 7
Chicken Salad Oriental, 44
Chicken Soup Base, 26
Chicken Tortellini Salad, 100
Crescent Chicken Squares, 81
Crunchy Tossed Salad with
    Chicken, 48
Curried Chicken Pita Pockets, 92
Easy Chicken Chili, 100
Hearty Black Bean Chili, 8
Hearty Luncheon Salad, 48
Hot 'n' Cheesy Chicken
    Sandwiches, 80
Mexican Chicken Salad, 45
Mulligatawny Soup, 22
Open-Faced Chicken Benedict, 88
Oriental Chicken Grill, 79
Perfect Chicken Salad, 49
Quick Mulligatawny, 105
Spicy Grilled Chicken Salad, 47
Spinach Cheese Soup, 37
Tarragon Chicken Salad, 44
Tarragon Chicken Salad
    Sandwiches, 91

CORN
Chunky Fish Chowder, 23
Confetti Soup, 35
Corn Chowder, 30
Fiesta Black Bean Salad, 55
Garden Chowder, 31
Hearty Hamburger Soup, 101
Quick Pantry Salad, 51
Sausage Soup, 30
Southwestern Vegetable Soup, 106
Spicy Corn Salad, 109

Succotash Salad, 67
Sweet Succotash Chili, 14
Zesty Chili-Cheese Soup, 31

CORNED BEEF
Irish Potato Salad, 64
Luncheon Mold, 71
Reuben Deli Sandwiches, 83

CRANBERRIES
Cranberry Cabbage Salad, 66
Cranberry Gelatin Salad, 77
Oregon Muffaleta, 97
Thanksgiving Sandwiches, 91

CUCUMBERS
Chopped Salad, 106
Cold Cucumber Soup, 39
Fire-and-Ice Salad, 59
Low-Fat Gazpacho, 39
Marinated Vegetable Salad, 64
Sour Cream Cucumber Salad, 60
Spectacular Shrimp Salad, 44

DIABETIC EXCHANGE RECIPES
*(Lower in salt, sugar and fat, and
    evaluated for diabetics)*
Apple Cottage Cheese Salad, 105
Apricot Aspic, 75
Beef 'n' Braised Onion Sandwiches, 81
Black Bean Soup, 15
Calico Tomato Salad, 65
Chicken Chili, 8
Chicken Salad Oriental, 44
Cold Cucumber Soup, 39
Dilly Beef Barley Soup, 14
Fiesta Black Bean Salad, 55
From-the-Garden Soup, 106
Fruited Turkey Salad, 49
Greek Rice Salad, 56
Green Bean Soup, 21
Grill-Side Turkey Salad, 48
Hamburger Soup, 26
Herbed Fish Soup, 18
Low-Fat Gazpacho, 39
Meatless Minestrone, 25
Mixed Greens with Mushrooms, 60
Pasta and Lentil Soup, 9
Rainy Day Soup, 19
Refreshing Turkey Salad, 76
Salmon Salad, 101
Sausage Soup, 30
Seafood Salad Sandwiches, 92
Spicy Grilled Chicken Salad, 47
Tropical Turkey Salad, 70
Turkey-Blue Cheese Pasta Salad, 107 ♂

DRESSINGS
Blue Cheese-Bacon Dressing, 65
Dijon Vinaigrette, 60
Ginger French Dressing, 67
Home-Style French Dressing, 64
Low-Fat Ranch Dressing, 66
Milly's Salad Dressing, 59
Poppy Seed Dressing, 69
Raspberry Vinaigrette, 71
Sweet-and-Sour Dressing, 61
Tangy Salad Dressing, 67

EGGS
Creamy Egg Salad Sandwiches, 93
Egg Salad Tacos, 95
Elegant Omelet Loaf, 89
Hot Tuna Buns, 107
Luncheon Mold, 71
Quick Pantry Salad, 51
Sour Cream Potato Salad, 66
Spinach Salad Ring, 70
Triple Tasty Sandwich Spread, 97

GELATIN SALADS
Apple Cider Salad, 70
Apricot Aspic, 75
Cranberry Gelatin Salad, 77
Creamy Citrus Salad, 76
Lime Pear Salad, 77
Luncheon Mold, 71
Mini Molded Salads, 70
Molded Cherry-Pineapple Salad, 77
Rosy Raspberry Salad, 77
Special Strawberry Salad, 74
Spinach Salad Ring, 70
Three-Ring Mold, 69

GRAPES
Anise Fruit Salad, 74
Cinnamon Fruit Compote, 75
Curried Chicken Pita Pockets, 92
Fresh Fruit Salad, 104
Fruit 'n' Spice Salad, 44
Fruit Bowl with Mandarin Dressing, 77
Fruited Turkey Salad, 49
Pork Salad Rolls, 92
Refreshing Turkey Salad, 76
Special Fruit Salad, 69

GREEN BEANS
Country-Style Stew, 15
Four-Bean Salad, 56
Green Bean Soup, 21
Herbed Fish Soup, 18
Sage 'n' Rosemary Pork Stew, 18

GROUND BEEF
Beef Barbecue Biscuits, 84

Beef Tortellini Soup, 18
Chalupa Joes, 89
Cheeseburger Soup, 105
Country-Style Stew, 15
Favorite Sloppy Joes, 104
Ground Beef Bundles, 81
Hamburger Soup, 26
Haystack Salad, 47
Hearty Black Bean Chili, 8
Hearty Hamburger Soup, 101
Hot Dogs with Chili Beans, 87
Hunter's Chili, 7
Mexican Bean Soup, 12
Mexican Beef Soup, 22
Potato Onion Soup, 22
Ravioli Soup, 17
Salad in a Bread Bowl, 47
Salsa Sloppy Joes, 100
Sausage-Stuffed French Loaf, 84
Shaker Herb 'n' Meatball Soup, 19
Southwestern Vegetable Soup, 106
Sweet Succotash Chili, 14
Wonderburgers for Two, 87
Zesty Meatball Sandwiches, 80

HAM
Barbecued Ham Sandwiches, 83
Confetti Soup, 35
Corn Chowder, 30
Country Bean Soup, 9
Creamy Wild Rice Soup, 29
Dijon Ham Salad, 44
Fruit 'n' Spice Salad, 44
Giant Picnic Sandwich, 95
Grandma's Harvest Soup, 23
Green Bean Soup, 21
Ham and Bean Soup, 13
Ham and Blue Cheese Pasta Salad, 53
Ham and Double Cheese
    Sandwiches, 91
Ham and Spinach Loaf, 96
Ham Salad, 43
Ham, Turkey and Wild Rice Salad, 53
Hearty Hash Brown Soup, 109
Italian Macaroni Salad, 12
Italian Market Salad, 55
Italian Submarine Sandwich, 93
Oregon Muffaleta, 97
Oven-Baked Bean Soup, 8
Pesto Pasta Salad, 56
Special Ham 'n' Cheese
    Sandwiches, 96
Spicy Summer Sub, 96
Succotash Salad, 67
Submarine Sandwich Salad, 45
Terrific Sub Sandwich, 91
Triple Tasty Sandwich Spread, 97
Turkey and Ham Salad with
    Greens, 43

LENTILS
Lemon Lentil Salad, 56
Lentil and Brown Rice Soup, 14
Mixed Legume Soup, 13

Pasta and Lentil Soup, 9
Roast Beef Soup, 27

LETTUCE SALADS
Cauliflower Lettuce Salad, 66
Crunchy Tossed Salad with
    Chicken, 48
Favorite Fruit Salad, 74
Haystack Salad, 47
Hearty Luncheon Salad, 48
Honey-Pecan Kiwi Salad, 104
Mary's Caesar Salad, 65
Mexican Chicken Salad, 45
Mixed Greens with Mushrooms, 60
Nutty Mandarin Salad, 75
Salad in a Bread Bowl, 47
Shrimp Salad with Creamy Pepper
    Dressing, 65
Spicy Grilled Chicken Salad, 47
Submarine Sandwich Salad, 45
Tropical Turkey Salad, 70
Turkey and Ham Salad with
    Greens, 43
Turkey Salad with Raspberries, 74

MUSHROOMS
Asparagus Soup, 27
Chunky Mushroom and Tomato
    Salad, 60
Grilled Blue Cheese Sandwiches, 85
Harvest Layered Salad, 64
Hunter's Chili, 7
Mixed Greens with Mushrooms, 60
Spinach Salad with Honey-Bacon
    Dressing, 59
Swiss-Barley Mushroom Soup, 34
Three-Bean Garden Salad, 51
Tomato Mushroom Consomme, 99
Vegetarian Chili, 14
Veggie Delights, 88

NUTS
Apple-Strawberry Peanut Salad, 75
Crunchy Pea Salad, 99
Curried Chicken Pita Pockets, 92
Grandma's Apple Salad, 76
Ham and Blue Cheese Pasta Salad, 53
Ham and Spinach Loaf, 96
Ham Salad, 43
Honey-Pecan Kiwi Salad, 104
Hot Turkey Pecan Salad, 45
Nutty Mandarin Salad, 75
Nutty Shrimp Salad Sandwiches, 97
Sweet and Savory Turkey Salad, 48
Turkey Cashew Salad, 49

OLIVES
Artichoke 'n' Olive Salad, 105
Chopped Salad, 106
Colorful Cauliflower Salad, 61
Fiesta Loaf, 95
Garbanzo Bean Salad, 53
Icy Olive Soup, 40
Italian Broccoli Salad, 66
Italian Submarine Sandwich, 93
Mini Molded Salads, 70
Minty Bean Salad, 53
Two-Bean Tuna Salad, 52
Vegetarian Chili, 14

ONIONS
Beef 'n' Braised Onion
    Sandwiches, 81
French Onion-Beef Strudel, 83
Golden Autumn Soup, 33
Potato Onion Soup, 22
Texas Turkey Soup, 26

ORANGES
Ambrosia Salad, 71
Anise Fruit Salad, 74
Cranberry Gelatin Salad, 77
Creamy Citrus Salad, 76
Favorite Fruit Salad, 74
Fluffy Fruit Salad, 71
Fruity Pasta Salad, 57
Nutty Mandarin Salad, 75
Raspberry Orange Soup, 40
Shrimp Salad with Creamy Pepper
    Dressing, 65
Simple Fruit Salad, 107
Special Strawberry Salad, 74
Spinach Salad with Orange
    Dressing, 61
Thanksgiving Sandwiches, 91

PASTA & NOODLES
Antipasto Pasta Salad, 51
Beef and Pasta Salad, 45
Beef Tortellini Soup, 18
Chicken Tortellini Salad, 100
Country Vegetable Soup, 22
Elbow Macaroni Medley, 52
Fruity Pasta Salad, 57
Ham and Blue Cheese Pasta Salad, 53
Italian Macaroni Soup, 12
Macaroni and Cheese Soup, 37
Minestrone in Minutes, 101
Mock Minestrone, 109
Oriental Friendship Soup, 26
Pasta and Lentil Soup, 9
Pesto Pasta Salad, 56
Quick Pantry Salad, 51
Ravioli Soup, 17
Spaghetti Soup, 99
Spicy Spaghetti Salad, 57
Spinach Cheese Soup, 37
Stroganoff Soup, 30
Texas Turkey Soup, 26
Tortellini Soup, 105
Turkey-Blue Cheese Pasta Salad, 107

Turkey Cashew Salad, 49
Turkey Noodle Soup, 23
Turkey Pasta Salad, 55
Turkey Shrimp Salad, 52
Tuscan Soup, 12
Winter Vegetable Soup, 8

PEACHES
Pineapple Peach Soup, 40
Simple Fruit Salad, 107
Turkey Shrimp Salad, 52

PEANUT BUTTER
Chocolate Peanut Butter, 96
Grilled "PBJ" Sandwiches, 87

PEARS
Fluffy Fruit Salad, 71
Lime Pear Salad, 77
Three-Ring Mold, 69

PEAS
Chicken Tortellini Salad, 100
Country Bean Soup, 9
Country-Style Stew, 15
Crunchy Pea Salad, 99
Dilly Beef Barley Soup, 14
Minestrone in Minutes, 101
Mixed Legume Soup, 13
Pea Salad with Creamy Dressing, 61
Pea Soup for a Crowd, 13
Perfect Chicken Salad, 49
Split Pea Soup with Meatballs, 12

PINEAPPLE
Ambrosia Salad, 71
Anise Fruit Salad, 74
Cranberry Gelatin Salad, 77
Creamy Citrus Salad, 76
Favorite Fruit Salad, 74
Fluffy Fruit Delight, 101
Fluffy Fruit Salad, 71
Fruited Turkey Salad, 49
Fruity Pasta Salad, 57
Molded Cherry-Pineapple Salad, 77
Pineapple Peach Soup, 40
Simple Fruit Salad, 107
Special Fruit Salad, 69
Spicy Grilled Chicken Salad, 47
Tangy Cabbage Salad, 61
Three-Ring Mold, 69
Tropical Turkey Salad, 70
Turkey Chutney Salad, 49

PORK
Green Chili, 7
Pea Soup for a Crowd, 13
Pork Salad Rolls, 92
Sage 'n' Rosemary Pork Stew, 18

Southwestern Chili, 9
Split Pea Soup with Meatballs, 12

POTATOES
Artichoke Potato Salad, 60
Carrot Soup, 33
Chicken and Bacon Chowder, 35
Chunky Fish Chowder, 23
Chunky Potato Soup, 33
Corn Chowder, 30
Dilly Cheese Soup, 33
Grandma's Harvest Soup, 23
Hamburger Soup, 26
Hearty Hash Brown Soup, 109
Irish Potato Salad, 64
Knoephla Soup, 34
Manhattan Clam Chowder, 27
Potato Clam Chowder, 37
Potato Onion Soup, 22
Sausage Soup, 30
Shaker Herb 'n' Meatball Soup, 19
Sour Cream Potato Salad, 66
Split Pea Soup with Meatballs, 12
Winter Vegetable Soup, 8

RASPBERRIES
Fresh Fruit Salad, 104
Fresh Fruit Soup, 39
Raspberry Orange Soup, 40
Rosy Raspberry Salad, 77
Turkey Salad with Raspberries, 74

RHUBARB
Ruby-Red Rhubarb Soup, 41

RICE
Asparagus Soup, 27
Cheeseburger Soup, 105
Chicken Salad Oriental, 44
Citrus Black Bean and Rice Salad, 52
Country Tomato-Rice Soup, 21
Curried Turkey and Rice Salad, 57
Creamy Wild Rice Soup, 29
Dijon Ham Salad, 44
Dilly Cheese Soup, 33
Fruit 'n' Spice Salad, 44
Greek Rice Salad, 56
Ham, Turkey and Wild Rice Salad, 53
Haystack Salad, 47
Italian Market Salad, 55
Lentil and Brown Rice Soup, 14
Mulligatawny Soup, 22
Refreshing Turkey Salad, 76
Tuna Rice Salad, 57

SANDWICH SPREADS
Chocolate Peanut Butter, 96
Triple Tasty Sandwich Spread, 97

SAUSAGE
Antipasto Pasta Salad, 51
Deli Club Sandwich, 99
Giant Picnic Sandwich, 95
Hearty Muffaleta Loaf, 92
Hot Antipasto Poor Boys, 104

SAUSAGE (continued)
Hot Dogs with Chili Beans, 87
Hunter's Chili, 7
Italian Submarine Sandwich, 93
Mock Minestrone, 109
Polish Sausage Soup, 101
Sausage Bean Chowder, 15
Sausage Soup, 30
Sausage-Stuffed French Loaf, 84
Spaghetti Soup, 99
Spicy Summer Sub, 96
Spicy Zucchini Soup, 17
Stuffed Pizza Sandwiches, 106
Submarine Sandwich Salad, 45
Terrific Sub Sandwich, 91
30-Minute Chili, 104
Tortellini Soup, 105
Triple Tasty Sandwich Spread, 97

SEAFOOD
(also see Shrimp and Tuna)
Cheesy Clam Chowder, 29
Chunky Fish Chowder, 23
Crab Bisque, 30
Easy Seafood Bisque, 107
Herbed Fish Soup, 18
Manhattan Clam Chowder, 27
Potato Clam Chowder, 37
Salmon Salad, 101

SHRIMP
Mini Molded Salads, 70
Nutty Shrimp Salad Sandwiches, 97
Seafood Salad Sandwiches, 92
Shrimp Blitz, 41
Shrimp Salad with Creamy Pepper
    Dressing, 65
Spectacular Shrimp Salad, 44
Turkey Shrimp Salad, 52

SPINACH
Beef 'n' Cheese Tortillas, 95
Ham and Spinach Loaf, 96
Hearty Luncheon Salad, 48
Mock Minestrone, 109
Oriental Friendship Soup, 26
Spinach Bacon Sandwiches, 85
Spinach Bisque, 35
Spinach Cheese Soup, 37
Spinach Salad Ring, 70
Spinach Salad with Honey-Bacon
    Dressing, 59
Spinach Salad with Orange
    Dressing, 61
Tomato Spinach Soup, 21

STRAWBERRIES
Apple-Strawberry Peanut Salad, 75

Cinnamon Fruit Compote, 75
Favorite Fruit Salad, 74
Fresh Fruit Soup, 39
Fruit Bowl with Mandarin Dressing, 77
Special Fruit Salad, 69
Special Strawberry Salad, 74
Succulent Strawberry Soup, 41

TOMATOES
Black-and-White Bean Salad, 55
Calico Tomato Salad, 65
Chili Sandwiches, 84
Chunky Mushroom and Tomato
    Salad, 60
Country Tomato-Rice Soup, 21
Fire-and-Ice Salad, 59
Fresh Tomato Soup, 29
Garbanzo Avocado Salad, 67
Green Chili, 7
Guacamole Mousse with Salsa, 76
Hot Antipasto Poor Boys, 104
Low-Fat Gazpacho, 39
Meatless Minestrone, 25
Mexican Bean Soup, 12
Mexican Beef Soup, 22
Minestrone in Minutes, 101
Open-Faced Mozzarella
    Sandwiches, 79
Pepper Lovers' BLT, 97
Southwestern Vegetable Soup, 106
Spicy Spaghetti Salad, 57
Taco Soup, 25
Three-Bean Garden Salad, 51
Three Cheese Tomato Melt, 83
Tomato Spinach Soup, 21
Tortellini Soup, 105
Tuna-Stuffed Tomatoes, 43
Turkey BLT, 80
Turkey Tomato Club, 96
Veggie Delights, 88
Zesty Meatball Sandwiches, 80
Zesty Tortilla Soup, 19

TUNA
Curried Tuna Melt, 89
Hot Tuna Buns, 107
Shoestring Salad, 43
Tuna Rice Salad, 57
Tuna-Stuffed Tomatoes, 43

Two-Bean Tuna Salad, 52
Vegetable Tuna Sandwiches, 93

TURKEY
Arkansas Travelers, 92
Creamy Turkey Melt, 100
Curried Turkey and Rice Salad, 57
Deli Club Sandwich, 99
Fruited Turkey Salad, 49
Greek Rice Salad, 56
Grill-Side Turkey Salad, 48
Ground Turkey Turnovers, 81
Ham, Turkey and Wild Rice
    Salad, 53
Hot Turkey Pecan Salad, 45
Hot Turkey Sandwiches, 89
Mustard Turkey Sandwiches, 84
Pepper Lovers' BLT, 97
Quick Pantry Salad, 51
Quick Turkey-Bean Soup, 100
Rainy Day Soup, 19
Refreshing Turkey Salad, 76
Spicy Summer Sub, 96
Submarine Sandwich Salad, 45
Sweet and Savory Turkey Salad, 48
Texas Turkey Soup, 26
Thanksgiving Sandwiches, 91
Tropical Turkey Salad, 70
Turkey and Ham Salad with
    Greens, 43
Turkey Barley Soup, 21
Turkey BLT, 80
Turkey-Blue Cheese Pasta Salad, 107
Turkey Burritos, 85
Turkey Cashew Salad, 49
Turkey Chutney Salad, 49
Turkey Gobble-Up, 79
Turkey Mornay, 88
Turkey Muffins with Cheese
    Sauce, 85
Turkey Noodle Soup, 23
Turkey Pasta Salad, 55
Turkey Salad with Raspberries, 74
Turkey Shrimp Salad, 52
Turkey Soup with Slickers, 17
Turkey Tomato Club, 96
White Chili, 9

ZUCCHINI
Calico Tomato Salad, 65
Country Vegetable Soup, 22
Cream of Zucchini Soup, 31
Garden Chowder, 31
Harvest Layered Salad, 64
Mock Minestrone, 109
Pesto Pasta Salad, 56
Spicy Zucchini Soup, 17
Veggie Delights, 88